The Nature of Good and Evil

Understanding the Many Acts of Moral and Immoral Behavior

Samuel P. Oliner

PARAGON HOUSE

First Edition 2011

Published in the United States by
Paragon House
1925 Oakcrest Ave, Suite 7
St. Paul, MN 55113
www.paragonhouse.com

Cover design by Liz Oliner, Oliner Graphics

Library of Congress Cataloging-in-Publication Data

Oliner, Samuel P.
   The nature of good and evil : understanding the many acts of moral and immoral behavior / Samuel P. Oliner. -- 1st ed.
      p. cm.
   Includes bibliographical references.
   ISBN 978-1-55778-896-2 (pbk. : alk. paper)
   1. Ethics--Psychological aspects. 2. Good and evil--Case studies. 3. Altruism--Case studies. 4. Genocide--Case studies. 5. Social psychology. I. Title.
   BJ45.O45 2011
   170--dc23
                              2011021506

The paper used in this publication meets the minimum requirements of American National Standard for Information Sciences—Permanence of Paper for Printed Library Materials, ANSI standard Z39.48-1992.

Manufactured in the United States of America
10 9 8 7 6 5 4 3 2 1

For current information about all releases from Paragon House, visit the website at http://www.paragonhouse.com

Contents

Acknowledgments

This book would not have been possible without the help of many people, including graduate students and colleagues at Humboldt State University. I am grateful to all of these individuals who supplied me with valuable input and support. Specifically, a number of graduate students who contributed to research, gave suggestions about what important information should be included in the chapters in this book, and edited at its initial stages. Among them are:

Jeffrey Gunn, currently completing his Ph.D. at the University of Oregon, has made an important contribution to chapter 2, "How Could They Do That? Understanding the Many Faces of Evil." Mark Bauermeister, who is also completing his Ph.D. from the University of Iowa, has had substantial input in chapter 3, "Silently Standing By: Why We Do or Don't Come to the Aid of Those Who Need Us." Jason Whitley, who has completed his master's degree in sociology, has done research from the inception of this book, and helped with initial drafts. Ali Chaudhary, currently completing his Ph.D. at the University of California-Davis, has critically evaluated chapter 4, "Paving the Way to Resistance: The Gift of Good during the Nazi Occupation 1939-1945" and chapter 5, "Preconditions of Resistance during the Armenian and Rwandan Genocides." Maral Attallah, who has completed her master's degree in sociology at Humboldt State University, and is currently an instructor at College of the Redwoods and Humboldt State University, has made valuable suggestions on the Armenian genocide and resistance, in which she is an expert. Matt Jelen, who received his master's degree in sociology, has helped with the research on resistance during the Holocaust. Amanda Bertana has completed her master's degree in sociology dealing with the exploitation of natural resources, which have ramifications for suppression of human rights in countries such as Sudan, Nigeria, and Angola. She has been deeply involved in editing the final version of the book, checking meticulously footnotes, spelling, and wisely suggesting changes of some words in the text and continuation flow of language in the book. I also want to acknowledge Jill Rothenberg, the former senior editor at Westview Press, who has made valuable suggestions including infusing the chapters with more anecdotes.

I want especially to express my deep appreciation to the eminent scholars who made generous observations about the value of this book: Professor John Roth who has written the Foreword for this book, Professor Michael Berenbaum, Professor Stephen Post, Professor Nel Noddings, Professor Everett Worthington, Professor Dacher Keltner, Professor Ronald Berger, and Professor Robert Krell.

Finally, I express my deep appreciation to Paragon House editor Rosemary Yokoi for her patience, guidance, and input.

Foreword

WRITING TO YOU

During the first week of November 2010, I received e-mail messages from two friends. One of them was from Rosemary Yokoi, an editor at Paragon House. She asked if I would review a manuscript for possible publication in the press's Holocaust and Genocide Studies Series, which I edit. The second message came from Nicola Wetherall, a gifted and determined teacher from England. At the Wootton Bassett School in Wiltshire, Nicola teaches her students about the Holocaust, Nazi Germany's genocide against the European Jews, and the importance of remembering how that catastrophe also targeted Roma and Sinti, Jehovah's Witnesses, homosexuals, disabled people, political dissidents, and other national and ethnic groups that the Nazis regarded as inferior. "I am writing to you," her message said, "to request that you send a letter to the Wootton Bassett students in support of the school's second annual Holocaust Day," a commemoration that Nicola initiated and that takes place in 2011 on April 28. I wrote back to Rosemary and Nicola, agreeing to do what they had asked.

The manuscript that Rosemary Yokoi asked me to evaluate became the book that is in your hands as you are reading these words of mine. Its author, Samuel Oliner, is another of my friends. As I studied Sam's manuscript, I thought about Nicola Wetherall and her students at the Wootton Bassett School. To the best of my knowledge, the two of them have never met, but they have the same ethical values, and both of them are especially concerned to transmit, in the words with which Oliner ends this book, the "education, moral role modeling, love, caring for diverse others, respect, and social and economic justice for all [that] may be the antidote for a divided world." So, here is the letter I wrote to Nicola's students, which, in turn, can help to introduce and contextualize Sam Oliner's important book, *The Nature of Good and Evil.*

To the Year 9 and Sixth Form Student of Ms. Nicola Wetherall at the Wootton Bassett School

Ms. Nicola Wetherall, my friend and your teacher, has told me about the outstanding work you are doing in studying and remembering the Holocaust and the other genocides that have done so much harm in our world. As a person who has spent more than forty years learning about and from such atrocities, I am writing to thank you and your superb teacher for taking the time and energy to do this hard work.

I know that your school's second annual Holocaust Day is coming on April 28, 2011. Before that, you also may be paying attention to the Holocaust Memorial Day observances that will take place on January 27, 2011. On both of those occasions, it is good to think about what Holocaust survivors have to tell us. Let me tell you about one of them, a good friend of mine named Samuel Oliner. He was born in Poland in 1930. I first met him fifty years later in San Francisco, and we have been good friends ever since.

Sam Oliner, who has written many significant books, has had a long and distinguished career as a professor of sociology. He is also a child-survivor or really an orphan-survivor of the Holocaust. When he was twelve, Sam's family was murdered by Germans in occupied-Poland. He managed to escape. He wrote about this in his book *Narrow Escapes: A Boy's Holocaust Memories and Their Legacy.* Importantly, Sam survived because various Polish families hid and helped him. Not all Polish families were like that, which made Sam especially grateful to those who assisted him. The fact that they had done so, while so many others had not, also raised questions that Sam has spent a lifetime pursuing: Why do some people help and rescue persons in need? Why are others indifferent to human suffering or even active in inflicting harm on people?

After the Holocaust, Sam Oliner found his way to the United States and became a social scientist. His studies, which often are carried out with his spouse Pearl, who is also a distinguished scholar, often focus on people who rescue women, children, and men from genocide and other crimes against humanity. Sam and Pearl Oliner want more and more people to be rescuers, so much so that the need for rescue would actually diminish because the world has become a kinder and gentler place. They believe, as I do, that studying the

Holocaust and genocide, difficult though it is to do, can sensitize us, make us more aware of the preciousness of human life, and help us to see that we need to stand with those who take the risks of rescue.

Sam Oliner is now in his eighties, but he continues to urge us to remember and honor those who do acts of rescue. Earlier this month, in fact, I read a new book by Sam. It is called *The Nature of Good and Evil*. For Sam Oliner, the difference between good and evil has everything to do with whether we respect or disrespect one another, whether we help or harm one another, whether we are kind or cruel to one another. He has asked me to write a foreword to his new book, which I am honored to do. As I do that writing, I am going to think of you at the Wootton Bassett School.

Not just on the Holocaust observance days that will take place in 2011 on January 27 and April 28 but each and every day, you have chances to be life-affirming, life-respecting rescuers in one way or another. I think your learning about the Holocaust and other genocides with the help of your wonderful teacher, Nicola Wetherall, is opening your eyes and your lives to that fact.

You may want to find out more about Sam Oliner. Try "googling" him on the Internet. Or look up his books on Amazon.com. In particular, you would find his *Narrow Escapes* well worth reading.

Thank you for letting me share some of my thoughts with you. I wish you all the best, and, again, I thank you for the good work you do, not only in your studies but also in your relationships with one another.

When Nicola Wetherall said "I am writing to you," that phrase stayed in my mind, particularly as I thought about Sam Oliner's *The Nature of Good and Evil*. His book is much more than an academic study, although it is packed with fine and wide-ranging scholarship as its clear writing explores not only the Holocaust but also the Armenian and Rwandan genocides and a discouragingly rising tide of hate crimes in our twenty-first century world. The tone and message of this book are intensely personal. Sam is writing to *you*, to *us*, bringing the insight and wisdom of his long and profound living to bear on our troubled times.

The world is besieged by destructive human behavior, but Sam testifies that it does not have to be that way, at least not so much, and he shows what is needed to make things better. More than that, while he does not shy away from the worst that human beings have done to one another, he points to people—many of them quite ordinary—who have stepped in to help and save when disaster strikes.

Oliner's book is action-packed and action-oriented. As he writes about events, he indicates that he takes *evil* to mean actions that have "negative moral consequences, which cause pain, injury or trouble to others." Such actions, he emphasizes, are "destructive, hurtful, corrupt and perverse." The *good* resists and combats the evil actions that seek to destroy it, and, for Oliner, the good means especially "helping others in need."

In writing to you, to me, to us, Sam Oliner simply and disarmingly asks people to help others in need. If everyone did so . . . well, that may be unrealistic and too much to ask, but maybe not, because if more people did so, the world might move closer to being a place where everyone did so.

E-mail that I receive from Sam Oliner often closes with one of his favorite quotations, which, he indicates, comes from an anonymous eighteenth-century source. I expect it is one that Nicola Wetherall would like as well.

> Life is short
> and we do not have too much time
> to gladden the hearts
> of those who travel the way with us,
> So be swift to love,
> Make haste to be kind.

Such is the hope and inspiration that can and should be found in the writing for you and me—for us—that Sam Oliner has done in *The Nature of Good and Evil*.

John K. Roth
Edward J. Sexton Professor Emeritus of Philosophy
Claremont McKenna College

Prologue

Psychologists, sociologists, historians, theologians, philosophers, journalists, novelists and others have written about the nature of good and evil. Though I and many others have dedicated our life's work to what motivates good and evil, the question remains: Why do some people choose one over the other? And more to the point, why should we revisit this question now? Though the rate of violent crime for the nation overall has gone down in recent years, hate crimes, by which I mean acts committed against another on the basis of race, ethnicity, social standing, or gender, show no signs of slowing down. In fact, they are on the rise.

For example, a recent report by *Southern Poverty Law Center* informs us that hate groups have increased since 2000 by 54 percent. That is substantial. There are now more than 900 different hate groups in this country, including the KKK, Neo-Nazi, White Nationalist, Racist Skinhead, Christian Identity, Neo-Confederate, Black Separatist, and other general hate groups.[1] Why the rise now? There are a variety of explanations, however, the following exemplifies a general reason for the increase which was, "fueled last year [2008] by immigration fears, a failing economy and the successful campaign of Barack Obama."[2] I believe the rise of these hate groups is related to a few factors working in tandem: we now have an African-American President for the first time in history, which ignited racist sentiment in many of these organized hate groups; an unprecedented economic crisis placed blame on Wall Street but reignited ethnic stereotyping of Jews; and the continuing disappearance of blue-collar jobs that are either being outsourced overseas or given to those workers who are willing to work for non-unionized, lower pay, such as legal and illegal immigrants.

So this book picks up where our other books left off at a much different time in history, when there have been both great strides made towards equality of opportunity for all, but also the resulting push-back of groups who feel threatened by this progress.[3] It is my hope that we can seek to understand why there is now a resurgence of hate crimes—human destructiveness against one's fellow man or woman—and also what motivates others to take the other, humane, moral path. This book will look to history, psychology, our previous research on goodness, and my personal experience as a twelve-year-old boy in Nazi-occupied Poland (throughout the book we use Nazi-occupied and German-occupied Europe interchangeably) where I witnessed good and evil. For example, the mass murder of my family, and being rescued by a compassionate Christian peasant woman. We will also analyze current examples of heroic behavior, which will help us understand what motivates, and drives people towards acting with compassion or to perpetrate evil.

By good we mean simply helping others in need of help from which the person in need benefits. A recent example of heroic behavior was exemplified in 2007 by Mr. Wesley Autrey who risked his life to save a student who fell onto the New York subway tracks after having a seizure. Another example took place in Washington, D.C. where Dimas Pinzon, a retired Marine, jumped on the subway tracks to save a man that fell.

By evil we mean an act that has negative moral consequences, which causes pain, injury, or trouble to others. It is an act of immorality that is destructive, hurtful, corrupt, and perverse. It is moral depravity. This type of pervasive, man-made behavior is found universally in most cultures and societies. A chilling example of evil was illustrated on July 13, 2010 when Michael Jerome Walker, after having an argument with his girlfriend while driving on a highway in Grapevine, Texas, pushed her child out of the car into oncoming traffic. Miraculously, the child did not die. We want to revisit the nature of evil and examine what is evil by giving examples such as the one above of unspeakable harm and hurt that ordinary human beings perpetrate upon others—ordinary people who were willing to follow malevolent authority and destroy innocent others. Throughout the book we will explore the nature of evil and how it has played out in several regions of the world, including the genocide in Rwanda, the Armenian genocide and the genocide, committed by the Nazis in Europe during World War II.

There is no single explanation for why people commit evil acts and there is no single explanation as to why people choose to risk their lives for others. Many social psychologists cite the impact of a person's childhood, while sociologists look at the importance of community and social and cultural norms.

Neither one provides a sufficient explanation on its own, but both are important. There are examples of how one who was brought up in a hate-filled environment can change when there is a compassionate intervention by others. For instance, hate-filled Klansman Larry Trapp (who was in a wheelchair) of Lincoln, Nebraska, greeted newly-arrived Rabbi Weisser with harassing messages calling him, "Jew Boy." The Rabbi decided to contact him asking him questions such as, "Larry, why do you love the Nazis so much? They'd have killed you first because you're disabled." One day Rabbi Weisser called and offered to help Mr. Trapp with his grocery shopping. Subsequent meetings resulted in Trapp apologizing to many groups he had threatened and denouncing the KKK.[4] This is one example of how caring and respect can transform someone full of hatred to one advocating against dehumanization of others.

We will also look at why people choose destructive behaviors and why they follow truly evil leaders—from Adolf Eichmann, the infamous Nazi responsible for officially transporting victims to their death to the followers of Jim Jones, the infamous cult leader. People are inclined to follow not only evil leaders, but evil ideologies as well. For instance, Heinrich Himmler, Hitler's right hand man, addressed the SS on October 4, 1943 and in that speech expressed Nazi ideology and encouraged the mass murder of Jews,

> ...I shall speak to you here with all frankness of a very serious subject. We shall now discuss it absolutely openly among ourselves, nevertheless we shall never speak of it in public. I mean the evacuation of the Jews, the extermination of the Jewish race.
>
> It is one of those things which is easy to say. 'The Jewish race is to be exterminated,' says every party member. 'That's clear, it's part of our program, elimination of the Jews, extermination, right, we'll do it.' And then they all come along, the eighty million good Germans and each one has his decent Jew. Of course the others are swine, but this one is a first-class Jew. Of all those who talk like this, not one has watched, not one has stood up to it.
>
> Most of you know what it means to see a hundred corpses lying together, five hundred, or a thousand. To have gone through this and yet—apart from a few exceptions, examples of human weakness—to have remained decent fellows, this is what has made

us hard. This is a glorious page in our history that has never been written and shall never be written.[5]

It is important to educate people about evildoers and mass murderers such as Tomas de Torquemada, also referred to as the Christian Inquisition's horror, was a religious bigot and cruel fanatic. He was made Grand Inquisitor by Pope Sixtus IV. He is known for torturing some 2,000 Jews by means of foot roasting, *garrucha* (suspension from the ceiling by the wrists) and suffocation. His hatred of Jews actually influenced King Ferdinand and Queen Isabella of Spain to expel all Jews who refused to embrace Christianity.

Robert G. Waite refers to Martin Luther, the founder of Lutheranism, and his book called *On the Jews and their Lies* (1543) that expressed hatred of Jews. It was influential in Hitler's hatred against Jews and was reflected in his book *Mein Kampf.* Luther promoted:

> First, to set fire to their synagogues or schools... Second, I advise that their houses also be razed and destroyed... Third, I advise that all their prayer books and Talmudic writings, in which such adultery, lies, cursing and blasphemy are taught, be taken from them... Seventh,.. Let whosoever can, throw brimstone and pitch upon them, so much the better...and if this be not enough, let them be driven like mad dogs out of the land.[6]

Ivan the Terrible was the first tsar of Russia. He constructed a Russian state and created an empire that included non-Slav states. During his reign he burned thousands of people in frying pans and impaled people.

Adolf Eichmann said, "The death of five million Jews on my conscience gives me extraordinary satisfaction." He was eventually hanged by the state of Israel for his part in the Nazi extermination of Jews during World War II.

Pol Pot was the Khmer political leader of Cambodia. He led a communist government that forced the mass evacuation of cities and he killed or displaced millions of people. During his reign the government was responsible for the death of one million people due to forced labor, starvation, torture, disease, or execution.

Mao Tse-tung killed between 20 and 67 million people. Despite his atrocities his picture still hangs in many homes and businesses throughout China.

The policies that were implemented during his leadership created anarchy and terror, which disrupted the urban economy. The industrial production for 1968 actually dipped 12 percent below that of 1966. The Revolution eventually led to a destruction of China's cultural heritage and an imprisonment of Chinese intellectuals.

Idi Amin was the president of Uganda from 1971–1979. He took the Uganda problem of tribalism to an extreme level by ordering the persecution of Acholi, Lango, and other tribes. He tortured and murdered between 100,000 to 300,000 people during his presidency. In 1972 he maintained that God had ordered him to expel Asians from Uganda. The reality of it was that he was retaliating against a prominent Asian family, the Madhvanis, in Uganda who refused to hand over one of their daughters to be his fifth wife. He ordered that political prisoners be decapitated on television. He also said the victims "must wear white to make it easy to see the blood." One of Amin's guards said that Amin used to lick the blood of his victims because he believed he wouldn't have nightmares if he did so.[7]

Joseph Stalin was a Soviet dictator for twenty-nine years. In the 1930s he ordered millions of peasants to either be killed or allowed to starve to death. During his dictatorship more than 20 million Soviets were killed. He induced famines to enforce farm collectives and eliminated perceived enemies through massive purges.

Genghis Khan was a Mongol warrior and ruler who eventually brought all the nomadic tribes of Mongolia under his military state. He massacred his defeated enemies in Asia and Europe in the early 1200s. When he attacked Volovoi he convinced the commander they would stop attacking if the city sent him 1,000 cats and several thousand swallows. He then tied cloth to their tails, lit the cloth on fire and sent the cats and birds back to the city lighting the city on fire. Genghis told his comrades, "man's greatest good fortune is to chase and defeat his enemy, seize his total possessions, leave his married women weeping and wailing, ride his gelding, use his women as a nightshirt and support, gazing upon and kissing their rosy breasts, sucking their lips which are sweet as the berries of their breasts."[8]

I have devoted a number of years to understanding the nature of good and evil. In 1990 Morton Hunt[9] visited Humboldt State University and interviewed me and some of my colleagues and friends attempting to understand why I am so focused on good and evil. Some colleagues who have read some of our published material have attempted to explain what "makes me tick." Among those evaluating me were Sociology Professor Paul Crosbie, who said, "Sam was an incredibly driven person...his intentions and his motives were so obviously good." Psychology Professor Jack Schaeffer said, "I have often wondered why Sam drove himself the way he did. My guess: Many Holocaust survivors have a sense of mission because they ask themselves why they're survivors while so many others died. Part of Sam's answers, I think, is to *contribute* something valuable." Rabbi Harold Schulweis puts it, "His work on rescuers was for him the therapy of knowledge. He found the spark of decency in human beings. It was a morally educative experience." Presbyterian minister Douglas Huneke says, "Sam had a sense of absolute urgency, of the great importance of the work. It was a sense of compelling passion with him, and a great fulfillment for him." Their evaluations may have some merit, and it may in some ways draw a profile of me. I don't believe I am obsessed, but I do feel strongly that not enough has yet been written about the nature of good and evil.

Chapter 1

Follow the Leader: Why Do People Go Against their Better Judgment?

ONE THING THAT CHARISMATIC LEADERS such as Stalin, Idi Amin, Pol Pot, or Jim Jones share is the ability to lead and to persuade people often against their own moral compass. For instance, during economic and political crisis, people long for a leader who will promise them a solution to their troubles. When Yugoslavia was in the state of dissolution of the federation, Milosevic found scapegoats and began to speak about the problems that were caused by the Islamic peoples in Kosovo. Using various propaganda tactics and cover-ups he attempted an "ethnic cleansing" of the Albanians of Kosovo. Among his tactics was his elaborate speech given at the Kosovo field where the battle between the Ottoman Empire and the Serbian Prince, Lazar Hrebeljanovic, took place in 1389. He implied that the Islamic conquest of the Balkans was tantamount to slavery of the Serbian people.

In their book, Covert Persuasion, Hogan and Speakman explain the reasons that lead people to follow a leader or an ideology that at an earlier time they might have found repugnant.1 These include the bandwagon effect. This is an approach which encourages people to join the "crowd" because it is an easy decision to go with the majority, as you get membership into a group who support one another's views, which extinguishes personal will and any sense of morality that came before. The bandwagon effect preys on the individuals who lack a sense of belonging and love in their family and social life. Jim Jones "preached a 'social gospel' of human freedom, equality, and love, which required helping the least and the lowliest of society's members. Later on, however, this gospel became explicitly socialistic, or communistic in Jones' own view, and the hypocrisy of white Christianity was ridiculed while 'apostolic socialism' was preached."2 The card stacking effect is a selective omission tactic used to manipulate people's reactions to a concept and convince them to follow an advocated action, or line of thinking. This tactic often tries to alter perceptions of the advocated action's consequences. During a war we only emphasize our victories, but omit our losses and defeats. This can be seen in every war that has been fought in order to convince people not to surrender. A recent example of a glittering generality used in political campaigns is a politician's tactic to "protect American jobs from immigrants." These are words that have positive meanings for the individual human being, but are linked to highly-valued concepts. When these words are used they demand approval, simply because such an important concept is involved. For example, in the defense of democracy in the United States many people would say it is "desirable to get rid of Communism because it inhibits individual freedoms." The *lesser of two evils technique* tries to convince people of an idea or proposal by presenting it as the least offensive option. It is often implemented during wartime to convince people of the need for sacrifices, or to justify difficult decisions by adding blame to an enemy, country, or political group. One idea or proposal is often depicted as the best option.[3] Name calling is the degradation of other people, products or ideas. It is also involved in contemporary society to demean the opposing group. Nazi Germany used the old canard, "the Jews, gypsies, homosexuals are our misfortune," which was used to demean these groups. Pinpointing the enemy is when one points out a group who causes "us" problems. Stalin pinpointed various individuals as enemies of the state opposing Soviet government policies. Jim Stachowiak, a longtime militia organizer, on his blog, calls Homeland Security Secretary Janet Napolitano a "Nazi-bitch."[4] Pinpointing using various media sources convinces the public, who is their enemy. For example, currently all Wall Street bankers have been blamed for the economic crisis that America is facing because of their greed and dishonesty. After 9/11, patriotism in the United States flourished and George W. Bush as well as other politicians used this to their advantage in initiating a war in Iraq by using the plain folks effect in order to emphasize that their agenda, to protect the American people from terrorism, was the same as the American people's. Plain folks effect are propaganda techniques which attempts to persuade the public that the views of the authoritative person reflect those of the common person because they are working for the same cause. Leaders employ this technique by using various tactics ranging from dressing casually, using simple words in speeches, or even incorrectly pronouncing words in order to portray themselves as the "Average Joe." This technique creates the idea that they are truly empathizing with the public, and in turn they receive support. Simplification, also known as stereotyping, is similar to pinpointing the enemy because it creates an "us" and "them" generalization for the public. "We" are good and "they" are evil, worthless, or lazy. During Hitler's regime, he stereotyped the Jews as greedy, and the cause of the problems in Europe. By stereotyping, Hitler was able to emphasize who the "enemy" was. Testimonials can also have a strong effect in a charismatic leader's arsenal. These are quotations or endorsements in or out of context, which attempt to connect a respectable and charismatic person with the idea of the product, the notion that "Fifty million Frenchmen cannot be wrong." Another example is the famous celebrity, Marie Osmond, saying, "Nutrisystem got me back on track, and I lost 50 pounds," or Tiger Woods saying, "Just Do It" as a spokesman for Nike.

Finally, the *transfer effect* is the idea that a person views an item in the same way they view another item, allowing the two to form a single subject in the person's mind. For example, just because there is a high incarceration rate for African-American men between the ages of 18 and 29, one would say all African-American men of this age were headed to prison. This method is often used to transfer feelings from one subject to another. In other words, when one condemns a member of a group, they usually condemn other members of that same group. Another example is the recent Wall Street scandals and resulting media pundits belief that if you know the behavior of one capitalist you know the behavior of all capitalists.

All of these reasons, or effects, in various mixes and proportions, lead people to follow leadership, to buy products, to condemn others, to stereotype others, to separate themselves from others, and to label people as "inferior" or "outsiders."

Evil is defined as an act that has negative moral consequences, which causes pain, injury, or trouble to others, it is not necessarily innate. It is an act of immorality; it is destructive, hurtful, corrupt and perverse. It is a kind of moral depravity. Philosophers, poets, theologians, social scientists, and others have spoken about the nature of evil.

Ervin Staub, in his book *The Roots of Evil: The Origin of Genocide and Other Group Violence*,[5] discusses the roots and nature of evil. He describes it as originating in a number of different sources of mistreatment of groups, which causes them grief, real or imagined. The examples that he offers are economic problems such as recession, inflation, and loss of jobs which threaten people's livelihoods. Hence, they retaliate against the immigrants because immigrants "take" their jobs. Cultural factors and personal pre-conditions, such as in-group/out-group feelings, as an aspect of culture, cause the in group to regard the out group as the enemy. Political factors, such as authoritarian or totalitarian governments may foster hatred and encourage genocide, as do evil leaders. Staub maintains that evil is not necessarily a scientific concept, but rather a part of a broadly shared human cultural heritage. It's part of our cultural heritage to oppose "evil" such as homosexuality. For example in 1998 Matthew Shepard was tortured and killed in Colorado by two men who targeted him because he was gay. Suffice it to say that the essential elements of evil are frequently the destruction of human beings. This does not only include killing, but the creation of conditions that materially or psychologically diminish a people's dignity, livelihood, happiness, and the capacity to fulfill basic material needs. But Staub, along with other social scientists, subscribes to the belief that humankind is capable of goodness and morality as well as selfishness and destructiveness towards others. And, along with other psychologists, Staub informs us that moral restraint is harder to achieve in groups than in individuals. Thus, people will commit more unspeakable horrors as members of groups than individual acts because of group dynamics that encourage violence and the role of anonymity.

It has been said in many different ways that man is an enemy-making animal. Not only is he an enemy-maker, but he is frequently an evil monster. For instance, Jeffrey Dahmer lured seventeen men and boys into his apartment and murdered them. Susan Smith, a thirty-year-old woman from South Carolina strapped her two young sons into the back seat of her car and drove them into a lake, drowning them. Hitler ordered the cold-blooded murder of millions, Pol Pot and the Khmer Rouge slaughtered 1.7 million in Cambodia, Timothy McVeigh murdered some 160 people in the Oklahoma City bombing, and thousands of other examples could easily be listed from various parts of the world where people hate and murder each other on a daily basis. One major explanation may be that there is something biologically awry in their brain circuitry, something at the level of instinct that induces violence, hatred, and megalomania in humans, especially by political ideologues such as Stalin, Mao, and Hitler. In Munich, Germany, there is a 1922 memorandum of a conversation with Adolph Hitler, who reportedly went into a rage on hearing the word "Jew." Hitler said:

> As soon as I have power, I shall have gallows after gallows erected. For example, in Munich in the Marianplatz, all Jews will be hanged, one after another, and they will stay hanging until they stink. They will stay hanging as long as hygienically possible. As soon as they are untied, then the next group will follow and will continue until the last Jew in Munich is destroyed. Exactly the same procedure will follow in other cities until Germany is cleansed, purified of the last Jew.[6]

Later, in the 1940s, he put his rage into practice by launching the destruction of European Jews. Bolsheviks, Jewish capitalists, and the bourgeoisie elites as well as the betrayal by the allies who brutally punished the German people for the Versailles Treaty gave Hitler the opportunity to scapegoat Jews, gays, gypsies, and those who politically opposed him.

Alice Miller describes Hitler's personality and the origins of his unspeakable cruelties in her book *For Your Own Good: Hidden Cruelty in Child-Rearing and the Roots of Violence*, she says,

> Hitler never had a single other human being in whom he could confide his true feelings; he was not only mistreated but also prevented from experiencing and expressing his pain; he didn't have any children who could have served as objects for abreacting his hatred; and, finally, his lack of education did not allow him to ward off his hatred by intellectualizing it. Had a single one of these factors been different, perhaps he would never have become the arch-criminal he did.[7]

Another example of evil is Osama bin Laden's attack on the United States on September 11, 2001, when three thousand innocent people died in the World Trade Center. Bin Laden has been quoted as saying, "Every American man is an enemy to us," and "Hostility toward America is a religious duty, and we hope to be rewarded for it by God . . . . I am confident that Muslims will be able to end the legend of the so-called superpower that is America."

James Aho, a sociologist, speaks of the enemy and how he or she is socially constructed, that is, he focuses on various aspects of evil, including groups of people who are enemy making which includes propagandists, ideologues, and organizations, which are involved in defaming others, for example, minorities such as Jews and gypsies during the Holocaust.[8] The focus of these hate groups is to defame others who they define as less than human.

In the twentieth century alone—a span of a hundred years—more than 100 million people have been slaughtered in various wars, rebellions, genocides and massacres. Modern military technology makes killing and mass murder antiseptic, covered up by euphemisms such as "collateral damage" when innocent bystanders are killed, as in the almost daily bombings in Afghanistan and Iraq. The Holocaust, perhaps the most documented human genocide in all of history, has exposed the capability of human depravity and shown how ordinary people can become killers.

There are many who explain how evil deeds and mass destruction can occur. It is very difficult for "normal" people to fathom the evil acts of destruction that some human beings are capable of. But they do occur. Opotow addresses the mechanisms of moral exclusion of certain groups of people.[9] Hilberg details the methodology of the destruction of European Jewry.[10] Browning describes how ordinary men can be made to murder the innocent, specifically in the extermination of Jews in Poland.[11] Goldhagen addresses that Hitler couldn't have committed this mass murder without the German people being willing executioners.[12] Felice describes how fascist ideology can be introduced effectively to people who have economic and political problems.[13] Gilbert, the British scholar, has a detailed history of the European Jews during the Holocaust.[14] Israeli scholar Bauer made an early contribution to the history of the Holocaust.[15] Wyman addresses how countries abandoned the Jews during their plight from 1941–1945.[16] Wiesel, a Nobel Prize winner and Holocaust survivor, informed the world about the devastating nature of evil.[17] Lipstadt has addressed a group of current pervasive individuals who have written that the Holocaust is a hoax and denied that it ever took place.[18] Dawidowicz has addressed the war against the Jews in various historical periods.[19] Malcolm Hay, British scholar Anthony Julius, and Robert Wistrich document the historical Christian hatred of Jews for the last two thousand years.[20] Baron has written on the history of the context of rescue during Nazi-occupied Europe.[21] Oliner has addressed the issue of how ordinary people can perform extraordinary acts to help others.[22]

EXAMPLES OF EVIL

By evil behavior I am referring to a deliberate harming of people who are considered by the harm doer as outsiders.

When people are bystanders, the implication is that no one cares about a poor minority group in a remote country. The world is largely made up of bystanders. This is true in the case of the Rwandan genocide of 1994 where 800,000 people were massacred.

On April 6, 1994 the Rwandan president Habyarimana and Burundi's president Ntaryamira held several peace meetings with the Tutsi rebels. Violence started when their plane was shot down on returning from the meetings, and for the next 100 days Hutu militias killed hundreds of thousands of Tutsis, often using machetes and clubs while the observers in Rwanda appealed to the UN several times to try to stop the killing. Without opposition, the Hutus embarked on an orgy of mass destruction. Not only did they kill innocent Tutsi men, women, and children, but also any Hutus who opposed the slaughter or who tried to rescue Tutsis from danger.

Responsibility for this massacre may clearly be placed on the shoulders of the UN and the leaders of the western democracies—the United States and Britain foremost—because of the abundant warning they had that such a massacre was impending, and because of their inaction as it was being conducted. The United States and Britain took the role of bystander as hundreds of thousands were dying, while peacekeeping soldiers were informing their own countries of the atrocities. The UN stood by because it wasn't in their interest to act. This was a definite lack of moral integrity.

Currently, there are attempts at reconciliation. The UN has finally publicly admitted that their leadership failed. Kofi Annan, Secretary General of the United Nations (1997-2006), personally apologized for the tragedy that occurred because leaders allowed caring, compassion, and social justice to take an extended holiday.

In the next chapter, "Manifestations of Radical Evil," we look more closely at the factors that led up to acts of horror as with the atrocities in Rwanda. First, we consider the psychopathological approach. Certain leaders, who are psychologically evil, are capable of mass murder because they feel that they are on the right side of history and "other" people need to be exterminated because they are considered to be a surplus population.

Another explanatory factor for evil is cultural factors, which consists of the values and norms of a culture that have contributed to the separation of people by labeling some as "others," or "they are not part of our people." Culture also produces certain personality characteristics, such as the authoritarian person who is rigid and may be producing individuals to obey authority and/or to internalize bigotry. The cultural components of evil have all kinds of sources including writers, priests, ministers and other people who are committing to paper ideas and ideologies, which claim infallibility and at the same time condemns those who are considered the outsider, such as homosexuals, for example, the pedophilia sex scandals of Catholic priests and the cover-up by the diocese.

Another factor we will consider is the importance of historical and cultural contexts and how they can be present in such a way that leaders can arise because of social and economic disruptions, or social problems. Leaders such as Hitler, Stalin, and Pol Pot were able to take advantage of the political, economic, and social distress and install themselves in positions of power. They seized power and decided that segments of the population were undesirable and were considered surplus populations who did not deserve to walk on this earth. When a situation arises where stereotyping and scapegoating become prevalent, evil leaders can encourage people to start destroying others. These situations of distress encourage violence, and utilization of modern technology such as the use of gas, and media to promote hatred and enable mass killings.

There are also individual characters that have pathological conditions and commit mass murder on an individual basis. For instance, Jeffrey Dahmer murdered a group of people and put them into his freezer after he cut up their bodies. Philosopher Martin Heidegger was propounding the Nazi philosophy that some groups are meant to be superior where other groups of people have slave mentalities.

In Chapter 2 we use narratives to understand evil from the Armenian genocide of 1915, the Holocaust, and destruction of other human beings. We also address social psychological philosophies of evil and how ordinary human beings commit extraordinary acts of evil. Experiments done by Philip Zimbardo as well as the famous Stanley Milgram Experiment of 1962 known as the Obedience Experiment conducted at Yale University showed that when people found themselves in a specific kind of role and were encouraged to perform acts of harm to others, they were more likely to do so.

Chapter 3 addresses the role of the bystander. One of the important observations that have been made in the literature by philosophers and other observers is that when people stand by witnessing a horror and injustice and do nothing, it encourages evil to be perpetrated. In a sense, bystanders give unspoken approval of the act of evil. The issue that this chapter concerns itself with is the different types of bystanders, reviewing the literature of actual events that have occurred where bystanders did nothing when others were being killed. For example, in 1964 Kitty Genovese was assaulted outside of an apartment building in Queens, New York, and despite people hearing her scream for help, no one did anything. There was another horrifying incident in 2009 where a fifteen-year-old girl was gang raped and beaten in Richmond, California, outside of her high school homecoming dance while more than twenty people watched.

There are also innocent bystanders of people who do not know much. This too causes a problem because nations act as bystanders by looking the other way while evil is being perpetrated. They find any excuse not to get involved in the internal affairs of other countries. The question that Chapter 3 addresses is how can we move people from the role and position of bystander to that of helper?

Chapters 4 and 5 address the nature of resistance to evil in several genocides. We also discern a number of different types of resistance, including rescue. Each of these genocides discussed have unique characteristics that reflect the specific historical and contemporary conditions present in each area. There are some common negative themes that lea to these genocides of the Twentieth Century (See Appendix 1). While chapter 4 primarily focuses on resistance during the Holocaust, chapter 5 focuses on resistance during the Armenian and Rwandan genocides. Historians and others make important observations that evil prevails because many people are bystanders.

Chapter 6 deals with the nature of goodness, in which we emphasize that there is no single explanation why people do ordinary acts of goodness as well as extraordinary acts of heroism. Essentially we divide goodness into different types. *Type 1* would be risking one's life for a stranger. *Type 2* would be intervention on behalf of oppressed people. *Type 3* is getting involved in actions that benefit the environment and all living things. *Type 4* is volunteering on a regular basis to help humanity in various settings. *Type 5* is typical acts of ordinary kindness towards human beings. As in the other chapters, this chapter gives examples of real people by the acts of kindness and persistence that made a difference. Examples of Rosa Parks, Bishop Tutu, Martin Luther King, 1992 Nobel Prize winner Rigoberta Menchu Tum, who publicized the plight of Guatemala's indigenous peoples during and after the Guatemalan Civil War, and others have been featured as moral exemplars that have tried to improve the world in which we live in.

Chapter 7 deals with heroism. We see a connection between moral heroism and general goodness. We divide heroism into different typologies from risking one's life for others to ordinary acts of helping. A particularly heroic act occurred in 2007 when a mentally-ill student named Seung-Hui Cho went on a shooting rampage at Virginia Tech. Romanian-born professor and Nazi camp survivor, Liviu Librescu attempted to protect his students from the shooter by barricading the doorway with his body. His students were able to escape through the window while he was gunned down. We focus on not only martyr heroes, but also Carnegie heroes who are recognized by the Carnegie Heroes Fund for risking their lives for a total stranger, and a variety of local heroes who have made a difference in society as well. We try to distinguish between moral heroes, that is, heroes that act on behalf of the welfare of others as well as evil heroes who act destructively for their own individualistic and psychopathological reasons.

In Chapter 8, we ask what road we have traveled in this book, and make some suggestions to help bring about a caring society. We know that evil will always exist and we cannot completely banish it. However, what we can do is try again and again to educate people on how they can contribute to a more compassionate, peaceful, and just society.

Chapter 2

How Could They Do That? Understanding the Many Sources and Faces of Evil

GENOCIDE, CHILD ABUSE, HATE CRIMES. Why do these occur? Is it biological, cultural, or a mix of both? What makes someone kidnap and imprison a young girl for nearly twenty years in his backyard? Why were so many killed and buried in mass graves in Rwanda? And why were so many Jews rounded up and sent to their deaths during the Holocaust?

In this chapter we will explore the attributes of evil as a way to make some meaning out of what seems to be the most aberrant of behaviors, yet have been with us for centuries.

We suggest a new approach to understanding evil using actual narratives. Human beings have always exhibited a variety of harmful behaviors toward other people and all other living things, including the environment. These harmful human behaviors range from denying human beings a livelihood to depriving dignity and justice. A few examples include slavery, prejudice, racism, sexism, and ageism, to exploitation of humans and animals. A contemporary example of exploitation is bringing young women from other countries to work as prostitutes and/or indentured servants to this country, and enslaving them with no means of escape. Regarding evil towards animals, I am referring to the extermination of animals by depletion of their environment for economic gain, such as with the BP oil spill, or deforestation in the Amazon for cattle pastures. Especially important today are the ever-present effects of global climate change, which are a result of blatant disregard for the treatment of the environment. Beyond the evils of human rights violations, we are increasingly seeing the effects on the earth in the form of floods, forest fires, desertification, and other forms of environmental degradation.

There is an age-old debate between what is regarded as universal morality and relative morality. Universal morality claims that morality is not flexible when it comes to perpetration of harm to the innocent. Good or evil can be determined by examining what is commonly considered evil amongst all humans. Moral relativism maintains that standards of good and evil are a product of specific culture, customs, and prejudices. There is also an attempt to find a compromise between the relative sense of morality and the universal sense of morality.

A psychological definition of evil by Phillip Zimbardo states, "evil consists of intentionally behaving in ways that harm, abuse, demean, dehumanize, or destroy innocent others, or using one's authority and systematic power to encourage or permit others to do so on your behalf."[1] This is a behaviorally-focused definition that excludes accidental or unintended outcomes and generic forms of institutional evil such as poverty, prejudice, or destruction of the environment. It also includes corporate wrongdoing, such as the tobacco companies marketing cancer-inducing products. The definition also includes agents of authority (military tyrants such as Pol Pot, and Idi Amin). Karl Marx pointed out that some people do not realize the state of their oppression, and suffer from false consciousness. For example, being a servant in Czarist Russia was accepted for centuries as one's status and destiny.

We seek to transcend the relativism that seems to underlie much of the discussion of evil today. Some groups claim that the term evil is relative or inappropriate. For instance, what was good for the German people when Hitler came to power was destructive to others such as the conquered peoples of Europe, specifically gypsies, Jews, gays, and intellectuals. We recognize a universally accepted definition of evil: deliberate acts which knowingly result in harm to innocent others, are universally reprehensible, morally corrupt, and destructive to life.

This can be understood on a continuum from typical evil to radical evil. We distinguish between "typical" and "radical" forms of evil. Typical acts of evil may be the murder of an individual, racism, or any such destructive harm or human degradation, such as bullying and hate crimes. Radical evil is "bigger" than one actor committing a single act, such as the Holocaust or the genocide in Rwanda, and other places. James Waller gives examples of radical evil perpetrated on victims in Mauthausen concentration camp and the mass killing of Jews in the ravine near Kiev called Babi Yar as well as other places.[2] For example, Maria Pia Lara's edited volume *Rethinking Evil* collects thoughts from several scholars who make an important distinction between *typical* evil and *radical* evil.[3] The distinction is not merely one of *scale*, although the consequences of radical evil are generally more widespread and are more serious. Rather, typical evil consists of acts that cause harm to others, but are not intended to dehumanize or murder an entire group. Typical evil might encompass, for example, robbery or assault, or perhaps the use of a racial epithet during a heated argument. Radical evil, on the other hand, involves actions of more than one person that the vast majority of humans would find reprehensible, such as genocide, ethnic cleansing, and race-based oppression. Radical evil transcends the individual.

Svetlana Broz gives examples of complicity of ordinary people and sometimes neighbors in the destruction of those considered enemies during the Bosnian war.[4] In Bosnia, this was the Islamic population, and in Rwanda, the Tutsis. Lionel Tiger addresses heinous crimes against others, dehumanization, and scapegoating against a group of people when societies experience economic troubles and humiliation such as the Germans did after World War I.[5]

Hannah Arendt described another form of evil which she called the "banality" of evil as represented by Adolf Eichmann who effectively transported Jews to their death into extermination and concentration camps.[6] He may or may not have been a racist or an anti-Semite, but uncritically obeyed a malevolent authority. The Holocaust may be viewed as a watershed in the phenomenon of evil that involved blind and unquestioning obedience to authority.

This chapter will also focus on the leaders who initiate and encourage radical evil. Adolf Hitler, Saddam Hussein, and Josef Stalin represent examples of ideological leaders who issued orders directly or indirectly, without feeling remorse, for the mass destruction of innocent human life. We argue that an important methodological approach to understanding the nature of radical evil is through narratives, as they help us to gain insight into the causes and consequences of moral and immoral behavior, and often serve as general metaphors for understanding society. It is through stories that we tend to think of the events in our own lives, and we tend to remember and analyze events best using narratives. We place the work published since the 1960s on dehumanization, obedience, roles, situations, and group dynamics into the context of a social-psychological framework to explain how some people commit banal and extraordinary evil. A contemporary example of this is the operations of the Taliban, who organize terrorist acts based on religious intolerance and their belief that their religion is God's true law.

PSYCHOPATHOLOGICAL APPROACH

We focus first on several types of explanations for evil. The first is a **psychopathological approach,** which explains how leaders with a disturbed personality and the right social conditions can motivate people to denigrate and murder others. This is true under the leadership of Pol Pot and the genocide in Cambodia, the Holocaust under Hitler, the destruction of the Kulaks under Stalin, and Pauline Nyiramasuhuko the Minister of Women in Rwanda, who ordered the systematic rape and murder of Tutsi women during the 1994 genocide. This process consists of dehumanization of people, based on their different religious beliefs, their gender, or their social class. Some leaders who act out evil are nearly always charismatic in their leadership and can arouse their populations to destroy innocent others. This sort of pathology is a top down bureaucratic structure based on central figures which leads to negative ends on a large-scale. In his book, *The Holocaust and Other Genocides in the 20th Century: Social Processes and Mechanisms that Lead to Mass Killings,*[7] Sippy Naveh provides a model of processes to help explain how leaders perpetrate evil against others.

(I) Cognitive process: (a) Instilling of ideology/propaganda—"the just cause"—and all the methods for achieving it are valid: "the end justifies the means;" (b) Dehumanization and demonization—perceiving the "Other" as an enemy, as inferior, evil, cruel, dangerous, threatening, and therefore deserving to die.

(II)   Affective (Emotional) process: Feelings of hostility, contempt, vengeance, anger, along with feelings of fear and peril.

(III)   Behavioral process (a graduated progression): (a) separation, distancing, isolation; (b) discrimination, denial of civil and human rights; (c) Humiliation, abuse, repression; and (d) physical harm, torture, murder, extermination.

Cultural Approach

The second are **cultural factors,** which help to understand traditional conflict and dehumanization of certain groups. Traditional beliefs of cultures can lead to destructive ends. The albino population in Tanzania is an example of the cultural murder of innocent people. In Tanzania there is a superstition that albinos (people lacking pigment in their skin) contain some magical essence and their body parts are sought after by witchdoctors for certain cultural rituals. There are less extreme examples of destructive cultural beliefs leveled against outsiders. Among them are such examples as ethnocentrism, xenophobia, racism, stereotyping, enslavement, and moral exclusionary practices. In order to transform Cambodian society, Pol Pot had to drive out urban people into rural areas making them farmers and peasants, which resulted in the murder and starvation of one and a half million Cambodian people. This is frequently regarded as auto-genocide, which means that some groups of people exterminate their own groups instead of outsiders. In the case of Nazis, it was superfluous members of the population that stood in the way of a new world order such as Jews, Bolsheviks, gypsies, and other undesirables.[8]

Punishment is the social medium through which the practices of social actors, groups, and institutions are meaningfully and effectively related to the category of evil. It is through punishment that evil is naturalized and recognized. Punishment essentializes evil, making it appear to emerge from actual behaviors and identities rather than being socially and culturally imposed on them. For example the Kulaks (well-off Russian peasants) who did not want to give up their land to collective farms in 1929 were severely punished by being expelled from the land to labor camps, imprisoned, or killed by the communist leaders when they took power.

There is an exhaustible amount of information that contributes to what scholars consider evil and its attributes. At this point a discussion of evil and its attributes is warranted. Among them are malicious acts that cause ruin, injury, pain, suffering, destruction and harm. In Buddhism this means acts that cause human suffering of various sorts. Plato argues that evil is merely ignorance and that which is good is what everyone desires.[9] Spinoza maintains that the difference between good and evil is merely one of personal inclination.

In political spheres, evil is caused by tyrannical and pathological leaders such as Josef Stalin of the Soviet Union who was paranoid and feared future enemies. Machiavelli favored a princedom that created a climate of fear in order to rule a population, instead of relying on popular support. He further maintained that deception and manipulation are the means to creating a prince's personal power, so the prince should have little concern for traditional moral and ethical considerations, essentially meaning the end justifies the means.

Robert Bellah, in *Evil and the American Ethos,* maintains that achievement and success for climbing up the ladder is part of the American ethos which divides us into "we" and "they."[10] Frequently, when people experience certain pressures, they separate from each other and sometimes become violent towards the out-group. Even today, all these years later, we can see this occurring with the Aryan Nation and White Supremacy in their attitudes towards minorities and new immigrants.

Roy Baumeister, *Evil: Inside Human Violence and Cruelty*, identifies the causes of evil as being displaced idealistic adherence to a creed or a doctrine to provide sadistic pleasure.[11] He applies this framework to analyze diverse evils: murder, rape, street crime, war, government oppression, and racial and ethnic hatred. He emphasizes evil grows and spreads when cultures stop restraining violent impulses that lead to *desensitization* and a desire for revenge.

Nevitt Sanford, co-author of *The Authoritarian Personality* and author of *Authoritarianism and Social Destructiveness*, sees that the kind of upbringing a person experiences can lead him or her to destructive impulses and acts against others.[12] Prejudice against an out-group is a central component of the book. Ethnocentrism, Sanford maintains, is rigorous adherence to conventional values, submissiveness towards the moral authority of the in-group, the readiness of the in-group to punish the slightest breach of conventional values opposing to the subjective, imaginative, or tender-minded, and inability or unwillingness to deal with the indefinite, ambiguous, or probable, such as the opposition to legalization of gay marriage.

Richard Rubenstein in *The Cunning of History* maintains that several situational factors are responsible for mass murder.[13] In order to understand more fully the connection between bureaucracy and mass death, it will be necessary to turn to the stateless or denationalization and loss of citizenship and their human rights. The Jews were among the first modern Europeans who had become politically and legally superfluous and were considered surplus populations for whom the most "rational" way of dealing with them was ultimately genocide.

According to the Nazis, Jews were the enemy of racially-pure Germans. This was the construction of Jews as an out-group and target for the anger and fear felt by so many after World War I.[14] The Nazis had taken advantage of historical anti-Semitism in much of Europe to successfully make Jews "the enemy." This campaign included some of the first organized, scientific attempts at propaganda, much of it aimed at reducing Jews to the status of animals.[15] One must look at only a few of these propaganda posters to see the insidious psychology at work. Whether Jews were pictured as rats or caricatured as degenerates trying to steal the innocence from fresh-faced German maidens, this was no intellectual argument over historical events, but rather the exacerbation of a centuries-old enmity between Jews and Christians. Jews were an easy target to be used as a scapegoat, and the German people, for the most part, swallowed the propaganda as fed to them by the charismatic Hitler and his total control of German education and mass media.

German culture and history played other roles as well. First of all, Germans were well trained to follow authority. After several Kaisers and a long line of authoritarian petty princes, the German people were divided along lines of class and were required to follow the rules. The Kaiser, although not considered "infallible" in the sense of the Pope, still commanded great loyalty, and was assumed to be the embodiment of the people. Traditional German culture helped Germany to develop into an orderly and bureaucratic society. German farmers raked the forest floor to keep it clean. Underlings were expected to implement the orders of their leaders. Strong leaders gave orders and expected them to be followed. And we cannot dismiss the long-term cultural effects of anti-Semitism. Malcolm Hay cites the existence of two thousand years of Christian hatred and oppression of Jews and documents the evil acts that such a system of beliefs has engendered, and Hitler's Germans inherited those feelings and beliefs.[16] Concentrated in pre-war Germany, and distilled through the chaos and hardships of that era, these social structural characteristics contributed to the propensity of its inhabitants to take up traditional German anti-Semitism and implement it as a national crusade to kill Jews.

Similarly, the Rwandan genocide of 1994, where Hutus massacred 800,000 Tutsis, arose from such underlying cultural and political factors. The United Nations ignored the many warning signs that Hutu nationalists were looking for any excuse to exterminate the Tutsi. The genocide began on April 6, 1994, and for the next 100 days Hutu militias killed hundreds of thousands of Tutsis, often using machetes and clubs. The Hutus claimed the Tutsi's possessed power disproportionate to their percentage of the population, and were favored politically by the Belgian colonizers. Historical tribal animosities present a sticky situation when examining contemporary evils. It would be oversimplified to label the Hutu actions as evil and destructive when viewed as a standalone event. Contextually we find a much more nuanced and complicated tribal conflict that dates back for centuries.

There was evidence that genocidal massacres were being planned by the Hutus. The UN dispatched a woefully inadequate multinational peacekeeping force of 2,500 soldiers to attempt to preserve the fragile ceasefire between the tribes, but Hutu extremists, who were violently opposed to sharing any power with the Tutsi minority, destroyed the possibilities for peace. Among the extremists were those who favored total extermination of the Tutsis. They were outraged that Rwandan president Habyarimana and the President of Burundi (a neighboring country with a Tutsi government) held several peace meetings with the Tutsis. While returning from such a meeting in Tanzania, on April 6th 1994, the two presidents were killed when shoulder-fired missiles shot down their small jet on approach to Rwanda's main airport in Kigali. This gave Hutu extremists the opportunity to unleash the simmering violence by spreading news that Tutsis had shot down the plane. It is now assumed that it was actually the Hutu forces themselves that killed the leaders who were seeking peace in the region. The violence started almost immediately. Leaders and observers appealed to the UN several times to try to stop the killing, but the small peacekeeping force was hopelessly outnumbered and completely unable to effect any sense of order. In fact, the Security Council voted unanimously to abandon Rwanda, and to immediately withdraw the small force to safety. Without opposition, the Hutus embarked on an orgy of mass destruction. Not only did they kill innocent Tutsi men, women, and children, but also any Hutus who opposed the slaughter or who tried to rescue Tutsis from danger. Responsibility for allowing this massacre to reach the crescendo it did may clearly be placed on the shoulders of the UN. The leaders of the Western democracies—including the United States and Britain—had abundant warning that such a massacre was impending, and it was their inaction that allowed it to happen. Many trace the reason for the inability of the West to act to a latent structural racism, and that is certainly of note here.[17] But the true horror of this genocide is the speed with which the latent hatred was translated into brutal machete killings.

Historical tribal animosity, the perception of oppression of one group by the other, and the encouragement by hate-filled political leaders all coalesced into the actual massacres of this genocide. Government-controlled Rwandan radio urged Hutus to act against Tutsi "vermin." One radio broadcast exhorted slaughter of the Tutsi:

> We have to kill the Tutsi. They are cockroaches. All those who are listening, rise, so we can fight for our Rwanda, fight with weapons that you have at your disposal, call on those who have arrows to use arrows, those who have spears to use their spears, we must fight. We must finish them, exterminate them, sweep them from our whole country, there must be no refuge for them. They must be exterminated, there is no other way. No mercy should be shown to them because mercy is a sign of weakness.[18]

The entire process of the Rwandan massacres is similar in some ways to that of the Holocaust. The Hutus went to great lengths to dehumanize the

Tutsis. Extreme ideological leaders authorized the destruction of these ene-mies, and the process became a daily routine until there were very few Tutsis left to hunt down.

Erich Fromm, along with Freud and Konrad Lorenz, maintains that human beings may have an instinct or predisposition for destructiveness.[19] Freud cites Lorenz's material which tells us that aggression is instinctive and can be con-trolled only under social conditions. Recently, much research focuses on vio-lence and aggression as being biologically based in certain individuals. On the other hand Skinner's neo-behavioralism shows stimulus responds to reward and punishment, which may affect human behavior. Along with sociologists and others, he maintains that our environment can influence evil or non-evil. For example the *Einzatzggrupen* (mobile killing units during the Holocaust) would be rewarded with liquor and cigarettes after mass killings, and those who refused to participate were punished by being sent to the Russian front. In 1941 a group of fourteen Yugoslav civilians were to be executed for resis-tance. German Corporal Josef Schultz refused to join his fellow soldiers in the killing unit. Citing his defiance, the commanding officer had him line up along with the victims and he was executed.

THE SITUATIONAL PERSPECTIVE

Philip Zimbardo maintains that there is an under-recognized power of social situations to alter the mental situation and behavior of individuals, groups, and nations such as the recent banking crisis in the United States.[20] Zimbardo focuses on how good ordinary people can be induced into unspeakable forms of destructive behavior. There are central conditions which provide some insight, rather than focusing on the individual and their pathology. The psychology of deindividuation, which is "anything that makes a person feel anonymous, thereby reducing personal accountability, responsibility, and self-monitoring,"[21] creates the potential for that person to act in evil ways.

The situational factors illustrated in the Stanford Prison Experiment in 1971 showed how the placement of roles (guards or prisoners) under assigned tasks had the potential to transform ordinary people into abusive authoritar-ian figures. Using realistic methods, a group of young men were placed in the roles of prisoners and guards in a mock prison. The experiment was intended to test the subjects' reactions to power dynamics in this extreme social situation, and researchers soon saw the lengths to which the guards would go to break the will of the prisoners. The experiment eventually had to be halted early because of the increasingly disturbing behavior of the guards such as cruelty, disrespect, and verbal abuse towards the "prisoners." Zimbardo found that—to a great extent—the role made the person. In a few days Zimbardo noticed the subjects in the experiment *became* guards and prisoners. The results from this experiment suggests that power can short-circuit the moral make-up of individuals, and can lead them to commit monstrous deeds within the demands of their role.

During a conversation with the most aggressive of the guards at a debriefing session held some months after the experiment, Prisoner #819, a leader in the revolt against the guards, makes some interesting observations. The guard admits to conducting his own experiment to see how far the prisoners would let him go in his brutality, and then asks the prisoner how he thinks *he* would have acted if he had been a guard. The prisoner replies that he hopes that he wouldn't have been so creative in his brutality, and that he would not have enjoyed it.[22]

In "A Situationist Perspective on the Psychology of Evil," Zimbardo shares a personal letter from a student who viewed the slide show of his prison experiment. He writes that the slide show had him in tears, and he compared the treatment of prisoners to the treatment he received at the hands of drill instructors in Marine Corps boot camp:

> One incident stands out in an effort to break platoon solidarity, I was forced to sit in the middle of my squad bay (living quarters) and shout to the other recruits, "If you guys would have moved faster, we wouldn't be doing this for hours," referencing every single other recruit holding over their heads very heavy foot lockers. The event was very similar to the prisoners [in the Zimbardo experiment] saying #819 was a bad prisoner...Other behaviors come to mind like the push-ups for punishment, shaved heads, not having any identity...[23]

Christopher Browning illustrates the situational perspective in his book Ordinary Men about Police Battalion 101 and the final solution in Poland.24

Browning managed to interview individual members of Battalion 101 who participated in the killing of Jews in several cities in Poland. Because of peer group pressure, and ideological indoctrinations such as, "Jews were poisoning German blood," they were willing to participate in the murder of the Jews. Jews were regarded as enemies by the Nazis who used the slogan first coined by historian and political writer Heinrich von Treitschke (1834-1896) *"Die Juden sind unser Unglück!" (Jews are our Misfortune)*.25

Psychologist Marshall Rosenberg claims that the concept of irrational labeling is the root of exclusion of others.[26] When we label a group as bad or evil, Rosenberg claims it evokes a desire to punish or inflict pain. It also makes it easy for some to turn off feelings toward the person who is being harmed. He links the concept of evil to the United States judicial system which seeks to create justice through punishment. He contrasts this approach with what he found in cultures where the idea of evil is non-existent. In such cultures, when someone harms another person they are believed to be out of harmony with themselves and their community—they are seen as sick or ill. Measures are then taken to restore that person to a harmonious relationship by actions such as counseling, and rituals dealing with the restoration of harmony as opposed to punishing them.

Other types of evil consist of personal actions that use others as a means to achieve one's own personal ends or fail to consider the lives of others. This sort of behavior is considered by some to be psychopathic or sociopathic. Scholars such a Zygmunt Bauman explain the Holocaust as one of the major evils of recent history. It is an extreme manifestation of technocratic modern rationality.[27]

Evil frequently evolves through stages. For instance, Holocaust scholars see the first stage of evil as the pervasive anti-Semitism and scapegoating of the other, including communists, homosexuals, and gypsies. The next stage led to establishing *Dachau* and throwing enemies into the concentration camp. *Kristallnacht* (1938) (The Night of the Broken Glass) further led to the sequential stages of evil, which then resulted in major genocide. Evil perpetrators or leaders emphasize the good in their own people and the evil in "others" creating an in-group out-group dichotomy. They use stereotypes and ignorance in order to convince people who the real enemy is. The use of clever propaganda and state-controlled mass media to dehumanize those considered inferior facilitates bystanders and enables evil to flourish.

In his book *Panoramas of Evil*, Leonard Doob gives us a variety of generalizations that could be defined as evil.[28] Disease, poverty, forces of nature, anything that we dread contrary to equality and mercy is correlated with evil. Interestingly, he also says that sometimes victims bring victimization on themselves by not combating the coming oppression. He does not blame the victim, but places a portion of the responsibility for the consequences on their shoulders because they did not act against retaliation. This evaluation is not plausible to all situations because there is evidence of resistance in cases such as the Holocaust, Rwandan, and Armenian genocides. He also talks about goodness and lists rationale and purposes in life, celebration of life, self esteem, recognition of beauty, and human rights.

Some scholars focus on the mind to explain evil. Sigmund Freud was perhaps the first to point to pathology of the mind that may lead to brutal acts, although he avoided the term "evil." He blamed unresolved, unconscious issues in the psyche for such acts. Paul Vincent maintains that the attributes of the "genocidal mind" are not necessarily psychotic, although some may be sadistic. The genocidal mind has acquired certain attitudes from his or her culture.[29] Vincent attempts to differentiate between pathology and a predisposition toward participating in evil. He argues that one of the attributes of evil may be adherence to an ideology that breeds illusions, fantasies, and forms of irrational behavior, devoid of spirituality, compassion, or moral mooring. Such a monistic or highly reductionist view of the world leads to racism, anti-Semitism, and other forms of oppression. While men do not commit radical evil by themselves, there is still no question that individuals are the perpetrators of mass genocide. Specifically, for radical evil to occur, it seems necessary for an ideology to be present. One example given is General George Patton being reprimanded by Eisenhower for statements he made about Jews who lived in Displaced Persons camps. Patton said, "I have never seen a group of people who seem to be more lacking in intelligence and spirit. There is a German village not far from here that is deserted. I am planning to make it a concentration camp for some of these god damned Jews."[30] The question that arises here is if Patton had been on the side of the Nazis would he have been a mass murderer? Being the center of power creates more power and monistic ideology. This means that one who believes that their perspective is the true way to live should eliminate those who stand in the way (what is good for me is good for the whole world).

In the twentieth century over 100 million people were slaughtered in wars, massacres, and genocides. We see this kind of violence continuing into the 21st century, with massacres and ethnic cleansing in Europe, Africa, and around the globe. Modern technology has made mass murder easier—almost antiseptic—and we gloss over it through the use of euphemisms, such as "collateral damage" or "ethnic cleansing." The Holocaust, the most documented human genocide in all of history, has exposed the human capability for depravity, showing how ordinary, or even upstanding, people can participate in genocidal killings—whatever their personal moral codes may be.

Many books detail the evil deeds that occurred in the Holocaust, and in other genocides. Still, it is very difficult for "normal" people to fathom the evil acts of destruction of which human beings are capable. But these evil deeds do occur, and "normal" people often commit them. In this sense, the Holocaust can be seen as a watershed in the concept of evil and its academic treatment. The problem of evil seems to lie at an intersection of disciplines including sociology, psychology, history, and philosophy. Frequently, people under the circumstances of need can sometimes turn to acts of injustice. For instance as I was hiding in the Bobowa ghetto in an attic while the Jews were being loaded into trucks, ordinary non-Jewish people who resided in a section of the Bobowa ghetto began to loot Jewish property. These people were neighbors, but when the opportunity presented itself they stole right out from under the noses of the Nazis who were clearing out Jews house by house in order to exterminate them at the forest. This I saw, and it was hard to understand because they were our neighbors.[31]

Evil has been defined in many ways over the centuries. Plato felt that evil was the result of external causation. He argued that man must be "made" evil, "For no man is voluntarily bad; but the bad become bad by reason of an ill disposition of the body and bad education, things which are hateful to every man and happen to him against his will."[32] Socrates assumes that evil people are driven by desires for domination and luxury. Although they are single-minded in their pursuit of these goals, he portrays them as deeply divided, because their *pleonexia*—their desire for more and more—leaves them dissatisfied and full of self-hatred (Aristotle), suggesting an "internal" source of evil.[33]

Evil is also seen as an almost inexplicable quality situated deep within our individual natures. These scholars point to mass killers and psychotic personalities seen in our society, and are quick to suggest that, although the causes may come from outside the individual, they are certainly not supernatural. According to forensic psychiatrist Dr. Park Dietz, who examined convicted murderer Jeffrey Dahmer, as well as Lyle and Eric Menendez, "As far as we can tell, the causes of their behavior are biological, psychological, and social, and do not so far demonstrably include the work of Lucifer."[34] For many philosophers and theologians, evil is located outside of individual humans, whether centered on a supernatural "devil" or not, and it operates to "take over" or corrupt what would otherwise be a fundamentally good person who would behave in a basically good manner. Dietz relates his feeling, "The fact is that there aren't many [such murderers] in whom I could not find some redeeming attributes and some humanity."[35]

Martin Heidegger was an admitted Nazi whose philosophy was based largely on the work of Kant, Hegel, and Nietzsche. One of the central features of his thinking that characterizes both Nazi ideology and postmodern thought is the elimination of "the other" from philosophical concern. Ideologically, this existence for one's self becomes an existence for the sake of the *Volk*; one can only be with others who are like one's self. Here, others are excluded—literally annihilated from consideration—and Jewish concern for the other, deprecated by both Heidegger and Hegel before him, is seen as the "slave mentality." Heideggerians (like some postmodernists today) are concerned with their own deaths, not the deaths of others.[36]

Nazi philosophers also stressed that man was the center of the moral universe, and these thinkers, such as Max Wundt, found the Jewish insistence on taking the part of the other to be the antithesis of Germany's natural "folkish" philosophy. If the Nazis were to be Nazis then they would have to eliminate the notions of a higher, divine image within every human being that places upon us infinite responsibility for the other human beings. And to do so, they had to eliminate the people whose presence in the world signifies such teaching.

Individual Leaders who Initiated Evil

There are several recent examples of individual leaders who initiate and encourage radical evil. One is Saddam Hussein, who came from an abusive home where there was no love from either his father or mother. Saddam was born in 1935 in the village of Takrit north of Baghdad. The family lived in dire poverty, and his father forced him to steal sheep and chickens to help support the family. His psyche was shaped by the fact that his parents rejected him. When his mother remarried, Saddam experienced further abuse from his new stepfather. His own father had deserted the family, and Saddam later found it necessary to manufacture a story that his father had died. Hassan, his stepfather, was heard by neighbors telling Saddam that he was "a son of a dog," and that he did not want him around. Later, Saddam served a stint in a detention center, before running away from home to his Uncle Tulfah, who lived in a nearby village. In his late teens, his uncle gave him a pistol and sent him back to Takrit to take care of himself. He joined the Ba'ath Party at the age of 24, and was involved in the assassination attempt of Abd al-Karim Qasim, the despotic ruler of Iraq. In 1979 Saddam became undisputed ruler of Iraq and murdered his own people and attacked Iran as well as Kuwait.

The abuse and misery of the childhood of Adolf Hitler was similar to that of Saddam Hussein. His father, Alois Hitler, was a minor civil servant in Austria, and an illegitimate child. There is speculation that he may have been fathered by a Jewish man, his mother's employer. More likely, he was fathered by an Austrian in the village in which his mother lived. His mother was a maid. Alois had been married to several different women, and it was his third wife Klara who bore Adolf, who took the brunt of his father's discipline. Adolf tried to run away from home because his father ridiculed his attempts to become an artist instead of studying for the Austrian civil service. Hitler was impressed with legendary Germanic heroes, and with Wagner's operas. He did not succeed at either art or architecture, but he exhibited a great ability to speak publicly, even as a teenager. He felt close to his mother, but lost her to breast cancer at a young age. Hitler's later rage against Jews and specifically Jewish doctors may be traced back to Klara's doctor, who was Jewish, and who Hitler blamed for his mother's death.

John Toland, in his detailed study of Hitler, claims that Hitler clearly manifested pathological inclinations.[37] By killing people, he tried to get even for hurts and humiliations suffered in his troubled early years.[38] Alice Miller describes him as a typical abused child:

> Constantly mistreated by his father, emotionally abandoned by his mother, he learned only cruelty; he learned to be obedient and to accept daily punishments with unquestioning compliance. After years, he took revenge. As an adult he once said, 'It gives us a very special, secret pleasure to see how unaware people are of what is really happening to them.'[39]

Similarly, an example of Hitler's philosophy is illustrated by the following quote:

> My pedagogy is hard. The weak must be chiseled away...young people will grow up who will frighten the world. I want a violent, arrogant, unafraid youth, who must be able to suffer pain. Nothing weak or tender must be left in them. Their eyes must bespeak once again the free, magnificent beast of prey... Thus will I place the pure and noble raw material...I do not want an intellectual education. With knowledge I will spoil the young. I would vastly prefer them to learn only what they absorb voluntarily as they follow their play instinct. They shall learn to overcome the fear of death through the most arduous tests. This is the historic state of heroic youth.[40]

A similar insight into Hitler's philosophy on mass murder may be found in his discussion of inferior races.

> We have the duty to depopulate as much as we have the duty of caring for the German population. We shall have to develop a technique for depopulation. You will ask what is depopulation? Do I propose to exterminate whole ethnic groups? Yes, it will add up to that. Nature is cruel; therefore we may be cruel too.[41]

He had signs of obsessive compulsive disorder, which was shown through washing his hands constantly. He had illusions of omnipotence, invincibility and infallibility, violent mood swings, rages, racing thoughts, and pressured speech.[42] Hitler received psychiatric treatment after World War I from Dr. Edmund Forster, and was later treated for these symptoms by Theodore Morell, his personal physician. Morell supplied him with amphetamines and cocaine for his depression, and was emboldened to say publicly in 1943 that the Fuhrer was a manic-depressive.[43]

Lieb also sees Josef Stalin as a depressed personality with low self-esteem who encompassed characteristics such as indecisiveness, pessimism, anxiousness, indifference, gloominess, and paranoia. His grandiose delusions and raging paranoia led him to order the destruction of millions of people he saw as personal threats. Any person could become a target, even his own family or members of his inner circle. Paranoid delusions of manic-depressives are infectious and as virulent as deadly microbes and can easily affect those in thrall to the host figure.[44]

Having scratched the psychological surface of these recent major purveyors of evil, we know that it is much more complex than pointing to specific childhood events as the explanation for the mental illness behind these murderous deeds. Many scholars agree that without Stalin, Hitler, and Saddam Hussein, the catastrophic genocidal massacres could not have occurred. But these kinds of leaders cannot operate in a vacuum and need willing followers to implement their programs. We believe that both social structural and individual social-psychological factors cause the genocidal massacres masterminded by these leaders.

UNDERSTANDING EVIL THROUGH NARRATIVES

Scholars have found a number of ways to study the causes of evil. Pure philosophy, laboratory experiments, comparative and historical analyses, psychological treatments including psychoanalysis, and other methods have brought us portions and pieces of comprehension. But experimenters cannot truly get into the minds of their subjects, therefore leaving the perpetrators and victims of real evil as those most able to shed light on causes and consequences. We feel that humans are best able to understand evil through narratives. Some scholars maintain that stories can have an important impact as they arouse not only emotions and images of the events, but also inform the reader, viewer, or listener *about* the event.[45] Narratives and stories can serve as a general metaphor for understanding human conduct. In part, this is because people think in narratives about their own lives. People remember stories or episodes better in narrative form.

Tulving distinguishes between semantic and episodic memory.[46] He maintains that people remember episodes better than abstract ideas, i.e. semantic memory. Listeners frequently identify empathically with a story. Besides being a popular and effective method for the dissemination of moral values, stories give the listener insight into a variety of human behaviors. These include evil, loneliness, fear, frustration, prejudice, arrogance, and the consequences of indifference, as well as pride, honor, courage, the consequences of caring, and social responsibility. We have found narratives to be crucial to our understanding of good as well. The authentic rescuer stories that we have accumulated over the years give us a dual message about evil committed by Nazis and other collaborating killers and provides insight into honor, altruistic inclination, compassion, empathy, social responsibility, and people who included diverse others into their sense of social responsibility. For example, John Rabe exemplified altruistic and heroic behavior during the Nanking Massacre in 1937, was a German businessman whose Nanjing Safety Zone sheltered some 200,000 Chinese from slaughter at the hands of Japanese soldiers.[47]

A narrative is really a subjective interpretation of reality. Stories attempt to explain people's actions, their intentions and their own experiences. Robert Coles frequently uses stories to teach moral values.[48] Alex Haley, in his book *Roots*, describes the evils of slavery in the form of stories.[49] Anne Frank's diary, circulated around the world in dozens of languages, teaches the nature of evil and the nature of caring and compassion.

Elie Wiesel tells stories in order to teach the consequences of indifference and the often tragic role played by bystanders. In his book *Night*, Wiesel describes the horror of being inside a cattle car with dying people.[50] But this is nothing compared to what he finds at the gates of Auschwitz. He sees flames from the crematoria and smells the odor of burning human flesh:

> Never shall I forget that night, the first night in camp, which
> turned my life into one long night, seven times cursed and seven
> times sealed. Never shall I forget that smoke. Never shall I forget

the little faces of the children, whose bodies I saw turned into wreaths of smoke beneath a silent blue sky. Never shall I forget those flames which consumed my faith forever. Never shall I forget that nocturnal silence which deprived me, for all eternity, of the desire to live. Never shall I forget those moments which murdered my God and my soul and turned my dreams to dust. Never shall I forget these things, even if I am condemned to live as long as God Himself. Never.[51]

His experiences in the camps, related in a straightforward manner, clearly indicate the ordinary nature of the situation, and the absurdity of that normality. As the prisoners were forced to watch the execution of a fellow prisoner, some were more concerned with getting the "ceremony" over with so they can get their daily soup. On the other hand, the killing of a single man in this manner had more impact than the assembly line killing of thousands in the gas chambers. This rings true, though it is dangerous to equate the routinized reality of the guards with the experience of the prisoners.

Valentina Iribagiza, a teenage survivor of the Rwandan massacre, experienced similar terror. She said, "They took stones and smashed the heads of the bodies. They took little children and smashed their heads together. When they found someone breathing, they pulled them out and finished them off." Having survived with her arms hacked off and other injuries, she said, "I prayed that I would die because I couldn't see a future life. I didn't think there was anybody in the country left alive to share a life as before. I thought everybody had been swept away."[52] It seems that one cannot begin to grasp an evil like the Holocaust or the Rwandan machete massacres other than through the eyes of witnesses.

Unfortunately, our world is composed largely of bystanders. This was true in the case of the Holocaust. For example, the Nazis did not have to replace police officials with Nazis:

On the contrary, throughout German society, there was a widespread social co-operation, collaboration, accommodation, and adjustment. Without social co-operation of various kinds, irrespective of motives, the anti-Semitic policies would have remained so many idle fantasies.[53]

Hitler once asked, rhetorically, "After all, who today remembers the genocide of the Armenians?" His point was that few outsiders care about one group of people destroying another group of people, unless the story is told and people are able to humanize the victims. But we do learn about ourselves and our capabilities when we read the stories of those involved in events like the Holocaust. Empathy for others, this ability to place ourselves in the shoes of others—committing acts of goodness or evil—is the root of being human.

GROUP DYNAMICS AND THE SOCIAL CONSTRUCTION OF THE ENEMY

Ervin Staub maintains that evil is not necessarily a scientific concept; rather, the idea of evil is part of a broadly *shared* human cultural heritage.[54] Staub pinpoints the sources of radical evil as the construction of out-groups and their mistreatment because of grievances, real or imagined. The examples that he offers involve economic tensions that threaten people's livelihood. What seems to be the deeply rooted response in such situations is to lash out against the outsider. Political factors such as authoritarian or totalitarian governments or psychopathic leaders may foster hatred and encourage genocide. The bottom line for Staub is that the essential product of evil is always the destruction of human beings. This includes not only the deaths of individuals, but also the creation of conditions that materially or psychologically diminish a people's dignity, livelihood, happiness, or the capacity to fulfill basic material needs.[i] A key factor for Staub is that moral restraint is less powerful in groups than in individuals. People, as members of groups, will commit unspeakable horrors against those perceived as their enemies.

Philosopher Richard Taylor distinguishes between good and evil— together with all morality—to human feelings, needs, desires, and purposes, rather than to human reason and intelligence.[55]

James Aho's "sociology of the enemy" looks at how human societies socially construct the enemies, thus laying the basis for radical evil.[56] His work focuses on groups of people and processes who "make" enemies: authors, organizations, etc., involved in defaming and dehumanizing others.

---

i.   It is only fair to mention that Staub also argues that humans are capable of goodness and morality as well as selfishness and destructiveness towards others.

Although in the Holocaust the Nazis were the perpetrators, it is clear that other constructions of the enemy also played a role in the destruction of European Jews. In Poland, for example, the Nazi occupation often ignited local pogroms against Jews who had been "neighbors." Jan Gross recounts one instance:

> What a terrible sight this [mass murder] presented can be gauged from the fact that the Poles had gone overboard. [The arrival of the Germans saved eighteen Jews] who had managed to hide during the pogrom...it was in this way that the Jewish community was wiped off the face of the earth after five hundred years of existence...[57]

Gross's book specifically addresses the fact that age-old group relationships between Catholic Poles and Jewish Poles contributed to the carnage.

One example of research conducted to test this idea of group construction and its consequences for evil behavior was the 1968 Blue Eyes/Brown Eyes experiment by Jane Elliott.[58] In response to the assassination of Martin Luther King, Jr., Elliott, a third grade teacher in Iowa, conducted the experiment with her eight-year-old students. None of the students had ever seen a person of color and had no real-life understanding of racism and discrimination. In order to allow students to get a sense of what such oppression feels like, she divided her class into a "superior" group of those with brown eyes, and a lazy and not-to-be-trusted group of blue-eyed students. Those with blue eyes were not allowed use of the inside drinking fountain, while the brown-eyed students were given preferential treatment at every opportunity, and allowed to boss around the others. It did not take Elliott long to become horrified at how her students were transformed into just what they were *told* they were. Brown-eyed students acted in a domineering and arrogant manner towards their blue-eyed peers in a very short time.

Just as the enemy is constructed—often with devastating results—so, too, is the in-group itself a human construction with more to it than meets the eye. The famous experiments on conformity by Solomon Asch in the 1940s and 1950s are instructive.[59] When a subject and several confederates were asked to judge the size of a line, the likelihood of subjects standing up for their choice (even though it was the right choice) was lowered significantly because the others were regularly making a different (wrong) choice. The definite and immediate sanctions from the group outweigh the vague and perhaps far-off positives of standing up for our perceptions; we often choose to "go along."

The in-group develops processes through which its own existence is solidified. One explanation for a group turning inwards for security is the concept of *groupthink*, popularized by Irving Janis.[60] Groupthink describes the social process through which individuals in a group can end up agreeing to radically different proposals and making very different decisions than they would likely have come to as individuals. The necessary conditions for groupthink include insulation of the group, high group cohesion, strong and directive leadership, homogeneity of group members' social backgrounds and ideology, and high stress from external threats (real or imagined). Members of groups thus generally strive for unanimity, with individual moral restraints often lost in the shuffle.[61]

A SOCIAL-PSYCHOLOGICAL APPROACH TO EVIL

There is a growing body of literature that attempts to place the concept of evil within a specifically social-psychological paradigm. Arthur Miller in *Social Psychology of Evil* brings together a group of scholars to address the nature of evil.[62] The authors discuss the complex interaction of individual, societal, and situational factors that produce good or evil behavior, the role of guilt, issues of responsibility and motivation, including why good people do bad things. Overall, the text provides theoretical perspectives, analysis, and synthesis that deepen an understanding of social behavior and how it is driven by internal motivations and influenced by relational, interpersonal, and contextual factors, but also serve to broaden our understanding of the importance of examining social behavior from a variety of philosophical, theoretical, and methodological perspectives.

It was through the exercise of considering the acts of Adolf Eichmann during the Holocaust that Hannah Arendt generated her theory of the banality of evil. She spent some months attending the Eichmann trial in Jerusalem for the extensive list of crimes against Jews during the war. The prosecution conducted a painfully complete survey of his crimes, and Eichmann admitted to all of it. "Despite all the efforts of the prosecution, everybody could see that this man was not a 'monster,'" wrote Arendt, "but it was difficult indeed not to suspect that he was a clown."[63] She dwells on his shallow intellect, his clichéd speech (which she interprets as a means of consoling himself), his infinite capacity for self-deception, and his profound detachment from reality.

Arendt portrays Eichmann as a "joiner," a conformist, describing him as "a leaf in the whirlwind of time."[64] It is this aspect of his character, according to her, rather than any deeply held convictions shared with the Nazi Party or a rabid hatred of Jews, that accounts for his actions during the war. "The prosecution had to assume that he was [aware of the criminality of his actions], as "all 'normal persons' would be."[65] But Arendt asserts that, "under the conditions of the Third Reich only 'exceptions' could be expected to react 'normally'."[66] With considerable insight and detail, Arendt explains how Germany's leaders went about creating these conditions, to the point that "conscience as such had apparently got lost in Germany."[67] There were individuals who resisted, she notes, but "their voices were never heard."[68]

The Holocaust stands alone as an example of radical evil. But in spite of a library full of works analyzing, de-constructing, and theorizing on the Holocaust, the definition of evil is generally left unaddressed by sociologists, and the word itself is used in such works as merely another synonym for "bad" or "terrible." The acts themselves may be spelled out in excruciating detail, and those who committed them analyzed in great social-psychological detail, but most authors are left asking the large questions rather than answering them.

Sociologist Jeffrey Alexander argues that we must base our views of evil culturally. At the same time he seeks to avoid the trap of cultural relativism. Alexander's insight is that the radical evil of the Holocaust can grow out of systematic tendencies in German culture. "Those murders of the millions of Jewish and non-Jewish people during the Holocaust must be seen as something valued, as something desired,"[69] on the part of those who planned and carried them out. The cultural components of evil may indeed be the foremost of causes.

While Alexander deplores the fundamentalism with which our post-modern society is beset, he admits both to the binary nature of these aspects of civil culture, and to the fact that "each code can be defined only in terms of the alternate perspective the other provides."[70] It is no surprise, then, that understanding the nature of institutions or structures is best accomplished through narrative. Alexander underscores the importance of the type of medium we use to carry out the messages that create and recreate our culture. In noting that the narrative may be used for perpetuating good or evil, he writes:

> George Washington and the cherry tree highlights honesty and virtue; English accounts of the Battle of Britain reveal the courage, self-sufficiency, and spontaneous cooperative of the British in contrast to the villainous forces of Hitlerian Germany; [and] no matter how apocryphal, French legends about the honorable, trusting, and independent patriots who resisted the Nazi occupation underlay the construction of the Fourth Republic after World War II.[71]

In his book *Hitler's Willing Executioners,*[72] Daniel Jonah Goldhagen addresses the effects of culture and ideology in Germany that enabled Hitler to come to power and to implement his racist agenda. He maintains that because it was a society inculcated with anti-Semitism and a "*Volkish*" ideology of racial superiority, instigating the destruction of non-Aryans was vastly simplified. While we know that ethnocentrism is found in all cultures, in Germany it developed into a destructive racist creed. The Nazi ideology was both a manifestation of the cultural milieu from which it was born as well as a direct reflection of the values of those who led the movement. For example, secrecy and strict obedience were valued over openness and cooperation.

DEHUMANIZATION AS AN ASPECT OF EVIL

The first step in Kelman's process of motivation for evil acts such as genocide is the dehumanization of the other. He addresses the profound question of how it is possible for "ordinary" people to perform extraordinary acts of violence seemingly without moral restraint. Kelman concludes that three processes are prerequisites to mass killing: *dehumanization* to the humanity of victims (some components of which are described above); *authorization* by government or other individuals in power; and, *routinization*, which makes genocide more efficient.[73]

The construction of groups works both to dehumanize the "enemy" while strengthening the rightness of the actions of the in-group. Heinrich Himmler, speaking to units of the SS in Kharkov in 1943, said, "Anti-Semitism is the same as delousing: getting rid of lice is not a question of ideology, it is a matter of cleanliness."[74] No matter the extent to which policies are determined from scientific underpinnings, from historical competition or enmity, or from ideology, the dehumanization of the out-group is an inevitable first step in any genocide. This tactic was shown in Philip Zimbardo's Stanford Prison Experiment where "guards" proved much more likely to use harsher force on "prisoners" who had been branded as animals than those described as nice. The most heinous of massacres have their roots in this kind of dehumanization, which gives perpetrators the ability to "morally disengage."[75] Not only in the Holocaust, but in virtually all radical evil—the extermination of Tutsis by the Hutus, the ethnic cleansing in the states of the former Yugoslavia, etc.—the necessary first step is to "dehumanize" the other and "desensitize" the perpetrator.

AUTHORIZATION TO COMMIT THE EVIL OF GENOCIDE

But desensitization to the humanity of others in itself is not enough to make "moral people" do horrific things. Generally, they must be externally "authorized" by leaders who take responsibility for the actions. Germans were ordered to blindly follow Hitler's instructions in all matters; in fact, they risked concentration camp or death for not obeying. Minister of Labor Robert Ley said, "The Fuhrer is always right. Obey the Fuhrer."[76] Stanley Milgram studied obedience to authority in the Milgram experiment at Yale University in 1961, where he had individuals administer electric shocks to "learners" (participants). He found that in some situations individuals are willing to act in ways that are at odds with their upbringing, and contradict their beliefs.[77] Milgram found that most of the "teachers" administering the shocks to the "learners" eventually reached their limit. As they approached their individual limits, however, the men were willing to continue administering the shocks—even when the learner was screaming, begging the teacher to stop—as long as the man in the white coat authorized it. Milgram says, "It is this ideological abrogation to the authority that constitutes the principal cognitive basis of obedience."[78] Milgram's notion of the "definition of the situation"—this willingness, in essence, to accept an authority's version of reality—is the foundation for subsequent action: "Because the subject accepts authority's definition of the situation, action follows accordingly." When an individual accepts an authority's situational definition, one's inner moral code or tendencies may be suspended. One is left to say, along with Auschwitz commandant Rudolf Hoess, "I had nothing to say; I could only say *jawohl* (certainly)!...[I] could only execute orders without any further consideration."[79]

Milgram also notes that the act of giving up personal responsibility in this way is self-reinforcing. Not only has blame or guilt been shifted, but loyalty has been even more strongly tied to the authority itself precisely because of the abrogation of responsibility. The subordinate person "feels shame or pride depending on how adequately he has performed the actions called for by the authority," not for the actions he took.[80]

The teachers did not seem to enjoy administering the shocks, and often tried to quit, but justified continuing by telling themselves that they were simply performing a duty. Mr. Braverman, one of the teachers in the original experiment, said, "This isn't the way I usually am. This was a sheer reaction to a totally impossible situation. And my reaction was to the situation of having to hurt somebody. And being totally helpless and caught up in a set of circumstances where I just couldn't deviate and I couldn't try to help."[81] Another "teacher" from the experiment said, "What appalled me was that I could possess this capacity for obedience and compliance...even after it became clear that it was at the expense of violation of another value, i.e., don't hurt someone else who is helpless..." The wife of one "teacher" summed it up when she told her husband, "You can call yourself Eichmann."[82] These and other recent experiments have found a human readiness to follow the path of blind, fanatical obedience to the group, or to fall easily into the pattern of distinguishing ourselves from an "out-group."

ROUTINIZATION

Kelman's third requirement is bound up with the idea of authority, the routinization of the actual evil acts. Although humans are clearly capable of terrible acts in the heat of the moment, or in a perceived defense of their own group, they may not be able to commit them on the day-to-day basis necessary for the massacres we have seen in the past century. At the same time, we may be reluctant to stray far from deeply held beliefs the first time, or the first few times we are faced with a serious dilemma. But once such activities are effectively made into a routine, with others including peers and leaders taking part—even the victims!—we are able to place those atrocities into a context that allows us to participate.* And even though moral concerns are bound to rise at some point in carrying out evil acts, routinization "reduces the necessity of making [moral] decisions, and helps the actor to concentrate "on the details of his job rather than on its meaning." According to Kelman, "Routinization creates a situation in which the person becomes involved in an action without considering the implications of that action and without really making a decision."[83] The role of language comes into play here. Just as the production of memoranda and formal discussion about heinous or immoral actions gives the actions themselves some legitimacy, so does the use of euphemisms help reduce the need for legitimacy—the acts are legitimated by the routine itself, the "real" meaning is simply put into code. "[Military] pilots euphemistically 'service' a target' rather than bomb it. Enemies are dehumanized as 'gooks' or 'hajis,' or infidels."[84] In Rwanda, the radio encouraged rampaging Hutus to "be strong and to cut down the tall trees."[85] Kelman says that using such euphemisms allow people to differentiate these actions from ordinary killing and destruction, and thus to avoid confrontation with their true meaning. The moral revulsion that the ordinary labels would arouse can be more readily suppressed and the enterprise can proceed on its routine course with all involved simply performing their duties.[86]

The Nazis were remarkably successful in making the killing of Jews and other desirables into a routine duty. The calm and formal bureaucratic language used by Nazi officers in the course of the liquidation of the Jews is telling. Reich Commissioner for Ostland, a man named Lohse, writing to his superior in Berlin, explained that he has "stopped the wild executions of the Jews in Libau because the way in which they were being carried out was totally irresponsible." He sought clarification of policy, asking whether a recent order should be "interpreted to mean that all Jews in Ostland are to be liquidated... without any consideration of age, sex, or economic interest..."[87] Similarly, Hutus referred to the bloody machete killing of unarmed Tutsi women and

---

* We can see just how unnatural this routinization is however, in the self-medication necessary for members of the killing groups studied by Christopher Browning (1992) on the eastern front. These troops needed to abuse alcohol in order to be able to perform mass murder.

children as merely "tiring work...If you didn't go they would beat you or fine you, therefore it was compulsory to go. Even if you were ill, you had to go or ask for permission to be excused."[88] Referring to past communications and to past policy considerations and discussions, and utilizing the formal language of bureaucracy all work together to help remove the horrible reality, reducing it simply to a process that duty demands.

It was precisely this problem of adherence to duty that sparked perhaps the best-known sociological debate on the nature of evil, namely the defense of Adolf Eichmann in his trial in Jerusalem for crimes he committed during the Holocaust.[89] Arendt came to the conclusion that evil is really quite banal, meaning ordinary, rather than some monstrous or supernatural phenomenon. It is Kelman's routinization component that shows how radical evil is banal. By definition, an activity cannot be routine without being banal. Arendt argued that Eichmann was not much different from the majority of people around the world. Although he did not have the moral compass that might have forced him to ask himself questions along the way, he merely fell into the routine of doing his job. For Eichmann, doing his job meant being as efficient and effective as possible, raising the notion that he would have been a valued worker in the modern corporate world. He was not a sadist or a villain. He simply had no anchor that prevented him from being swept along with the strong tide of anti-Semitism and the ruthless plan.

Rudolph Hoess, infamous commander of the Auschwitz concentration camp, plainly spelled out his duties and accomplishments at the camp where he estimates more than three million died under his command. In his confession he boasts of "improvements" he instituted such as larger crematoria, more streamlined sorting of arriving prisoners, and better acting on the part of the Nazi participants. Hoess matter-of-factly outlines how they sought "to fool the victims into thinking that they were to go through a de-lousing process" rather than being gassed, and how that charade improved efficiency of the process.[90] There is an ongoing debate centered on both Arendt's methods as well as her conclusions on the banal nature of Eichmann and others, but there can be little doubt that many of the German perpetrators of the Holocaust fell back on the mundane idea of "duty" to explain their actions. Hoess referred to himself as "a minor cog in the wheels of Himmler's organizational machinery."[91]

Creating an evil routine is not easy. To the contrary, much effort is needed to make an evil routine. That the evil acts were routine is not to say the process was mindless. For example, the Rwandan massacre was extremely well organized. In a recent interview, Gerard Prunier, author of *The Rwanda Crisis,* said:

> I think the most [mistaken word to use] is 'mindless.' It was anything but mindless. It was extremely carefully planned and well executed violence, because if you use mostly machetes to kill off a million people, which is roughly the estimate, in the space of two and a half months, [it] is admirable. It requires extreme organization, extreme care, and extreme perseverance. This was not like the Germans with gas chambers and death squads with machine guns, 90% of the people were killed with blunt instruments and with machetes, which means that day after day after day, crews of peasants including women were marshaled and taken to the fields exactly as if they had been reaping a crop and were killing people.[92]

Many participants in such crimes report that they were able to "wall off" or *compartmentalize* these deeds from the rest of their lives. R. J. Lifton addresses the issue of the mass murders committed by Nazi doctors, focusing on the process of *doubling,* which separates the personality, making continued and routine horrors possible.[93] For Lifton, this involved a process that creates two opposing selves that are walled off from each other to avoid internal conflict. The doubling process of Nazi doctors was heavily buttressed by anti-Semitic Nazi ideology that made it easier for the perpetrators of mass murder to accomplish their mission. The catalog of atrocities committed by the Nazi doctors is long and varied, and assuming the usual, genuine intention of serving fellow humans generally found among doctors, some sort of compartmentalizing of evil would be necessary to allow them to maintain their sanity.

Albert Bandura explains how humans have developed the ability to "short-circuit" personal moral codes:

> Self-sanctions can be disengaged by reconstruing conduct as serving moral purposes, obscuring personal agency in detrimental activities, disregarding or misrepresenting the injurious consequences of one's actions, and blaming and dehumanizing the victims.[94]

Even in cases of typical evil, humans demonstrate this ability to reconcile behavior that goes directly against people's moral codes. In a study of college students taking an accounting examination, the students were able to justify cheating in a variety of ways. "The decision to cheat is the product of a variety of factors, some internal and some external," explains University of Arkansas professor Tim West, one of the authors. "However, there is one variable that is nearly universal—all cheaters develop mechanisms that allow them to justify their actions." Students made comments such as, "I think it's hard for people not to [cheat by] looking at an answer manual if it is available" and, "I really don't consider [cheating by] working with another person that unethical." One even reasoned "Everyone was doing it."[95] The surprising finding in the study was that those who scored highest on a standard test of moral judgment were most likely to cheat in real life. Clearly, the more "moral" of the students in the group were able to rationalize or justify their actions in ways that allowed them to temporarily suspend strong personal values that should have prevented the behavior.[96] It seems that routinization is facilitated by the human capability for rationalizing just about anything.

CONCLUSION

In this chapter we have sought to define evil and to briefly sketch its radical manifestations. We examined the roots of evil and differentiate between typical evil and radical evil. We also sought to examine briefly what others have said about the development of evil. There is not a widespread theoretical understanding of the causes and consequences of radical evil. Instead, it is an amalgam of factors explained by subjective experience and personal narrative. Paul Vincent sums up the difficulties for social scientists in "establishing verdicts of right and wrong." He argues that we must give great weight to "our class position, our race, our religion, our education, our gender, [and] our cultural and political traditions" in determining how and why evil happens.[97] While acknowledging the importance of working within an empirical framework in analyzing evil, Vincent underscores the importance of moral evaluation: researchers in the social sciences "differ from those of [physical] scientists in that the judgments they entail—be they moral, political, cultural—are intrinsic to their subject matter and not, as in the [physical] sciences, external to it."[98]

In addition, while there may be genetic or biological bases for aggression, obedience, violence, and other aspects of individual and group behavior, we believe that the cultural environment is most closely associated with the manifestation of radical evil. Structural conditions such as political upheaval, poverty, unemployment, or alienation may make a society ripe for a charismatic leader to rise. A leader may arise and try to implement his psychopathic ideology as social policy as we suggested in the cases of Saddam Hussein, Adolf Hitler, and Josef Stalin. Radical evil is the result of a combination of individual pathology and complicated structural forces. Those who look at the horrors of the Holocaust or the Rwandan massacres may join Elie Cohen in pointing to the "cool, calculating manner in which it [was] inflicted."[99] The massive evil of the twentieth involves both psychological and sociological factors.

If we agree that deliberate and conscious harm to human beings is the consequence of psychological and environmental influences, what can alleviate this? It would be naïve to claim that we—or anyone else—know the "answers," although many scholars have grappled with this problem. There is enough evidence about human behavior to suggest how to discourage such evil. Societies must do a better job of alleviating hunger and poverty. It is important to educate the young about the dangers of conformity and blind obedience, and to emphasize tolerance and empathy. The formative years of an individual's life produce leaders like Hitler, while structural and social-psychological factors makes blind followers out of "normal" people; any approach to evil must come from these underpinnings. Without a Hitler, a Stalin, or another evil charismatic leader, we are convinced that the ordinary people involved in the various massacres and genocides would not have committed those heinous acts. At the same time, it is just as clear that without the people who were willing participants in these acts, the horrible policies and goals envisioned by these psychopathic leaders would have remained symptoms of mental illness rather than constituting the suffering and misery they did. It is possible to "manufacture" the causes of individual pathology, as well as the social-psychological and structural causes of group behavior that can support it. This makes it imperative that we inculcate the values of caring for others and the ability to take the part of the other, and to remember the consequences of indifference. "Violence by groups of people against other groups of people is not going to disappear tomorrow," argues Ervin Staub, but we can make a difference "by attending to both direct immediate, practical approaches like activating bystanders and working to heal historical antagonisms [as well as] long term approaches like child rearing."[100]

Chapter 3

Silently Standing By:
Why We Do or Don't Come to the Aid
of Those Who Need Us

"All that is necessary for the triumph of evil is that good men do nothing".—Edmund Burke

WHETHER IT WAS THE SCORES OF GERMANS who stood by as millions of Jews were rounded up and taken to the gas chambers or witnesses to the beating of Rodney King by Los Angeles police, the question is: why do some people come forward and others turn away? This chapter focuses on why bystanders to often horrific situations either intervene—or not. The most widely-known case of bystanders not helping their fellow human beings are those who stood by during the atrocities of such events as the Holocaust and most recently, the Rwandan and Darfur genocides. Past research has identified definitions and typologies to help understand the reasons why individuals and groups choose to remain bystanders rather than the opposite, upstanders: those choosing to speak up, acting in order to deny personal, human, and societal atrocities to go unchecked. This chapter builds on the research identifying bystanders, revealing an encompassing syndrome involving some members of society. By broadening the conventional understanding of bystanders to include a number of social, political, and environmental injustices affecting our contemporary global society, there may be a clearer path toward a more caring and just society.

In the midst of the horror taking place in German-occupied Europe, there were countless individuals who failed to meet the ethical challenge of standing up to the genocidal acts they were witnessing. Most often referred to as *bystanders*, we can understand them in this case as people who "had done nothing out of the ordinary during the war either to help other people or resist the Nazis."[1] In their publications on rescuers of Jews in German-occupied Europe during World War II Oliner and Oliner (1988) divided the population of 300 million European people into four groups.[2] These consisted of *perpetrators* (killers and collaborators), *victims* (Jews, gypsies, homosexuals, priests, ministers, and others), *rescuers* (heroes, helpers), and *bystanders* (the largest group). It is an unfortunate characteristic of modern society that the largest number of people fell into the bystander group. Many individuals could have been involved with saving lives in Nazi-occupied Europe, but did not. Although the "good Germans" who did not directly participate in the killings were originally considered to be non-guilty bystanders, it is only through the complicity of bystanders—who were guilty of unquestioning obedience to evil leaders— that the Holocaust was possible.[3] What are the social-psychological developments that remove a person from the role of bystander to that of an upstander? According to scholar Uwe Kitzinger, an upstander is described as having,

> [T]he courage of the non-conformist...it is the courage that risks social disapproval, the capacity to resist by thinking critically with one's own mind, and the will to be an active participant in life, not a passive bystander. Regardless of their differences in age, gender, literacy, religious affiliation, ethnic identity, or wartime roles, upstanders share the bravery to risk their lives rather than commit or be complicit in a crime. When so many other people choose to compromise their morals in order to survive, the upstander's actions suggest that we must not allow ourselves to be debased by circumstances: To retain our dignity, we must sometimes refuse to live life at any cost.[4]

Are there enough upstanders among us today unwilling to stand-by and allow genocide to continue in Darfur or a witness to intervene in a brutal rape or mugging of an innocent person? Are we able to broaden our understanding of bystanders in order to stand up to the array of contemporary atrocities taking place today? For example, how much longer are we able to stand by while the soldier and civilian body counts rise in the Middle East? And for those soldiers returning stateside who suffer from undiagnosed symptoms of Posttraumatic Stress Disorder (PTSD), do we stand by?[5] In the same light, are we able to stand by while the U.S. and much of the global population face barriers to adequate health care?[6] Additionally, how do we stand-by knowing the health of our ecosystem is continually compromised and degraded by our consumptive culture pushing for dominance and allocation of natural resources?[7]

This chapter will focus on finding the difference between bystanders and upstanders in a number of cases, both historic and in more recent times. Essentially, the questions posed here are: how can we identify and understand our bystander role in order that we may reduce our ignorance and indifference to stand up against the numerous atrocities taking place in our world? How can we begin to take the proper steps to ensure we are actively working toward a more caring and just world?

BYSTANDERS

The most readily understood definition of *bystander* comes from the works of scholars who have studied the phenomenon of human (in)action toward atrocities.[*] [8]

The definitions offered by these scholars differ in some degree but remain applicable when understanding what we call the social (in)action of society. What turns bystanders into rescuers and heroes, however, is difficult to say, for every person has their reasons for extending their hand in kindness. Oliner found that 76 percent of the rescuers in Nazi-Occupied Europe offered "[p]ity, compassion, concern, and affection" as reasons for rescuing those in need.[9] More often than not, these rescuers or upstanders were helping strangers, not just friends and loved ones.[**]

---

[*]   Action and inaction must be understood as the choices made by the individual or group; the action of remaining silent may be understood as inaction, therefore qualifying the person as a bystander. Whereas the action of standing up for a victim(s) may be interpreted in the literal sense of taking action. For an in-depth analysis of (in)action see Vetlesen (2000) and May (1990).

[**]   Likewise, it is important to understand that the rescuers and heroes' upbringing had much

Bystanders and upstanders are relative terms that apply to each and every one of us; we are both bystanders and upstanders in our own lives, households, and communities (locally and globally). One of the first steps in understanding the bystander is to identify us *all* as being bystanders. This claim will be problematic for many, as there are countless people in this world who are choosing to stand up to a variety of social ills, such as unjust wars, genocide, poverty, racism, sexism, environmental degradation, and more. Everyone at one time or another has chosen not to help out of fear, lack of knowledge, or simply not caring. However, the job of the upstander is never complete; by upstanding in one arena there remains neglect in another. On a daily basis we witness in one form or another a person or group of people in need of help. Those in need of help may include our family, neighbors, local community members, the global community, and ourselves. If we choose not to do anything for those in need, then we are choosing bystander status. For if one has the opportunity to stand up for a victim or group of victims, but fails to do so, then they are indirectly supporting the perpetrator(s).

However, some bystanders choose to maintain their inaction for fear of being punished, such as the cases found in the responses from bystanders during the Holocaust.[10] Many bystanders also claimed a sense of powerlessness to take action;[11] they simply did not feel they could make a difference. There are others who have argued and suggest gender may affect an individual's inclination to stand up because of their physical ability.[12] *Indifference* toward the victims also slowed the action of standing up against the Third Reich.[13] Factors of indifference ranged from modernity such as urbanization and isolation between people[14] to prejudice and ethnocentrism.[15] This creates disconnect in community and therefore produces indifference towards another, blaming them (the victim) for their economic and political plight, whereas the latter is an embedded indifference such as anti-Semitism in Nazi Germany, or apartheid in South Africa.

Conversely, research details how some European states, such as Bulgaria, stood up to the Nazis, refusing to hand over their Jewish populations.[16] Unlike

---

to do with their outlook on humanity; those who were verbally and physically abused were not as inclined to stand up and help those in need. For a more in-depth view of rescuers and heroes during the Holocaust, see Oliner (2003) and Oliner and Oliner (1988).

all other German-occupied countries excluding Denmark and Bulgaria managed to save the majority of their Jewish population during World War II from deportation. In the case of Bulgaria, 48 thousand Jews were saved with the help of Ditmar Peshev, Minister of Justice during World War II, Bulgarian church officials, and ordinary citizens.[17] Also, within Germany there were communities that stood up to the killing of the physically and mentally handicapped, so bystanders and indifference did not always prevail.

In more recent years, the world witnessed in Rwanda the contempt and subsequent massacre inflicted upon the Tutsis by the Hutus. However, this contempt was not a shared sentiment felt by all Hutus. In fact, many Hutus put their lives on the line to guard the lives of a number of Tutsis.[18] Likewise, today the genocides taking place in Darfur are gaining international attention[19] resulting in actions to identify those responsible for the atrocities.[20]

But how can it be explained that some stand by while others stand up? It is as much a psychological phenomenon as it is social embedding us into the bystander role. If we are to understand how one becomes a bystander, then it should be just as likely that we may understand how they may become upstanders.

Based on the work and research of Latané and Darley, a five-stage model was developed to identify bystander intervention.[21] For the bystander to intervene, they must first identify the problem or struggle, and secondly they must interpret it as an emergency. The third stage, and possibly the most crucial, is for the bystander to assume personal responsibility; this is often where most bystanders either decide to help or to remain in the bystander role.[22] In the fourth stage, the bystander will gain the feeling of competence to help, leading to the fifth and final stage, to help. Unfortunately, oftentimes individuals are affected by their peers (their in-group peers) and others around them; the individual will shrug off the responsibility, so to speak, onto others in order that they will not have to help, or "An individual's likelihood of giving help decreases as the number of other bystanders also witnessing an emergency increases."[23]

More often than not, an individual who is an "in-group" member will be more likely to help others who are part of their Group And Less Likely To Help Those From An Out-group. In-group members, are people identifying each other as representing the same group, i.e., race, nationality, social class, religion, etc.[24]

As group behavior proceeds, it can be assumed an individual within a group will not feel they are in a position to help an "outsider" of the group simply because the group in which they are a member does not act to aid the outsider. Hence, the group member is choosing to "go along" with the group or collective. This closely parallels what Arne J. Vetlesen refers to as being a part of *collective inaction*, "the failure of a group that collectively chooses as a group to remain inactive but that could have acted as a group—aka, 'putative groups,' in which 'people are sometimes capable of action in concert but in which no formal organization exists and, as a result, there is no decision-making apparatus.'"[25]

Collective inaction is directly related to the well-known concept *bystander syndrome*, which affects individuals as well as entire groups,[26] and often arises in the third stage of bystander intervention as a *diffusion of responsibility* or *social loafing*. The latter is the individual behavior of "slacking" when there is work to be done; in this case "the work" is standing up to intolerance and social injustice. Diffusion of responsibility ties the hands of the individual within the group as they are looking for other group members to take action, therefore, they as individuals are not responsible for not stopping the atrocity; the group did not act, so therefore it is "okay" that the individual did not act.[27]

The three concepts relate to the influence of a collective or group upon an individual's choice of (in)action; if the individual feels they are one of many and they have no more responsibility to aid a victim than the next person in the group, then they will silently stand by.

In a study conducted by researchers Darley and Latané, subjects were told they were to discuss problems about university life.[28] To assure their anonymity, they were placed into separate rooms and instructed to only communicate via intercom. During the conversations, one of the "subjects" began acting out an epileptic seizure, pleading for help through the intercom. The study found that when subjects believed they were the only other person in the discussion, 85 percent left the room to seek help for the victim, whereas the subjects in groups of four or more people, only 31 percent went for help. The members of the group were frozen by inaction, thinking someone else would help.

In a similar study by Latané and Darley, a group of men were asked to fill out a survey individually or in groups of three.[29] The individuals and groups were separated in order for the researchers to measure their response to the imminent dangers of a staged fire in the building. While they were filling out the survey, smoke began to spill out of the ventilation shafts and into each room. After four minutes of witnessing this, 75 percent of the individuals reported the smoke to the researcher, whereas only 13 percent of the groups' members notified the researcher. Again, people freeze, or act differently as a group than when they are alone responsible.

These findings offered social science a clearer picture of collective (in)action, however, the realization of these findings within society are disturbing. The following examples of collective (in)action are profound. One of the most well known cases took place in 1964 when Catherine "Kitty" Genovese was brutally assaulted and murdered near her Queens, New York, home, outside of an apartment building. The assault lasted for a half-hour, and during that time thirty-eight people either witnessed or overheard Kitty's struggle, but did not come to her aide.[*] Her perpetrator even fled the scene, but came back to continue his assault. The police were eventually summoned, but she died before arriving at the hospital.[30]

On February 12, 1993, two-and-half-year-old James Bulger was abducted at a Liverpool, England shopping mall. The captors were John Thompson and Robert Venables, both 10-year-olds. Again, a reported 38 individuals witnessed the child struggling with the boys, leading some to inquire about their relation with Bulger. The boys lied saying Bulger was their younger brother, and they were taking him home. However, the boys drug Bulger many miles from the shopping mall to a railway line where the child was murdered. Witnesses explained during the trial they believed the child to be related to the two adolescents, and therefore did not intervene in the struggle.[31] The witnesses offered their dismay for the abuse of the child, but were unable to save the young James Bulger.

---

[*]   The accuracy to the number of bystanders witnessing Kitty's assault is problematic, however. Parts of the story may have been fabricated by reporters on the case (See Manning et al. 2007). Nonetheless, Kitty Genovese's story has motivated research in social psychology, helping to understand group behavior and the bystander effect.

Another harrowing example involved a group of mountaineers who ignored British climber David Sharp's need for assistance as they continued past him to the summit of Mt. Everest. Climbing enthusiasts are eager to reach the summit of Everest to snap a picture of their grand feat, but at what expense? How glorious is the climb if you have to step over, and ignore, a dying fellow human being in order to snap that summit picture?[32] Mr. Sharp perished on the snowy slopes of Everest.

What caused these individuals to forsake Kitty Genovese, James Bulger, and David Sharp? In Nazi-occupied Europe, rescuing victims from Nazi brutality was a crime punishable by death, therefore it is important to understand that during WWII potential upstanders were fearful for their lives. However, in the case of Genovese, Bulger and Sharp, saving their lives would not have been a crime. On the contrary it would have been viewed as an honorable act. The aforementioned findings of personal fear and indifference may offer clues to help us identify some of the barriers individuals and groups may endure when faced with a decision whether or not to aid another in dire need.

Ultimately, these findings may help offer clues to contemporary indifference surrounding genocide, prejudice, sexism, and environmental degradation. We may also have a better understanding of the apathetic nature our society holds in regards to a less than adequate health care system in the U.S. and around the globe, indifference toward "collateral damage" in foreign wars, as well as a lack of immediacy to the residual effects of Post Traumatic Stress Disorder (PTSD) experienced by returning soldiers from these wars. The list continues when we consider the social injustices that prevail in our world due to people's indifference.

INNOCENT BYSTANDERS

"What can I do? I don't even live near those people. I have my own problems to deal with." How many times have we thought this? How many times have we overheard someone in conversation rationalizing their (in)action? We offer excuses not to help because we "didn't know," "we don't live anywhere near 'them,'" etc. We are essentially claiming our innocence as a bystander. But are we really innocent?

Arne Vetlesen refers to innocent bystanders as *passive bystanders*—those who claim ignorance or are emancipated from guilt by their geographical and spatial positioning in context to the atrocity;[33] the individual or group becomes aware of the atrocity through media coverage or word of mouth. What I am proposing here is the absence of innocence, passivity, or ignorance. The levels of atrocities and victimization encompassing the world is not defined solely on the basis of state and media attention to genocide or individual crimes, but rather the everyday nuances that create the larger structures of our society and its shortcomings. What the *passive bystander* fails to recognize are the numerous crimes, as well as social and environmental injustices surrounding their lives. We as individuals are complicit in these crimes through our silence, indifference, and/or direct support of the crimes. Understanding these atrocities may remove the passive bystander status, urging individuals and groups to develop into upstanders. Standing up to an injustice can be as simple as demanding healthier school lunches for your children, or refusing to work for or patronize a corporation that exploits its labor force. On the other hand, upstanding can be as grand as putting one's life on the line to save a victim of assault or genocide. Whatever the case may be, the bystander is never innocent when there is an opportunity to stand up, break the silence, and demand change. However, standing up is not always an easy task for one to undertake. As we already know, collective inaction is very dependent upon the individuals' inability to "break free from the pack."

INDIVIDUAL BYSTANDERS

Individualism in America, according to Staub, is a "double-edged sword;" there is the independent thinker who will not follow blindly.[34] In the same light that individual may occasionally find themselves alone, facing difficult times and therefore falling in line with a certain group that offers them security and a sense of worth. As research has proven, an individual is more inclined to help and stand up for another when they (the individual) are not influenced by a group.[35] "Individuals often give up autonomy, responsibility, and decision making to their group and leaders"[36] often occurs in groups of conformity such as the military and gangs.

The advantage of group cohesion can have its benefits; allowing individuals to feel a sense of belonging by dividing their difficulties amongst the group, directly reducing their responsibility. However, we also know that group behavior is detrimental, as it has created factions between groups, i.e., Nazi Party and Jewish communities. Group behavior will therefore determine how the individuals within the group act. Hence, bystanders are born. If we can understand group behavior, then we may be able to correlate group behavior in scenarios around the globe: genocide, environmental degradation, racism, sexism, and jingoistic fervor. Individuals in groups are greatly affected by the ebb and flow of the group; if the group acts, the individual tends to act according to the group—"mass behavior," the "rule of the mob."

INSTITUTIONAL BYSTANDERS

For the individuals in Nazi-occupied Europe "[i]t was easier for individuals to conform to their institutional role if they could see this as purely part of their job, as something distinct from the private realm in which they were good spouses, churchgoers, and so forth; '[T]he essentially private person, anxious to make a good life for his family and totally lacking in any attachment to the idea of citizenship, is the perfect cog.'"[37]

Institutions such as churches and schools are often responsible for the socialization of its members. Therefore, individual socialization of group members will directly determine the group's collective behavior. Unfortunately, group interaction can involve the inculcation of prejudice and xenophobia, which may hinder group (in)action.[38]

Germany, for example, was in a stage of economic downturn after WWI. When a strong military regime arose rooted in German historical ideals buttressed by a scapegoating, anti-Semitic propaganda, the German people were socialized by the Nazis into complicity with the Furher's actions.[39] Religious institutions in Europe were also complicit with Nazi policies for reasons of pragmatism, safety, as well as anti-Semitism.[40] In 1998 Pope John Paul II publicly apologized on behalf of the Catholic Church for its cooperation with the Nazis.[41] The Holocaust may never have taken place had it not been for the pervading anti-Semitic sentiments and subsequent indifference held by the world's individuals and its institutions.

Tice and Baumeister, as well as others, offer the institution of gender as another component of socialization.[42] Men and women tend to take on roles instituted at birth, which sociologist Mary Douglas maintains are reinforced by labeling throughout their lives; traditionally the woman is the caretaker, the emotionally acute human to her male counterpart, denoted as the rational thinker, leader, and provider for family. Ridgeway offers examples to support Douglas' labeling theory, building upon her theory by identifying reciprocating roles within social settings.[43] Yet, Ridgeway also challenges Douglas' institutional gender roles, for she identifies gender as a two-way street. For example, we have all witnessed a group setting at work, at dinner with friends and family, or in a classroom, where the person leading the discussion or professing knowledge of a certain subject will overrule the opinion of others. When a person professing knowledge of a subject proclaims expertise, they control the setting while the other gender tends to acquiesce.

INTERNATIONAL BYSTANDERS

The international community became aware of the Holocaust through networks, such as religious groups between the U.S. and Germany.[44] Barnett states that the allied countries and its organizations claimed to not know of the genocide in Nazi-occupied Europe until 1943. However, that claim was found to be untrue. The Red Cross knew of the genocide, but was reluctant to oppose Nazi authority for fear they may not be able to continue their duties as an organization. Likewise, religious networks between the U.S. and Germany were communicating prior to 1943. Certainly there was indifference to the Jewish plight. Some circles around the world held anti-Semitic attitudes, and were therefore unwilling to help. Barnett adds, "[t]he question was not knowledge—those who wanted to know could... Perhaps some of the limitations were emotional. Throughout the world the predominant reaction to reports from Europe was disbelief, indifference, passivity, and a sense of powerlessness."[45]

Samantha Power discusses the absence of nation-states' roles in opposing genocidal acts as *systemic bystanding*.[46] In more contemporary times, this concept may best be understood in regards to the lack of intervention on the part of the U.S. during the Rwandan genocide. Between April and July of

1994—about 100 days—nearly one million people were massacred, mostly
Tutsis, but the toll also included Hutus who were sympathetic to their Tutsi
neighbors. The Hutu government explicitly encouraged this genocide and
organized a group called the *Interahamwe*, an informal militia to methodi-
cally kill Tutsis, as the government-controlled radio broadcasted to its citizens
to continue mass killing. Many Hutus claimed they were forced to join the
Interahamwe gangs because the military threatened their lives if they did not
kill Tutsi neighbors.[47]

The U.S. and a great portion of the world were aware of the genocide,
however, only a small United Nations peacekeeping troop were dispatched.
The U.N. was simply put in place to "keep the peace" between the Hutus and
Tutsis, and were not necessarily choosing the side of the Tutsis who were greatly
outnumbered. Arne Vetlesen labels the U.N.'s bystander role as *bystanders by
assignment*—they are assigned physical presence at the scene, but not necessarily taking sides.[48]

Additionally, nation-states, such as the U.S., have historically been blamed
for their lack of recognition, intervention, and prevention of genocide based
upon economic and political interests.[49] Another example is the flooding
in New Orleans. In New Orleans, the poorer people, who happened to be a
majority black population, were in the neighborhoods that were exposed to
natural disaster. Due to an inefficient response by the government, these communities were neglected and most affected by Hurricane Katrina. This lack of
intervention may help us draw conclusions to why hundreds of thousands have
perished in Darfur, with more than two million having been displaced from
their homes.[50] In early 2003, the Darfur region of Western Sudan entered a
horrific state of affairs as largely nomadic Arab tribes (Janjaweed), believed to
be funded by the Sudanese government, began what has now been determined
by the U.S. Congress to be genocide.[51] President Bush later acknowledged the
mass displacement, murders, and sexual assaults as genocide, however he also
stated, "The United States will continue to provide financial and logistical
assistance, but not U.S. troops, to help stop the genocide."[52] Samantha Power,
details in her book, *A Problem from Hell*, the lack of government inclusion
in stopping atrocities such as genocide is a trend among powerful nations.[53]
Jerry Fowler, staff director of the Committee on Conscience, reflects on U.S.

inaction, "We don't intervene because the political risks of not acting are less than the political risks of acting."[54] By not acknowledging the immediacy of intervention the Darfur genocide requires, the U.S. Government is opting to stand by while death pursues innocent lives. We have learned from Rwanda it takes more than the U.N. to intervene, begging the question, how much longer will the international community stand by as genocide persists in Darfur?

BYSTANDERS: SOCIAL-PSYCHOLOGICAL INTERPRETATIONS

Social psychology clarifies the processes individuals and groups undergo when choosing to stand by. This chapter has already given some clues to group interaction and its effects on the individual (eg., in-groups and out-groups). Furthermore, Shotland and Stebbins offer *limited altruism* as a concept to identify the social-psychological phenomenon of a low need/high cost or high need/low cost condition necessary for people to help others.[55] "Need" and "cost" are perceptions of the bystander and will greatly determine their subsequent (in)action; the higher the perceived physical, emotional, or economic cost, and the lower perceived need of the victim, there will inevitably be less help offered from the bystander. On the other hand, if there is low cost and high need, the likelihood of helping is greater. Both Power[56] and Glazer's[57] assessment of the lack of U.S. and international involvement in recent genocides may correlate to *limited altruism*. Stepping back further, we can see how limited altruism parallels the third stage of bystander intervention; there is a cost assessment to one's ability to intervene.

If a person, or nation, decides not to intervene, what develops is the *free rider problem*, which mirrors the diffusion of responsibility; where individuals within groups believe the victim(s) problem is someone else's responsibility, not theirs.[58] Essentially, the bystander has been socialized to believe that the person in danger is not worth their time and effort, and that effort that may cause harm or burden to the upstander.

Staub offers the idea that people may be indifferent due to their beliefs that the victim(s) may have "had it coming to them."[59] This is known as the *Just World Hypothesis*: if a person believes that an individual or group is leading a life of "negativity" then that individual or group in turn can expect to have negative consequences befall them. Therefore, in a just world, people get what they deserve. He offers the example of a drunken man falling in a subway and that of another man, reliant upon a walking cane, falling in the same environment. In his research, Staub points out the general indifference one will have for the alcoholic, believing the cause of his fall being the result of consumption. Therefore, the alcoholic could have avoided the spill, whereas the handicapped individual is not held responsible for his fall and merits more sympathy. The tragedy in these contrasting views is the socialized prejudice embedded within our society; we are taught to believe alcoholism is a drag on society, not a physical and mental illness warranting public attention.

Conservative ideology has been linked to the *Just World Hypothesis*, as well as prejudice.[60] In the aftermath of Hurricane Katrina, many blamed the *victims* for their desire to live in a city that was predicted to become a disaster area, and others mentioned that the hurricane hit New Orleans because there were more bars than churches![61] They offered divine intervention as a rationale for poor structural foresight and state disaster preparation. When we consider an institution's role in socialization,[62] it is understandable how individuals and groups may take on the collective behavior held by the institution. However, the indifference in bystanders is multifaceted; on the individual and group levels, the literature speaks of personal fears, powerlessness, as well as prejudice, xenophobia and racism. *Personal fears* and the sense of *powerlessness* are distinct sentiments of bystanders in cases of totalitarian governments like Nazi Germany; as mentioned earlier, it was a crime to harbor Jews and others sought after for elimination by the Nazis.[63] Fear of personal harm may have taken hold of some of the bystanders in the Kitty Genovese case as well.

The social psychological traits of prejudice and xenophobia relate more closely with a *Just World Hypothesis*, which helps explain individual and group factors for standing by. Along that line the socialization process lends weight to what author Vishavjit Singh labels as *bystander syndrome*.[64] Singh offers the term bystander syndrome in relation to years of oppression and violence in Indian culture. The case study revolves around the brutal sexual assault of a woman in a subway system. Nobody came to her rescue as this type of episode and general debasement of women has become all too common. The fear of personal injury and involvement with police, as well as public indifference are reasons offered for their inaction to stop such atrocities.

Bystander syndrome is the result of the numerous acts of violence and injustice, which bombard the psyche of the world populations; it is a world disease, not just that of India. Essentially it is *programmed indifference*;[65] a "numbing affect" individuals and groups undergo due to the socialization of violence, indifference, and social stratification surrounding them. Much like the socialization of anti-Semitic propaganda pumped out by the Nazis prior to and during the Holocaust, which was buttressed by the 2000 years of anti-Semitic sentiments prior to Nazi occupation.

REASSESSING THE DIVISION OF LABOR

From a social-psychological viewpoint, collective behavior helps us understand the indifferent nature of society. Historically, collective behavior theorists have been able to shed more light on the human phenomena of indifference. Herbert Blumer utilizes symbolic interaction to describe group behavior.[66] He claims, using a social-psychological framework, individuals are unable to choose to defect from group action, therefore allowing the group to determine the individual's behavior. However, there is evidence of upstanding citizens who have broken away from group conformity in an effort to make a positive change.[67] Shaffer and Oliner interviewed hate group members who defected their group, because they were mistreated by the leadership and discovered that the ideology of the group was false.[68] Additionally, a loving person such as a girlfriend, or friend, was able to talk them out of the group. How else are we to explain upstanders if we are to assume that group behavior has the final say for individual action?

But still the question remains as to how we are able to comprehend the macro-level bystander (i.e., systemic bystander). Is it simply a matter of conservative economic and political interests? Emile Durkheim viewed modern society as having organic solidarity, where beliefs and values support individualistic attitudes, specialization, and differentiation of activities in institutions.[69] The problem arises when many of these individualistic behaviors and specializations undermine human well-being. In a sense, the division of labor, or the separation of roles has failed to cohere society, not allowing it to function in a manner where social, economic and environmental equality is possible. When society is unable to maintain its cohesion, a sense of lawlessness forms, producing anomie: a social-psychological condition stemming from the rapid increase in economic change, creating a general dissolution of moral regulation that would otherwise help keep pace with social changes. This is generally where we begin to see indifference and hopelessness occur, as was shown in the fall of the Czarist Empire in the beginning of the twentieth century, after the rebellion against the unjust treatment of the working people and peasants.

Durkheim believed the necessary changes for a more cohesive society are based in education. Only then may we begin to see maintaining the division of labor and controlling the subsequent anomie that threatens to undermine our society as a whole. However, we must see society as it is: a conglomeration of roles developed to create some sort of economic fluidity. Unfortunately, as we stand as a society today, we typically fail to meet the social and environmental factors necessary to create a balance in the division of labor. Within the division of labor that Durkheim spoke of, we can understand the individual's complementary task toward a more cohesive society. Better understood, we all have our own interests, and it could be inferred that each individual has an inclination toward bettering their part of the world, in one form or another. Therefore, one individual may work toward bettering the economic livelihood of their neighborhood, while another individual in that same neighborhood seeks to ensure safe drinking water for its residents, while another seeks to educate the underprivileged.

If this pattern were to be inculcated and networked throughout society to reach the macro level, then we may hypothesize that individual and group responsibility will ensure that bystander status discontinues its current reign in society. An example of solidarity on the macro level could be equated to the development of the international court system, which in 1998 sentenced former Rwandan Prime Minister, Jean Kambanda, to a life imprisonment for his role in the deaths of 800,000 Rwandans. This U.N. tribunal in Tanzania was the inaugural step toward convicting anyone for genocide, and the first to hold a head of government responsible.[70] More recently, the Bosnian War Crimes Court convicted seven Bosnian Serbs of genocide in the 1995 massacre of Bosnian Muslims at Srebrenica. Serb political leader, Radovan Karadzic was tried and sentenced in a separate U.N. war crimes tribunal in the

Netherlands.[71] If a collective group or groups are willing to stand up for social justice, there will be less opportunity for atrocities to go unaccounted for, so that they will be dissolved before they occur.

EXPANDING OUR UNDERSTANDING OF BYSTANDERS

What needs to be stressed is that the reassessment of social stratification and inequality in society will not cure the bystander epidemic. There are simply too many atrocities surrounding our daily lives locally and internationally: environmental degradation, corporate greed, institutional racism, sexism, spousal battery, child abuse, casualties of war and its "collateral damage," including the mental and physical anguish of returning soldiers suffering from Post-Traumatic Stress Disorder (PTSD). Let us not forget the innocent civilians who are displaced from their homes, families torn apart, and lives lost. Are these innocents accounted for? Are the returning soldiers receiving adequate mental and physical health care? Expanding this question: how does the *rest* of the U.S. and world fare when considering the lack of adequate health care? How are we bystanders when corporate interests move production to "developing" countries in order to exploit labor, while concomitantly the previously employed laborers of these corporations are laid off and faced with personal hardships? Are we concerned about the health of people who consume chemically-treated, mass-produced, processed and prepackaged foods? Or the global food commodity system that undercuts indigenous producers, forcing them off their land and into the streets to sell consumer goods?[72] What about the numerous U.S. farm families who have been forced from their farms due to their inability to financially maintain the pace of the commoditized grain and livestock production within the industrial/agricultural system?[73]

Could these indirect displacements of culture be considered a form of genocide? How willing are we to expand the deep-rooted definition of genocide in order to bring about awareness of the severity and evil of our current social ills? This is a contentious question, but one where we are able to see some of the linkages to the internationally agreed upon definition of genocide. In Resolution 260, the U.N. defined genocide in 1948 as any of the following acts committed with the intent to destroy, in whole or in part, a national, ethnic, racial or religious group, as such: Killing members of the group, causing serious bodily or mental harm to members of the group, deliberately inflicting on the group conditions of life calculated to bring about its physical destruction in whole or in part, imposing measures intended to prevent births within the group, or forcibly transferring children of the group to another group. We could argue that "collateral damage" in Iraq is mainly innocent civilians who are driven from their homes. Likewise, U.S. farm families are pushed off their land in order to make room for corporate agriculture to make more money with fewer farmers and more land; farm kids who once had visions of farming their great-grandparents' land are now forced into an urban workforce. Ironically, as this same corporate agriculture system displaces U.S. farmers, it is concomitantly displacing indigenous farmers in the southern nations of Latin America as well as in Africa and Asia. From an environmental point of view, the degradation of the soil, water, and deforestation taking place around the globe, oftentimes to expand agricultural production, reduces the quality of life of those dependent upon those natural resources, while displacing farming communities and indigenous villages.

The scope of this chapter is not intended to expand upon genocide, but rather to bring to light the necessity of standing up to contemporary atrocities. If we were to consider the depth of injustices around the globe and in our backyards, and how their circumstances are comparable to atrocities such as genocide, we may be willing to be held more accountable and not claim the innocent bystander status. We must ask ourselves, are we bystanders if we purchase the goods that directly support the aforementioned atrocities? Do we directly or indirectly support these social and environmental injustices through indifference? Are we willing to take responsibility in order to stand up to the numerous injustices that pervade our world?

If we recognize the fact that we are all bystanders in some form or another, it may be easier to take action and lessen the burden of those historically and presently affected by our indifference and inaction. If we choose not to take action, remain silent and indifferent to local, national and global atrocities—both environmental and social—we are then no different than the historical understanding of bystanders. We must find a balance of values benefiting a more peaceful and caring global society, one promoting personal and group accountability.

International Bystanders: Environmental Negligence

But how do we begin to create accountability on a global scale? We already know there is social inequality, but how is this linked to environmental inequality? How can we identify bystanders in this arena? If we consider the economic benefits to be gained for a small percentage of individuals, we can understand that self-interest can present itself as a political sentiment similar to the previously discussed cost-benefit analysis of limited altruism. Labor and land exploitation are not a new phenomenon in the world market. Inequality of labor and allocation of land and its resources seem to be necessary components for maintaining a nation's economic stability and competitive edge in the world market. Authors Sprinz and Vaahtoranta explain the interest-based stance of international environmental policy as having two parts or "unit-level factors"; the country's vulnerability toward pollution, and the economic costs of pollution abatement.[74] The latter is a factor determined by the country's gross domestic product (GDP) and gross national product (GNP); if the abatement of environmental degradation affects the ability of the country to compete in national and international markets, there appears to be reluctance for the country's political parties to adhere to international environmental policies. Thus, there is a conflict of interest for those concerned about economic benefits, whether for the betterment of the country or set of individuals, than there is for the well-being and health of the environment and global citizens.

For countries with highly polluting industries, but reaping high returns on the product sold nationally and internationally, there is a direct cost to abate these practices. There is little benefit to be gained in the short term. As a result, counties are now becoming more concerned with the "downstream" affect of pollutants: country A's factories are upstream/upwind from country B. There is little country A would want to do to incur a cost for abating their industrial measures to concede with country B's demands for stricter environmental regulations for the benefit of their natural environment and public health.

Sprinz and Vaahtoranta consider the following model to help identify the four classes into which a country may fall based on its political-economic relation to international environmental policy.[75]

Ecological Vulnerability

		Low	High
Abatement Costs	*Low*	(1) Bystander	(2) Pushers
	High	(3) Draggers	(4) Intermediates

In cell 2, "Pushers" are going to be those countries at high risk or most vulnerable to the consequences of ecological degradation, but yet they are not necessarily high competitors in the international market (low abatements). Therefore, they will "push" for more stringent environmental policies because their country may be "downstream" of a country falling into category number three. "Draggers" are those countries reluctant to follow environmental standards for the high abatement will endure to restructure their outputs. They are not feeling the environmental stresses felt by the "Pushers" and the "Intermediates," hence, these countries will "drag their feet" so to speak, showing no immediate concern for the "Pushers'" plea. The "Intermediates," find themselves needing to adhere to environmental policies, but due to the high abatement costs, they may not be willing to make adjustments to their economic and production policies. Finally, "Bystanders" with both low ecological vulnerability and low abatement costs, will find a position of indifference, although they may take a more ambitious stance than the "Dragger."

How is it possible to turn the "Bystanders" into "Pushers?" It may be understood from an economic standpoint. The "Draggers" and the "Intermediates" will not recognize the international environmental policies and pacts for reasons of high abatement costs, which would hamper their viability in the national and international markets. It may not be a matter of requiring countries to follow strict environmental guidelines, for if history repeats itself, and normally it does, we will see "Draggers" searching for improved environmental standards.

Until recently, there were no environmental scientists who were able to accurately monitor the degradation of the planet's natural resources. Today we regard the current use of polluting agents, such as carbon monoxide emissions, as being a detriment to the atmospheric and global health. There are arguments against these findings, which say many of the effects of global warming we are experiencing have happened as natural phenomenon in the past and will continue into the future. However, our high usage of carbon and petroleum-based fuel have influenced the natural cyclical phenomenon of global warming/cooling. What lacked in the years past was a global consciousness based on scientific findings that human actions are directly affecting the environment.

Environmental sociologist Sing Chew's findings of timber pollen counts over the past five thousand years lends evidence to mass harvesting of timber to fuel nation-states of the past.[76] Countries and empires over the past five thousand years have waxed and waned depending on their ability to harvest timber as a fuel to expand their empires' wealth and borders. Consequently, ecological degradation ensued as mass erosion and siltation choked vital waterways, arable lands gave way to desertification, and societies lost their means of economic reproduction. What Chew found was those societies and their empires with degraded natural environments lost power and were no longer able to compete in their global system of commerce. Five thousand years ago, people began to destroy the environment and nations and groups continue to allow this degradation to happen and, in some cases, partake in it.

Today, oil and other carbon-based fuels are sought to reproduce society; it is the fuel primarily used for maintaining a country's strong GNP and GDP. As a consequence, landscapes and societies are still being ravished by empires searching for oil and other forms of carbon based fuels, which contribute to air, water and soil pollution just as mass timber harvesting desecrated the landscapes in previous empires. Today's economic gain from environmental exploitation takes precedence over environmental protection.

FROM BYSTANDER TO UPSTANDER: EDUCATION FOR RAISING AWARENESS

Just as Durkheim suggests, the creation of a cohesive society may be established with education and a reevaluation of how the division of labor is constructed. In this section, I want to reinforce this idea of how education can be the catalyst for a transition of a bystander to upstander. Oliner and Oliner in

1982 established the Altruistic Personality and Prosocial Behavior Institute at Humboldt State University, which has been educating students and global community members for almost thirty years about the social psychological behavior of individuals and their groups, such as the heroes or (upstanders) of World War II. Oliner's own story and that of his rescuers has been told in the numerous books and articles that he and his wife Pearl have co-authored together. His dedication to telling his story, and the stories of others like him, attempts to remove the silence and bystander status from society through education.

Beaman et al. show that informing people about bystanders can indirectly influence them to help.[77] A study was conducted where one class was lectured about bystander affects, and another class was not. Shortly after the lectures the participants were reported to have witnessed a person slumped over on a park bench. Of the students who had not heard the lecture, 25 percent stopped to help, but 50 percent of the students who had attended the lecture offered to help. Therefore, by simply lecturing to a class about a specific topic a student could recognize and apply to their daily life, the chances of helping and not remaining a bystander doubled.

In another account, a group of adolescents have been introduced to the educational concept of understanding history to understand one's self. Barr details the program, *Facing History and Ourselves*, which is based in viewing the beginnings of the Third Reich and how an adolescent boy became a member of the Hitler Youth.[78] The program allows youth to understand the pressures of in-groups and how these groups tend to ostracize out-group members. Kids are able to relate to these pressures by studying the in-group pressures youth have faced throughout history, and directly apply it to their own experiences. The students are encouraged to account their personal stories in journals in order that they may reflect on their own subjugation to social injustice, and how they can learn from past mistakes by seeing themselves in contemporary situations. One of the main goals of the program is to show students the correlation between social isolation and the need to belong. As a result, we begin to see how people go along to get along with their in-group peers, even if it means to debase one's personal conviction for social justice. In short, the students are able to understand through personal experience how in-group interactions can lead to social injustice towards out-group members.

The qualitative research established throughout the course of the program details the positive impact on students' capacity for critical reflection that has broadened the students' understanding of themselves and their relationship to others in society; self-reflection, pro-social awareness, and personal involvement were all demonstrated when analyzing student journals.[79]

In another educational setting, a Toronto-based English teacher and students sent more than 1,500 letters to the U.N. demanding relief for the victims in the Darfur genocide. These students became aware of the atrocities of genocide by watching the film *Hotel Rwanda*, which depicts the genocidal horrors of Rwanda. The students did not want to be referred to as "silent bystanders,"[80] and their letters were aimed to urge government representatives and the U.N. to intervene in the violence. By making their voices heard, these students felt they were doing their best to help stop the Darfur genocide.

This example is important when considering the mass media's involvement for educating society as a whole; the media's great influence on collective behavior is relatively well-known.[81] However, more research is necessary to gauge a tangible shift in group behavior after media exposure to make an accurate statement as to whether or not society is taking the multitude of social and environmental atrocities seriously. On the other hand, there is proof of a shift in ecological values in specific areas of the U.S. and throughout the world, which may be attributed to the roles of the media. In 2007, the California State Legislature introduced a bill that would phase out the sale of incandescent light bulbs, opting for the more eco-friendly compact fluorescent bulb.[82] California was setting a trend of ecological stewardship through their action. Lloyd E. Levine, Chair, Assembly Utilities and Commerce Committee, and author of the Assembly Bill 722 says,

> Six days after I announced AB 722, similar legislation was intro-
> duced in Connecticut. A day later, [San Francisco] Mayor Gavin
> Newsom announced an initiative to improve the efficiency
> of lighting technologies used in commercial buildings in San
> Francisco. Two days after that, a Republican Assembly member
> from New Jersey introduced legislation that calls for his state to
> switch to fluorescent lighting in government buildings over the

next three years. And then, a month later, Australia's Minister of Energy announced that Australia will phase out all incandescent bulbs by 2010.[83]

This trendsetting is exactly what needs to happen in order for the U.S. and other national communities to recognize that we are sharing the same environment. No longer can they claim bystander status based on ignorance, for political leaders, the media, and progressive organizations are educating the public on a mass level. Empirical studies regarding the plight of the ecosystem have been underway for quite some time.[84] However, when those studies are accessible to a wider audience we may safely predict that this transfer of knowledge will have a lasting effect on collective action. Reducing the amount of ignorance in the world will limit the number of passive bystanders, which will theoretically aid the advancement of a more cognizant and caring society.

CONCLUSION

By examining schemata, the social psychological cues of bystanders and group interaction, this chapter begins to help us understand how bystanders are created and maintained in a number of settings. The atrocities of the Third Reich brought to light the need for public recognition and monitoring of genocide. The numerous bystanders who chose silence for a variety of social psychological reasons, have been emancipated by time, but their legacy pervades our contemporary times. There are a number of social and environmental ills surrounding us today that warrant more resistance from the global populations; every day we are witness to a multitude of needs that fall short of help due to our indifference and silence.

It is our hope that this discussion can help light a path for how bystanders may become upstanders. Furthermore, there is an opportunity for us to expand the definition of bystanders, namely in the area of environmental degradation and its connection to social and economic injustice. With rising food shortages and fuel expenses, there seems to be an interesting fate on the horizon for global communities. How will the low-income populations find healthy foods? Learning from the past has not been adequate, for today we still are witnessing genocide, wars are still fought for natural resources, and the mismanagement of those natural resources continues to degrade the integrity of the earth's ecosystem and its people's livelihoods.

However, there are individuals and groups who choose to stand up, who are affected by the need for change and the need to realize a more caring world. They refuse to choose silence. By means of education and media outreach, proactive attempts to bring about awareness have proven to create change, but there is still plenty of work to be done before the world is free of evil, free of hate, free of fear, and free of silence.

Chapter 4

Paving the Way to Resistance: The Gift of Good during the Nazi Occupation 1939-1945

THE CONTEXT IN WHICH THESE EXAMPLES of genocide and resistance took place was World War II. The root causes of the war have been examined and theorized by many academics looking at various areas of interest. However, most would agree that there are three main components to the explosion of World War II. The first is the economic plight of the German people after the First World War and the environment of desperation that these economic conditions created. It is with this sense of hopelessness that the German people were manipulated into seeing the Nationalist Socialist Party as their best option. The second component is widespread anti-Semitism that existed throughout the occupied territories, resulting in high numbers of bystanders turning a blind eye to the genocide occurring around them. The third component to the explosion of World War II was the inability of the allied forces to take the Nazi aggression seriously. It was not until Germany invaded Poland that the allied forces started to recognize the real threat that the Nazis represented. Had this threat been taken seriously it is possible that the Nazis could have been stopped before they committed the greatest genocide in human history.

JEWISH RESISTANCE

One of the most vital and historically important organized efforts to do good in the face of evil and the threat of death was the resistance movement in Europe during the reign of the Nazis. As a boy in Poland during this time I was a direct beneficiary of this resistance to evil when a Polish family took me in and disguised my Jewish identity, thus saving my life and propelling me on a lifelong journey toward understanding this impulse to do good in the face of certain death.

Resistance can be defined as an organized movement, expressed in underground efforts to resist a government or occupying power regarded as oppressive and unjust. Examples of resistance can be found in a variety of historical contexts. Barbalet informs us that there can be no adequate understanding of power and power relations without the concept of resistance.[1] He goes on to say that most social relations and institutions invoke a variety of power relations, including an often small minority who go against the majority opinion, despite the risks. In this section, we shall review and analyze acts of resistance ranging from extreme cases (individual acts of violence and armed revolts) to subtle acts (sabotaging production lines, stealing, and feigning sickness) by those who were forced to work for the Germans under the *Arbeitseinsatz* (Work Contribution) as well as keeping lines of communication open through illegal press that combated Nazi propaganda, and writing resistance songs and poems.

To best understand the conditions that led to the eventual destruction of European Jewry, and later the Armenian and Rwandan genocides, a theoretical framework is needed. For this we draw from Thalhammer, O'Loughlin, Glazer, Glazer, McFarland, Stoltzfus, and Shepela's *Courageous Resisters: The Power of Ordinary People*.[2] The authors provide a theoretical framework of three key factors that explain courageous resistors. The first factor is *preconditions*, one's own attitude and personal feelings to the current situation at hand, implying that the individual is already sympathetic to the injustices that are occurring. *Networks* are relationships that someone has with groups and/or organizations that provide inside information to the people in danger, so they can keep them safe. An example of a *network* is someone who works in the concentration camps, is sympathetic to the resisters, knows important information, and may warn Jewish people in hiding that Nazis are going to come to their house soon. The final factor is *context*. This is the actual situation at hand. It is the resources available at the time, when other resources may be made unavailable. For example, a German running an orphanage may be able to hide Jewish children by saying they are German orphans. The factors that contribute to courageous resisters are the values the person already holds, who they know, and the resources they have available to resist the evil that is going on around them.

What follows is a discussion of the above-mentioned genocides that inspired both individuals and organized groups to resist the state-sponsored evil. In each of these examples we can see compelling similarities between these divergent conflicts. The societies where these conflicts occurred had ethnic, religious, and sectarian divisions already embedded in their culture. These pre-existing divisions encouraged the dehumanization and scapegoating of the out-group, as the Nazis did with the Jews. This eventually led to the perception of the minority group as an enemy.

Harvard scholar Herbert Kelman studied several genocidal massacres and found three important explanatory variables; *dehumanization, authorization,* and *routinization.*[3] The people in power *dehumanized* the victims by referring to them as cockroaches or cancer. The state *authorized* the oppression and/ or killing, provided the means to kill the victims, and *routinized* the methods of killing—making the process organized to the point of people not questioning authority and their own actions. Additionally, each of these societies had either an occupying force or state apparatus that encouraged, facilitated, and perpetrated a campaign against a particular ethnic or cultural group of its citizenry. In conjunction with these preconditions and networks of genocide, each of these societies had individual citizens and organized groups that were determined to resist the attempt by the state to "ethnically cleanse" the perceived "inferior race." The particular manifestations of resistance varied depending on the context of the genocidal campaign. However, in each historical period there were individuals and groups who, in the face of death, stood up and resisted in a variety of ways, including force of arms, rescuing of innocent victims, and protest.

PRECONDITIONS OF RESISTANCE DURING THE HOLOCAUST

We will begin our discussion of resistance to genocide with an examination of the distorted image of Jewish passivity during the Nazi occupation of Europe. Austrian-born American historian Raul Hilberg in his work, *The Destruction of the European Jews,* asserts that the Jewish leadership, also referred to as the

Judenrat, cooperated in their own destruction.[4] Hilberg stated that Jewish reaction to threat and certain death during the Holocaust took five forms.[5] The first form, *armed resistance*, was violent and confrontational challenges to persecution, such as ghetto resistance to Nazi extermination of Jews. *Alleviation* was the activity to avert danger, such as petitions, protection payments, and ransom payments. *Evasion* was flight, concealing Jews, and hiding in order to escape the Nazis. *Paralysis* was the inability to respond at all, brought on by a psychological numbness to dread and fear. The final form was *compliance,* the acceptance of the requirements of the authority in order to avoid penalties. He emphasizes that they passively accepted their demise stating:

> Finally, in the supreme moment of crisis the primeval tendency to resist aggression breaks to the surface. Resistance then becomes an obstacle to compliance, just as compliance is an obstacle to resistance. In the Jewish case the cooperation reaction was the stronger one until the end.[6]

Yehuda Bauer, a renowned Israeli historian, argues that there is a great volume of evidence that the Jews resisted against the Nazis.[7] In his book, *A History of the Holocaust*, he provides specific stories of resistance, and maintains:

> Although no comprehensive historical analysis of these rebellions exists, fairly adequate descriptions of most of them are available. Armed and unarmed rebellions occurred in Sachsenhausen, Auschwitz, Sobibor, Treblinka, Kruszyna, and Krychow. Organizations intending rebellion that in some cases brought about escapes existed at Plaszow, Ostrowiec Swietojarski, Budzyn, Poniatow, Trawniki, the Jewish POW camp at Lublin, and elsewhere.[8]

The *Judenrat* in particular refused to cooperate and resisted the Nazis, contrary to Hilberg's assertion.

The most distorted and inaccurate image of the Holocaust is of European Jews calmly and passively walking to their deaths. This myth has been recently corrected in the media by such depictions of heroic resistance by the Rosenstrasse women and others mentioned below. Frequently, people ask,

"Why didn't they fight back?" The reality is that many did resist, in many places and in different ways. Jews actively fought the Nazis among partisan units, they revolted in death camps and ghettos, they evaded and hid from the Nazis, interfered with war production and factories, and led and participated in resistance groups in a number of countries including Bulgaria, Poland, Ukraine, Belorussia, Yugoslavia, Belgium, Greece, France and others.[9] Jews were also involved in rescuing other victims of Nazi persecution by smuggling them across the borders from France to Spain, and into Switzerland.[10] The myth of passivity has been a powerful force in the interpretation of the Holocaust and has functioned to not give the resisters the attention they so richly deserve. For anti-Semites it reinforces the stereotype of the cowardly and treacherous Jew who was unable to buy his way out and was incapable of resisting the Nazis.

The Jewish survivors of the Holocaust came up with a motto, "Never Again!" The state of Israel was the dream of Theodor Herzl (1860-1904), considered to be "The Father of Zionism," who wrote a book titled *A Jewish State*. Due to the lingering anti-Semitism in Europe, Holocaust survivors wanted to establish the state of Israel in order have a secure homeland. The establishment of the state of Israel in 1948 allowed the Jews to be secure enough to use military force, fight, and refuse to concede to the demands of a hostile world. Israeli leaders such as Ben Gurion and others sought to contrast European Jews and submissive weakness with Israeli heroism by resisting the immediate invasion of several Arab armies immediately after Israel's declaration of independence. Leon Poliakov described a new "Jewish dynamism" in his book *Harvest of Hate*.[11] He claimed the aftermath of the Holocaust produced "a new kind of Jew, physically and morally." Once Jews concluded that the Nazis were determined to exterminate them, they joined a number of partisan groups in Nazi-occupied Europe in Poland, the Soviet Union, Yugoslavia, France, Belgium, and others.

The last, and probably the most widespread, acceptance of the myth of Jewish passivity came from the interpretation of the Holocaust in the Christian metaphor of sacrifice. The term "Holocaust" carries with it some of its original religious meaning; an offering that is consumed by fire. The Holocaust was "punishment" for the Jews' obstinacy in not accepting Christ.

Interpreting the Holocaust in religious terms has not been limited to Christians. Rabbi Ignaz Maybaum is most frequently remembered for his controversial view in *The Face of God after Auschwitz* where he maintained that the suffering of Jews in the Holocaust was vicarious atonement for the sins of the rest of the world.[12] He connected the Jewish people to the figure of the "suffering servant" of Isaiah in the *Tanakh* (the Christian Old Testament). In the same work, he employed Christian imagery speaking of Auschwitz as the new Golgotha and the gas chambers as replacing the cross. He also saw Hitler as an instrument of God who was used to cleanse, purify, and punish a sinful world; the six million Jews that died an innocent death died because of the sins of others.[13]

The longstanding tradition of anti-Semitism in Europe and its role in creating an environment that would allow Jewish genocide to occur cannot be overstated. Throughout European history anti-Semitism has been a central theme and justification for brutally oppressive policies such as the expulsion of Jews from Spain during the Inquisition of 1478, pogroms of Czarist Russia from 1903-1906, and creation of ghettos designed to confine and restrict the movement of European Jewry, which was originally established in Venice, Italy in 1516. Most of these early examples of anti-Semitism have religious origins that justify discrimination of the Jews. These anti-Semitic views derive mainly from Christianity in stories that blame Jews for crucifying Christ. Throughout the last two thousand years, teachings of contempt against Jews by bishops, priests, ministers and others was evident. One of the most potent examples of religious intolerance is seen in the teachings of Martin Luther and is best expressed in Luther's inflammatory pamphlet titled *On the Jews and Their Lies (1543)*. His writings and sermons advocated the destruction of Jewish synagogues, the Torah and other religious relics. These religious and cultural traditions allowed the Christian communities of Europe to justify the dehumanization and brutal oppression of the Jewish people. For instance, *The Protocols of the Elders of Zion*, a forged book of anti-Semitic propaganda first published in the late 19th century alleges to be evidence of a world-wide conspiracy by Jewish and messianic entities to covertly control the world through dominating banking and intellectual institutions. Although this book has been widely debunked as nothing more then an anti-Semitic hoax, it has been and continues to be utilized to justify anti-Semitic policies and genocidal campaigns. It is important to understand that the Holocaust rose up in this historical context and that these Jews provided an additional barrier for resistance against nationalism.

NATIONALISM

The threat of Jewish dominance has deep roots in Europe. During the Napoleonic Wars from 1799-1815, Napoleon freed the Jewish communities from segregation and ghettoization in many parts of Europe, attempting to engender the Jewish people to his cause. After Napoleon was defeated, resentment towards the success of European Jews in the areas of business and commerce gained new traction in the public discourse. Wilhelm Marr, a famous anti-Semite who coined the term anti-Semitism, introduced the idea that Germans and Jews were in a longstanding conflict, the origins of which he attributed to race, and that the Jews were winning. He argued that a climate of liberalism had allowed greedy Jews to control German finance and industry.[14] These successful Jews were perceived to represent a threat to the success of non-Jewish citizens. Additionally, the post-Napoleonic period coincided with the emergence of communism. The fact that some Jews played a central role in these events further supported the idea that Jews were a threat.

Following the 1918 World War I defeat of the Kaiser's forces in Germany and the acceptance of the terms of the Treaty of Versailles, the German people were demoralized both by the extent of the punitive elements of the treaty and in the loss of the empire. The treaty stated that Germany was to accept blame for the war, pay reparations, surrender their colonies, and adhere to limits on their military. In the face of this economic crisis, high unemployment, violence between political parties, and a weak Democratic Weimer Republic (the post-war German government) the German people elected Hitler, a charismatic leader, as the chancellor and ushered in the reign of the Nationalist Socialist Party.

The final precondition which led to the genocide of the Jewish people was the pathological hatred festering inside Adolf Hitler and his desperate need to externalize that hatred toward the Jews, communists, gypsies, homosexuals and intellectuals of Europe. Hitler's desire to see the total destruction of European Jewry was first articulated in his highly influential book, *Mein Kampf*, which he wrote during his time in prison just after WWI. In this book, Hitler fanned the flames of European anti-Semitism by citing the *Protocols of the Elders of Zion* as evidence for the need to adopt his plan of destruction of European Jewry. Although these books were fundamental in articulating the Nazi ideology, it was the explosion of World War II and the inability of the allied forces to take the threat of Nazi aggression seriously that allowed the greatest genocide in modern history to take place.

Several authors, among them Raul Hilberg, Hana Arendt, Bruno Bettelheim, and Leon Poliakov, have expressed in various ways that the Jews were incapable of resistance due to the fact that they were living in Diaspora and had a history of being persecuted.[15] Bettelheim argues that the Jewish genocide was really a form of Jewish suicide, placing the major responsibility on the victims.[16] He maintains that Jews could have marched as free men, rather than grovel, wait for their own extermination, and walk themselves into the gas chambers. Bettelheim attributes the success of the Holocaust in part to the victims by not realizing their fate and perhaps even buying into euphemisms.[17] These widely-read books transformed the myth of passivity from the historical to the psychological realm, where they have continued to influence the interpretation of the Holocaust.

Fortunately, in the name of historical accuracy and balance, another group of historians studying the Holocaust present a more balanced view of Jewish behavior. Rubin Ainsztein's work, *Jewish Resistance in Nazi Occupied Europe*, written with the purpose of refuting the myth of Jewish passivity, provides a detailed documentation of formal resistance, but tends to overestimate its effectiveness as well as minimize Soviet anti-Semitism.[18] Lucy Davidowicz's, *The War against the Jews*, and Yehuda Bauer's, *A History of the Holocaust*, sought a more balanced approach by examining earlier works and incorporating newly-discovered material of resistance.[19] Helen Fein in *Accounting for Genocide* relates Jewish victimization to the response of the nations in which it occurred.[20] Martin Gilbert's *The Holocaust: A History of the Jews in Europe during the Second World War* excels in the use of survivor recollections and provides ample evidence of individual resistance.[21]

These works have refuted the idea that Jews went passively to their fate.

Lawrence Langer spoke of the many temptations that beckon from the pit of the Holocaust, "One of the most engaging is the instinct to invent myths of more favorable outcomes, as if the parched imagination might somehow transform irrevocable extinction back into potential survival."[22]

The European Jews were faced with the determination of the Third Reich to exterminate them. According to scholars the Jews had three behavioral options.[23] First, they could *collaborate* in hopes of saving themselves. Second, they could adopt *defensive acquiescence,* hoping that by complying with Nazi demands they could survive. Lastly, they could *resist.*

The definition of resistance is crucial to understanding Jewish behavior during the Holocaust. Hilberg referred to the use of arms against the Nazis as resistance.[24] Bauer's definition of resistance includes active and conscious organized action against the Nazi command policies, or wishes, by whatever means: social organization, morale-building operations, underground political works, active unarmed resistance, or, armed resistance.[25] Bauer's definition is broader and can be used to review and analyze resistance in the Armenian and Rwandan genocides as well. Whereas Hilberg's definition of resistance refers to those that use violent means, Bauer provides sufficient examples of non-violent resistance that can be just as effective.

Although other scholars including Wener Rings[26] describe resistance, we use Ainsztein's conceptualization of resistance (1) *partisan activities,* (2) *revolts and underground activities in ghettos,* (3) *revolts and underground activities in camps,* and (4) *actions in defense of lives and human dignity.*[27] Examining each of these typologies of resistance separately will provide a greater understanding of the nature and variety of resistance to not only the Jewish Holocaust, but to the Armenian and Rwandan genocides also.

NETWORKS AND CONTEXT OF RESISTANCE TO GENOCIDE

The networks that allowed the Nazis to engage in the most sophisticated and diabolical genocide in human history are a result of the bureaucratization of the Nazi death machine. This bureaucratization allowed the Nazis to engage in genocidal practices with the cold impersonal precision of a successful corporation. The actual networks that physically allowed the genocide to take place can be divided into three major areas. The first is the appropriation of the railway system throughout the occupied territories and their use in the deportation of Jews to the extermination camps. These camps were administered by the SS (Schutstaffel) which were the elite of the Nationalist Socialist Party. Second, the Nazis created the SD (Sicherheitsdienst) which was the intelligence service of the party and was responsible for discovering and destroying any covert attempts to destroy or damage the Nazis. The third important network used by the Nazis was the Gestapo (the secret police) who were responsible for the daily maintenance of life in the occupied territories. Along with these bureaucratic institutions, the Nazis used an intricate system of informants and spies who alerted the party to any suspicious behavior such as people hiding Jews, communicating with allied forces or questioning Nazi policies.

The Partisans

Following Ainsztein's typology there were three types of partisan resistance groups found in the forests of Eastern Europe: (1) individuals hid together in forests linked by friendship or family, without any central leadership or any means of defending themselves; (2) family camps allied with a group of armed men and women under the leadership of a single charismatic personality; and (3) fully armed partisan fighting battalions, known as *otriads,* which were organized on military lines. Some were composed of all Jews and some were Russian partisan brigades that reported to Moscow and received substantial support in the form of training, troops, ammunition, and medical supplies.[28]

Throughout Europe during WWII there were many partisan resistance organizations, both Jewish and non-Jewish. In some instances there was cooperation between Jewish and non-Jewish partisan groups. However, particularly in Eastern Europe, there was a high degree of anti-Semitism, which resulted in many non-Jewish partisan groups denying Jewish requests for material support and strategic alliances. In some cases non-Jewish partisans participated in the murdering of Jews. The most important and influential non-Jewish partisan group in Eastern Europe were the Russian partisans who were comprised of local non-Jewish citizens and Russian officers who were parachuted into the Belarusian forest and received both material and strategic support from the Russian Army. Another important non-Jewish partisan group, Armia Krajowa (Home Army) were made up of mostly ex-Polish army officers, soldiers, and non-Jewish Polish citizens who resided in Poland and the eastern forests.

Although there were instances of anti-Semitic acts by the Home Army, there is indication that the Home Army did try to help Jews resist the Nazis. Witold Pilecki, a member of the Home Army, disguised himself as a Jew, called himself Tomasz Serafinsk, and entered an Auschwitz concentration camp in order to begin a rebellion from the inside. While in Auschwitz, he kept contact with the outside world, and sent reports to the United States and Britain, confirming that the Nazis were in fact attempting to exterminate the Jewish people. He organized resistance groups within the camp and had planned to have the Allies liberate Auschwitz, after he learned of the existence of the gas chambers. Despite the details Pilecki provided to the United States and Britain from 1941-1943, the Allies did not interfere, and after two and a half years of voluntarily being in Auschwitz, Pilecki escaped. He fought in various uprisings, but in 1948 he was tried by the Polish Communist Regime and executed. Michael Schudrich, the current Chief Rabbi of Poland, recognized Pilecki as "an example of inexplicable goodness at a time of inexplicable evil. There is ever-growing awareness of Poles helping Jews in the Holocaust, and how they paid with their lives, like Pilecki. We must honor these examples and follow them today in the parts of the world where there are horrors again." Pilecki and the other members of the Home Army that resisted the Nazi regime are stark reminders that regardless of race, religion, ethnicity, and gender people resisted.[29]

There were two central ghettos among many others that participated in resistance across Nazi-occupied Europe and functioned as key recruitment centers for Jewish Partisan organizations. The largest of these were the Warsaw and the Vilna Ghettos. In both locations, partisan groups organized and used the ghettos as centers for arousing the Jewish population to resist Nazi extermination at all costs.

One Jewish partisan organization stands out for its high rate of success. This partisan group was formed in June of 1942 in the Belarusian forest near the Vilna Ghetto and was organized and commanded by the Bielski Brothers (Tuvia, Alexander, and Asael). After their parents and two other siblings were lead away by the Nazis and killed, the Bielski brothers fled to the Belarusian forest, with which they were familiar, and set up a hidden camp for Jewish victims.

Nechama Tec's *Defiance: The Bielski Partisans*,[30] which was recently made into a feature film called *Defiance*, describes the leader of the Bielski partisan, Tuvia Bielski, and how he ran his camp in the woods. Tuvia Bielski assumed full control over the external and internal policies of the camp and the overall arrangements of the *otriad* (community in a forest).[31] He was a gifted, charismatic leader who set out to neutralize the surrounding dangers by cooperating with different partisan groups, specifically the Soviet partisan detachments.[32] This collaboration extended to food collection and joint military ventures. Different partisan groups were assigned to different villages from which they would confiscate provisions. Peasants were forced to be the main suppliers of food. While food was gathered separately by each group, attacks by men from various partisan units were carried out on German officers and their collaborators for the purpose of collecting arms and goods. The men also participated in sabotaging activities such as cutting telephone wires and blowing up bridges and trains.

From the very start, the Bielski brothers insisted that all Jews, regardless of age, sex, state of health, or any other characteristic, would be accepted into the camp. This policy stood in direct opposition to every other active partisan unit in the Belarusian forest because the other partisan groups only wanted fighters and the strong. The Bielskis were able to successfully build a large camp in the forest, which at the time of liberation housed 1,200 people. This camp was highly sophisticated with a variety of workstations ranging from arms repair and manufacturing, to a camp kitchen, cloth and shoe repair, and a working sausage factory. The Bielski partisans engaged in many forms of resistance, including revenge attacks aimed at killing Nazi officers and their sympathizers, destroying rail lines, sabotaging military convoys, rescuing Jews out of the ghettos before liquidation, and resisting Nazi tyranny by surviving the Nazi's intention to exterminate all the Jews of Europe. After resisting the Nazis and living in the forest for nearly two years, the Bielski camp was eventually liberated by the Soviet army in the summer of 1944.[33]

The Ghettos

Some of the fundamentally important elements of the history of Jewish resistance to Nazi tyranny were the various underground organizations that functioned in the ghettos. Ghettos were reestablished by the Germans to separate and concentrate Jews into specific locations. The purpose was to have them available for slave labor, and to exterminate those who were not fit to work, primarily the elderly and children. A survivor of the Warsaw ghetto, Nelly Cesana, was four years old when she lived in Warsaw. She described life in the ghetto as, "I remember the fear, of never feeling safe. You had to hide constantly. And the hunger..."[34]

These resistance organizations, primarily run by the youths of the ghettos, were initially ideologically based, but when the true intentions of the Nazis prevailed, it shifted to a militant form of resistance. The group Hashomer Hatzair (a socialist-Zionist movement founded in 1913 in Austria-Hungary) focused in the first stages of World War II on activities aimed at maintaining a moral, spiritual, and educational continuity of community life, as well as repatriation of Jews to pre-Israeli Palestine. Eventually, it evolved into military driven organizations. Hashomer Hatzair organization originally focused on maintaining an active underground press, holding educational classes for the children of the ghettos, holding religious services, keeping open lines of communication between the various ghettos, and archiving the horrific crimes committed towards European Jews.

Once it became clear that the objective of the Nazis was to exterminate all the Jews in Europe, the focus of Hashomer Hatzair shifted to a militant style of resistance, which led to the creation of the FPO (United Partisan Organization) and the ZOB (Jewish Fighting Organization) formed in July, 1942. This shift to military tactics and the acknowledgment of the aim of the Nazis was met by resistance from many elders in the various ghettos. It was inconceivable to many Jewish elders that the Nazis would completely destroy their own cheap labor force. These elders felt that they had survived previous eras of oppression such as the expulsion of Jews from various parts of Europe and a millennium of pogroms all over Russia, Poland, Spain, and other places in Europe in which Jewish communities and businesses were destroyed. They believed that like these previous eras, "this too shall pass," and the best thing to do to ensure the survival of the Jewish people was to do as the Nazis commanded. This position stood in direct opposition to beliefs and goals of the various underground resistance organizations.[35]

Nowhere is this conflict more evident than in the story of the Vilna ghetto and the betrayal by the ghetto president, Jacob Gens, and his turning over to the Gestapo Yitzahak Wittenberg, the leader of the FPO. The Vilna ghetto was a hotbed of resistance activities and important source for resistance leaders such as Abba Kovner, Yitzahak Wittenberg and Mordechai Tenenbaum. Eric Sterling provides an account of the betrayal of Wittenberg by the head of the *Judenrat* of the Vilna ghetto, Jacob Gens.[36] According to Sterling the Vilna Ghetto military resistance movement started January 23, 1942, after approximately 33,500 of the 57,000 Jews in Vilna were executed and buried in huge excavated pits located in the Ponar Mountains.[37] The FPO members cleverly and courageously smuggled weapons into the ghetto in order to battle the Nazis. At some point Bruno Kittel, Gestapo officer in charge of the Vilna ghetto, became aware of the resistance movement and the identity of the leader, at which time he ordered Gens to turn over Wittenberg. This transpired in the wake of the Warsaw Uprising, resulting in Nazi concern about preventing another successful and costly uprising.[38] The strategy of the FPO was to inspire the 20,000 remaining camp residents to rise up and attack the Nazis. To further this plan they had started collecting arms and preparing a revolt in the spirit of the Warsaw ghetto. Wittenberg and other FPO fighters such as Abba Kovner wanted to create a revolt that would have historic and national significance and might also enable some to escape. Three weeks before the creation of the FPO one of the founding members, Abba Kovner, who later became the poet laureate of Israel, gave a speech on behalf of the resistance group in which he stated:

> No one returned of those marched through the gates of the ghetto. All the roads of the Gestapo lead to Ponary. And Ponary means death. Those who waver put aside all illusion: your children, your wives, and husbands are no more. Ponary is no concentration camp. There they all were shot! Hitler aims to destroy all the Jews of Europe. It is the lot of the Jews of Lithuania to be the first line. Let us not go like sheep to the slaughter.[39]

It is with this backdrop of organized resistance that the demands of the Gestapo were met with outrage and courage. However, unlike the youth represented by the FPO, the elders of the community refused to believe the truth about the Nazis' plan for the Jews of Europe. They believed that the only choice they had was to turn over Wittenberg, in hopes that this would avert a liquidation of the ghetto. In the end, Gens and the *Judenrat* decided to follow this line of thought and after several days of debate turned over Wittenberg to the Gestapo. This choice was a tragedy and signaled the decline of the FPO in Vilna and the eventual exodus of all resistance fighters to the forest, where they renamed themselves the "Avengers." To highlight just what a tragedy this betrayal was, it should be noted that the majority of the "Avengers" survived the war. On the other hand, only a small percentage—two to five percent—of the rest of Vilna survived the war.[40] The Vilna partisans avenged the loss of their commander by blowing up trains and burning bridges, rescuing other Jews from various ghettos, and killing Nazi officers whenever possible. In light of the cruelty on the part of the Nazi guards the prisoners had very little to lose by avenging their pain and attacking the guards.

Perhaps the best known resistance during the Holocaust was the Warsaw Ghetto Uprising from April–May of 1943. This was not only the most organized and sophisticated of all Jewish resistance events during the war, but was also the longest lasting of such events—lasting for twenty-seven days—and the first major civilian revolt against the Nazis in all of occupied Europe. Warsaw was the biggest ghetto in all of Europe, housing at its peak as many as half a million Jews with an average of seven people per room. It was enclosed with a wall more than ten feet high, topped with barbed wire, and surrounded by guards. At the time of the uprising only about 60,000-75,000 people remained in the ghetto; the rest had been deported to execution and labor and death camps.

The Nazis, through their various informants in the ghetto, became aware of the Warsaw Ghetto resistance movement. They planned and organized, waiting for the right moment to liquidate the ghetto and transport the Jews to killing centers. Nazi central command sent Waffen-SS General Jurgen von Stroop to the Warsaw ghetto.

Stroop and his troop of over 9,000 plus men were heavily armed and prepared to battle the estimated 750 Jewish resisters in the Warsaw ghetto. Not only were the Jews heavily outnumbered, but their only ammunition was comprised of Molotov cocktails, hand grenades, and a few automatic guns with little ammunition.

On April 19, 1943, the Nazi forces moved into position to begin the final liquidation of the ghetto. The Nazi officer in charge of this first action, Oberst von Sammern, did not expect the Jewish fighters to resist and ordered his troops to march straight into the central ghetto. The Nazi soldiers were stopped dead in their tracks by a concentrated attack from the Jewish fighters, who were hiding in windows, attics, and balconies of the surrounding buildings. The unexpected intensity and concentration of the attack sent the German soldiers fleeing in panic. In response to this defeat, Sammern reported to Stroop that "all was lost in the ghetto" and that they had sustained substantial casualties and requested that Stroop order bombers to be flown in from Krakow to level the ghetto.

Stroop dismissed this idea, stating that taking that step would be an embarrassment to the Reich and would be an admission of defeat. To demonstrate to his troops that he was in command of the situation and in an attempt to finish the liquidation quickly as a "present" to Hitler, Stroop assumed tactical command of the campaign. Over the next twenty-six days, the Jewish fighters waged a fierce battle, forcing Stroop to eventually call in air support from Krakow. During the battle, the Jewish fighters caused heavy casualities on the Nazis and it took the total destruction of the ghetto on a house-by-house basis to quell the uprising. The goal of the people remaining in the ghetto was to combat the evil in front of them and survive. Viktor Frankl expresses this idea best in his book, *Man's Search for Meaning*, in which he said, "Everything can be taken from a man or a woman but one thing: the last of human freedoms to choose one's attitude in any given set of circumstances, to choose one's own way."[41]

All of the Jewish fighters that participated in the uprising exhibited a level of bravery and heroism. However, there is an individual in particular that stands out, Mordechai Anielewicz, the recognized leader of the uprising and of the ZOB, who came from the leadership of the Hashomer Hatzair youth movement and had uncommonly close relationships with his comrades. In many accounts and reflections on his character, particularly in the writings of Emmanuel Ringelblum, the chief archivist of the uprising, he is portrayed as a kind, understanding, and courageous leader, ready at any moment to lay down his life in defense of his comrades remaining on the front lines of the uprising all the way up to the last moments of the final day of battle. He met his end in the underground bunker at 18 Mila Street, which had functioned as a head-quarters for the underground movement, where he was shot on May 8, 1943.[42]

The Vilna and Warsaw ghettos were not the only ghettos to engage in uprising events and underground activities. There were also full-scale revolts in other ghettos such as Bialystok, Marcinkonys, Lachwa, and Tuczyn.[43] Although these underground activities did not always result in a full-scale uprising, Jewish resisters nonetheless carried out many brave and courageous acts both in terms of self-defense and in the defense of others.[44] Regardless of the intensity and sophistication of any particular organization or event, it is important to understand that the Jewish peoples of Europe stood up and resisted all forms of Nazi terror. In the face of the greatest evil, they decided that fighting for their lives and for a greater good could make a difference in the end.

The Camps

By the time Jews were sent to the labor/death camps they had witnessed hor-rors beyond imagination and had undergone a continuous and terrifying cam-paign of dehumanization. This left many without the will to go with no hope for the future, either for themselves or for the Jewish people. However, there were three incredible and spectacular events in three different camps, includ-ing Treblinka, Sobibor, and Auschwitz, that defied the will of the Nazis and exacted a modicum of retribution for the millions of lives lost in these camps. These uprisings are an example of a small group of determined people doing good in the face of the utmost brutality.

Treblinka was, before the war, a small and relatively unknown railway station near the town of Sokolow, which was located about fifty miles from Warsaw. However, by the end of the war it was the largest extermination camp after Auschwitz. The execution camp of Treblinka was responsible for the deaths of about 800,000 Jews. Emmanuel Ringelblum, the chief archi-vist for the Jewish underground in Warsaw, called it the *"slaughterhouse of European Jewry."* We know about the Treblinka revolt from the account pro-vided by Samuel Rajzman, a participant and one of the few survivors. After the Treblinka revolt on August 2, 1943, Rajzman hid in the forest of Wengrow and documented his experience. His journal was smuggled out of occupied Europe and submitted as evidence at the hearings before the House Committee on Foreign Affairs on the prosecution of war crimes. His is one of the only first-hand accounts of the revolt to survive the war. From that brave day he recalls,

> At 3:45 p.m. we heard the signal—a rifle shot near the gates of the Jewish barracks. This shot was followed by the detonations of hand grenades hurled at previously "disinfected" objects. An enormous fire broke out in the whole camp. The arsenal exploded and everything was burned, except the "bath" cabins, because it proved absolutely impossible to get near them. The victim of the first shot was Obersharführer Kittner, the chief of the guards and the leading camp spy. The flames devoured all the storerooms for clothes and shoes.[45]

Between July and September of 1942, over 300,000 Jews were brought to Treblinka from Warsaw and other ghettos around occupied Europe. Samuel Rajzman was on one of these transports to Treblinka and would eventually become part of a camp-wide secret resistance movement. This group of camp inmates had pledged to take revenge for the thousands of murdered Jews. Originally, this group of brave resisters was lead by Dr. Julian Chorazyski. Unfortunately, Chorazyski, through a momentary slip in discipline, drew his concealed knife after being brutally struck by Camp Director Unterstrumfuhrer Franz for failing to properly salute. Franz survived and ordered Chorazyski captured alive. However, Chorazyski consumed a concealed poison tablet and died before the Nazis could capture him and force him to reveal details about the underground movement. As a result of this setback, the revolt was postponed indefinitely because the rest of the underground organization did not feel capable of leading the group.

Less than two weeks later on May 1, 1943, Dr. Leichert, who was a Polish army officer from Wengrow was brought to the camp. He assumed leadership of the underground organization soon after arriving and between May and August the secret resistance planned and organized an armed revolt, waiting for the right moment to spring their plans. On August 2, 1943 they were able to break into an armory, gaining access to the camps arsenal. The underground organization, under the guise of doing their daily activities, planted several bombs, which they had stolen from the German armory, and doused most of the buildings in gasoline. On that same day, the revolt began with the other members of the underground setting fire to the buildings in the camp, signaling the final escape attempt. Of the 700 workers on the camp grounds, 150 to 200 succeeded in escaping. Of those only twelve individuals survived the war. During the revolt as many as twenty Germans officers and guards were killed.[46]

The second of these uprisings took place in Sobibor. Of the six death camps the Nazis built in Poland, Sobibor is one of the least known. However, it was the setting for one of the most dramatic events of Jewish resistance, which was considered the most successful of the three death camp revolts. Our most complete and accurate account of this event comes from a pamphlet written in Yiddish by Alexander Pechersky, the organizer and leader of the revolt, who amazingly survived the revolt, escaped the camp, and survived the war.

Pechersky arrived in the camp on September 23, 1943, and was selected to become a *sonderkommando* (Jews selected to remove the bodies from the gas chambers and transport them to the crematoriums). In his first moments in the camp, Pechersky spoke with one of the other *sonderkommandos* who had been there for some time, and he learned the true purpose of the camp. As an officer of the Russian Army, Perchersky was suited to organize an armed revolt. Between September 23 and October 14 preparations were made and plans were set in motion. On the day of the revolt, a dozen Nazi officers were separately called into various barracks and workshops under false pretenses. Inmates working as tailors called officers in for fittings, and once inside they were assassinated with stolen hatchets. While this was taking place, most of the rest of the camp was preparing to escape. Once Perchersky had received the signal that all of the officers had been killed, he raised the alert signaling to the rest of the camp to storm the gates. In an attempt to escape, all 600 camp inmates stood up against the Nazis and stormed the gates, and about 400 successfully broke out of the camp. Many perished in the land mines surrounding the camp, while others were hunted down by the SS. Of the 600 brave resistors that staged the escape and revolt, only about fifty to seventy people were able to avoid capture and join partisan groups in the forests. Amazingly, Alexander Pechersky was among those who survived and his recollections of these spectacular events provide us with this riveting firsthand account of the revolt at Sobibor.

As a direct result of the events of October 14, only two days after the revolt, Himmler ordered the total destruction of the camp. This decision ended the terrifying history of Sobibor, where 800,000 Jews were murdered during its operation. This event stands alone as the most successful execution camp revolt and the only one that resulted in the closing of a camp.[47]

The third uprising took place at Auschwitz, which was one of the most sophisticated of the underground movements in the death camps, although they were not able to mount a successful revolt that included all members of the camp. However, *sonderkommandos* were able to destroy Crematorium III, damage Crematorium IV beyond repair, and kill several SS guards before being executed. This desperate act was preceded by the courageous efforts of several female camp inmates. Rosa Robota, from the Birkenau camp, exhibited an unbelievable amount of courage and bravery by her involvement in the events that led up to and followed the destruction of Crematorium III in Auschwitz.

In preparation for an armed uprising, underground members began to look for ways to smuggle weapons and explosives from the munitions factory to other parts of the camp. The underground leadership chose Israel Gutman and Jehuda Lerner to establish contact with the Jewish girls in the Birkenau camp who had access to explosives they would need. This proved to be nearly impossible since the girls were under constant surveillance. Rosa was contacted by Noah Zabludowicz, another member of the Auschwitz underground, to act as intermediary between the women working in the munitions factory and Gutman and Lerner. Rosa agreed, wanting desperately to avenge the death of her family in the gas chambers of the camp. Within a short time she had more than twenty women smuggling explosives hidden in secret pockets sewn into their blouses. But before the camp underground could mount a successful revolt, one of the resistance leaders was caught with a detailed plan of the revolt. This led to the Nazis increasing the security protocols in the camp, which prevented a camp-wide armed revolt.

Once rumors spread that the SS was going to exterminate the existing *sonderkommando* unit, new plans were set in motion to stage a revolt. The SS had done this previously in order to get a fresh crop of workers; it was safer for the Nazis to exterminate the workers on a regular basis. The *sonderkommando* at Crematorium IV set fire to the crematoria and attacked the SS guards with hammers, axes, and stones. The flames signaled the rest of the camp to revolt, and the *sonderkommando* at Crematorium II moved into action, killing a kapo (a prisoner selected by the camp authorities to keep order among the prisoners in exchange for special privileges such as food and living quarters) and several SS men. Several hundred prisoners escaped, but most were recaptured and murdered. The two hundred prisoners who took part in the revolt were executed. The stolen explosives were traced back to Rosa along with three others women, Ester Wajcblum, Ella Gartner, and Regina Safirsztain. Each was arrested and brutally tortured, but they did not divulge who their co-conspirators were. The four women were hung in the camp's center in front of all the other inmates.[48] Rosa and the other three women met their death in the spirit of defiance and strength, especially Rosa, whose last words were, "Be strong and brave."

DEFENSE OF LIFE AND HUMAN DIGNITY

The Wilhem Bachner Story

The story of Wilhelm Bachner is a prime example of Jewish resistance: the defense of lives and dignity.* Bachner saved more than fifty people from the Jewish ghettos of Poland and almost all of them survived the war. He did it unarmed with only his skill, courage, intelligence, and determination.

He was born on September 17, 1912 in the Polish town of Bielsko (German Bielitz), part of the Austro-Hungarian Empire, Bielsko was culturally German, joining Poland only after World War I. Bachner's surname and the fact that he grew up speaking German reflected this German heritage, which benefited him during the war. He studied engineering in Brno, Czechoslovakia, graduating in 1938. After a short stay in his native city, he

---

*   See Samuel P. Oliner and Kathleen Lee, 1996. *Who Shall Live: The Wilhelm Bachner Story*. Chicago, IL: Academy Chicago Publishers. In 1982 I interviewed Wilhelm Bachner as a rescued survivor. To my surprise, I found him to be a Jewish rescuer. P.M. Oliner and I decided then that when we finished *The Altruistic Personality* we would undertake research on Jewish rescuers, which we began in 1991.

went to work in Warsaw in the spring of 1939 and soon married. By then the Warsaw ghetto had been established.

Hungry and afraid, Bachner slipped out of the ghetto and applied for a position as an engineer with the Kellner Firm, a local German architectural firm that had recently opened an office in Warsaw. The Kellner Firm was under contract with the German railroad Deutsche Reichsbahn and was provided with a construction shop on rails—a *Bauzug*—that carried its own tools, supplies, food, and sleeping quarters for railroad work crews. Their task was to rebuild destroyed bridges, rail lines, barracks, and railroad stations. He impressed the firm's owner, Johannes Kellner, and before long Bachner was supervising more than eight hundred people, and was in charge of the hiring process.

Bachner was eventually able to rescue over fifty Jews from various ghettos by hiring them for the Kellner Firm. These included his wife—who he passed off as his mistress—and other members of his family. Soon after the Nazi invasion of the Soviet Union, Bachner convinced Kellner to open branches in different parts of newly conquered Eastern Europe, most importantly in Kiev. In Kiev he obtained a house with the help of his trusted non-Jewish friend Tadek Kazaniecki and converted it to a safe house for the Jews he had rescued from the Warsaw and Krakow ghettos.

With careful planning and anticipatory action, he deflected suspicion from himself and those Jews he hired. All were given false identity papers, and worked alongside the 750 Poles and Ukrainians under Bachner's supervision. In this manner fifty Jews survived the war on the Eastern Front until Bachner surrendered himself and his crew to the American forces who arrived in Germany in 1945.

In 1982 Oliner interviewed Wilhelm Bachner in Moraga, California, to find out how and why this modest man and several of his rescued survivors were able to accomplish this feat. Wilhelm Bachner's success in eluding discovery was due to a complex combination of innate and acquired qualities. But for Jews in Nazi-occupied Europe, survival was as much a matter of luck as of skill and environment. Recounting the story of his many brushes with death, Bachner admitted, "If I go through my whole story, it looks like God in heaven had nothing else to do; only to look after Willi Bachner with all his family and with all the Jewish friends he saved."* But growing up in Bielsko meant that he had absorbed German culture. Bachner's socialization into German culture also gave him a German outlook: "I was used to organizing everything in a perfect, German way," he said, "which was very appreciated by the Germans who were guarding or supervising us."** Appearance also helped. Though slight in stature, the photo on Bachner's work permit shows a handsome, dark-haired man with a neat mustache. Had Bachner been born with obvious Jewish features, speaking German like Goethe could not have saved him. Dressed in a black leather jacket and boots, discussing construction plans in elegant German, Bachner's Jewish identity was never suspected.

Fast thinking and sheer luck also played a role. In September 1942, shortly after Bachner had brought the last of his people from the Warsaw ghetto to Kiev, he found himself facing the Gestapo, who had been alerted by an informer. They showed up at his office with guns drawn and accused him of hiding Jews. Hania Shane recalled the incident during our interview: "Willi, very calm, was yelling back at them, 'How dare you say this; if you are so sure, why don't you go find them yourselves.' While he was arguing with them and prolonging the heated discussion, my friend Heniek left the office and went to the train station where his crew was working and quietly dispersed the Jewish workers, just in case."

These were some of the factors that made him effective, but it was character, courage, and his values that motivated Bachner to act. When asked what induced him to risk his life to rescue others beyond his immediate family, Bachner said, "I did it to show—if you are nice to people, God maybe will be nice to you."

Oliner also interviewed Bachner's cousin in Israel. He described their grandmother telling them they had the responsibility to do good and that they would receive their reward in heaven. Bachner grew up in a family that emphasized the importance of helping your neighbor. Bachner himself demonstrated caring for others even after the war. He continued to be deeply involved with those he had rescued, even with his German boss, Kellner, who only after the war learned that Bachner and many members of his crew were Jews.

---

*   Wilhelm Bachner interview, July 15, 1982.
**   Ibid.

The Aron Grunhut Story

Aron Grunhut's story also represents resistance in the form of the defense of human dignity. Before the war, Grunhut was a wealthy goose liver merchant from Bratislava, but by the end of the war he had become a successful and daring rescuer of Jews. Grunhut is credited for successfully engineering half a dozen rescue missions that resulted in more than 2,000 lives being saved. In one of his most daring rescues, Grunhut chartered two steamships to take 1,350 Jewish refugees to Palestine. He was able to secure their safe passage through the British blockade of immigration to Palestine by agreeing to undertake a secret mission for the British Consul in Bratislava. This technique of negotiating with advisories to save Jewish lives characterizes all of Grunhut's efforts during the war.[49]

In another instance, during the winter of 1938–39, he negotiated with two Nazi brothers to allow him to lease a closed restaurant to use as a hiding spot for Jews. He traveled to Nazi-occupied Austria, where he met with a Gestapo lawyer and secured the release of Juda Goldberger, a Bratislava clothing merchant kidnapped by a Gestapo officer. He was able to successfully help Goldberger and his family flee to America on a rabbinic passport.

Although he had many opportunities to stay in Palestine, safe from the horrors of the Holocaust, he chose to fight Nazi terror. Indeed, Grunhut remained in Europe as the Holocaust was at its peak, helping charter a train in 1943 to take Jewish children from Budapest to Teheran. While in route from Budapest he paid off the train engineer to reroute the train to Palestine and by doing so saved another 350 lives. Aron Grunhut survived the war and eventually immigrated to Israel where he died of old age in 1974.

The Janusz Korczak Story

Another powerful example of the defense of life and human dignity is that of Janusz Korczak, a renowned Jewish physician and children's author, who was in charge of Poland's orphanages for Jewish and non-Jewish children. He was expelled from his position when the Nazis invaded Poland in 1939 and he was forced into the ghetto in Warsaw. There he tried his best to keep the Jewish orphanage alive. Korczak found the children of the ghetto who had lost their parents to starvation and murder, and took them to his orphanage. Unfortunately, the orphanage experienced continuous shortages of food and medical supplies. Korczak would have to go to the Gestapo headquarters and beg for additional food and supplies for the children, sometimes these trips would be successful and other times he would be humiliated or beaten. When the time came for the liquidation of the Warsaw ghetto, Dr. Korczak had no choice but to obey orders. His non-Jewish colleagues begged him to leave the ghetto, which was a possibility because of his professional credentials. They offered to help him out of the Nazi-occupied territories, but he refused and chose to stay with the orphans.

On the day of the liquidation of the Warsaw ghetto he lined up the children in columns and marched them to the trains, singing songs with the children to help them to remain hopeful and diminish fear. Worriedly, the children asked him where they were going. Although Korczak did not know for sure, he was able to keep the children's spirits up. They found themselves at *Umschlagplatz*, a railroad station where Jews were rounded up for deportation to the labor and death camps. Korczak and the children were loaded on to trains and sent directly to the Treblinka death camp. When they unloaded at Treblinka, the children were in a state of terror, and Korczak did his best to comfort the children, carrying some who were no longer able to walk. On their way to the gas chamber, a child asked if it would hurt, and he reassured them that it would not. Korczak faced his death with bravery, walking into the gas chamber hand-in-hand with two hundred children.

Other examples of resistance to the genocide include grown children who chose not to leave their disabled or sick parents who were unable to escape into the forest and join the various partisans. They felt themselves morally obligated to care, love, and provide for their parents, even if that meant death. In some ways the choice to stay with one's aged or disabled loved ones who could not escape is a form of resistance and altruistic, heroic behavior.[50]

Zionism as a Resistance Movement

The emergence of Zionism as a driving ideological force for European Jewry should be understood as the seed for the future resistance to Nazi Tyranny.

Theodor Herzl stands out as the central figure at the head of this movement, playing a central role in the development, articulation, and dissemination of Zionist ideology. Prior to Herzl's ascendance to the head of the Zionist movement, Zionism was considered a minor cultural feature of Judaism. However, while covering in 1891 the Dreyfud Affair in Paris (a notorious anti-Semitic case involving the wrongful conviction of a French Jewish captain for spying for the Germans) Herzl underwent a radical transformation, coming to the conclusion that the only way for the Jewish people to have freedom from anti-Semitic discrimination was to create an independent and free Jewish State. Herzl spent the rest of his life traveling Europe, lecturing and writing on this mission, successfully transforming the Zionist movement from a fledgling ideology to a fully articulated political and social movement. The emergence of Zionism as a central feature of Jewish discourse created a politically articulated ideology that would evolve into the backbone of the resistance movement.

In addition to this ideological motivation, two other factors need to be understood as central to the preconditions for resistance. These factors are the emerging awareness of the truth about the Nazis' plan of extermination and the deeply-held need to alert the world to this truth. Throughout the occupied territories, accounts filtered into the ghettos about the atrocities committed by the Nazis and their plan for total extermination of the Jewish people. As conditions continued to worsen throughout the occupied region it became clear that the accounts filtering into the ghettos were not mistaken. Once this truth was understood two decisions were made: the first was to resist extermination of Jews by every means available and the second was to alert the world to this horrific truth. These physical and ideological motivations acted as the catalyst for a fully articulated resistance movement that was active throughout the occupied territories from the Belarusian forest to the ghettos and villages, to the underground bunkers and secret hideouts of the resistance movement.

The networks which facilitated resistance by the Jewish people was most clearly represented by the fighting organizations FPO, the ZOB, and the various partisan groups in the Belarusian forest of Eastern Europe. Both the FPO and the ZOB evolved from the Zionist youth movement Hashomer Hatzair—sharing the same ideological base enabled them to work closely with one another. In fact, it was the infrastructure developed by Hashomer

Hatzair that resulted in a sophisticated set of networks that the Jewish youth in the occupied territories were able to convert into networks of resistance. In addition to these ideologically-based networks, the partisan organization also developed complex networks that facilitated resistance. However, these groups were more directly connected to non-Jewish resistance groups, receiving material and strategic support from the Russian partisan organizations. These relationships provided the networks of support necessary to engage in an active and sustained resistance campaign.

The bravery of the people and groups discussed in this chapter are great examples of individuals and groups choosing not to be bystanders to their own deaths and the death of others. They show the triumph of good against evil, even on a small scale. They still made a difference.

Eyewitnesses Escape from Auschwitz

For most of the war the Allied forces and the rest of the world, including the Pope, refused to acknowledge the truth about the Nazis' intention to exterminate European Jewry. This unwillingness was due to how inconceivable the nature of the Nazis efforts were, as well as a lack of credible firsthand accounts of what was going on in the death camps. This all changed in April of 1944, when two courageous camp inmates Alfred Wetzler and Rudolf Vrba successfully escaped from Auschwitz determined to alert the world to the truth about the Nazis' plan for the total extermination of European Jewry.

On April 7 of that year, Wetzler and Vrba escaped from Auschwitz and made their way to the nearby town of Zilina in Slovakia, about one hundred miles from the camp, by utilizing the generosity of strangers. It took them two weeks to walk the distance, but once in Zilina they made contact with the local representatives of the Jewish council. Both Wetzler and Vrba spent two years in the camps and were forced to work in every part of the camp. This extensive firsthand experience made them uniquely qualified to provide a detailed account of the inner-workings of the camp. To ensure that they collected a comprehensive account, the Jewish authorities recorded both Wetzler and Vrba's recollection of events in the camp separately. These two interviews, numbering around sixty pages of transcripts, were then compiled to create a composite report, which was translated into German and Slovakian. The original intention of the authorities was to send copies to the Jewish authorities in neighboring Hungary where the last large concentration of Jews was left in Europe. Unfortunately, through a series of unexplained decisions and mishaps, the report never made it to its intended destination. Over the next year, 400,000 Hungarian Jews were deported to their deaths in the execution camps in Poland. While the report never made it to Hungary, a copy of the report was smuggled into neutral Switzerland where it was simultaneously sent to the World Jewish Congress and the Swiss press. From here the report found its way into all the major western newspapers.[51]

Until this report surfaced, the Allied powers were able to dismiss previous "rumors" of Nazi atrocities as unsubstantiated and likely exaggerated accounts. Once this report was published with extensive descriptions of the Nazi death machine, there was no credible way to dismiss the horrific truth. Historians have debated the reasons for the inaction of Allied forces to stop the wholesale slaughter outlined in this report. However, no historian can debate the fact that after this report was published, the railways, gas chambers and crematoriums were never bombed. Had these facilities been destroyed, the capacity of the Nazi death machine would have been severely reduced.

There was another daring escape from Auschwitz on July 21, 1944, motivated by nothing else but love. Jerzy Bielcki, a German- speaking Catholic Pole walked into Auschwitz in a stolen SS uniform to rescue his Jewish girlfriend, Cyla Cybulska. He was twenty-three years old at the time and more than sixty years later he recalled in an interview, "It was great love. We were making plans that we would get married and would live together forever."[52] Bielcki was able to save Cybulska and escape to Krakow where they were able to survive the Holocaust.

RESISTANCE BY GERMAN CIVILIANS

Rosenstrasse Protest

It has been noted by many academics and historians that if more German people had chosen to resist the Nazis rather than remain bystanders, it would have been nearly impossible for the Holocaust to have taken place. Instead, most of the German people, either out of fear, complacence, ignorance, or sympathy for the Nazi cause, chose to remain passive bystanders. The Rosenstrasse Protest by the non-Jewish wives to release their Jewish husbands is an important example of the impact of protest when one chooses not to be a bystander. Rosenstrasse has the honor of being the only successful nonviolent civilian resistance in Berlin during the war.

On February 27, 1943, the Gestapo in Berlin, in what they called the "final roundup," conducted a massive arrest of all the remaining intermarried Jews in the city. To the dismay of the Nazis, not very many intermarried Aryans sought voluntary divorce to avoid arrest. On the following day at Rosenstrasse 2-4, where the remaining two thousand Jews who were awaiting transfer to the death camps were being held, the German wives of the incarcerated Jews gathered together and demanded that the Nazis return their loved ones. This protest was carried out by mostly women numbering several hundred chanting "Give us our husbands back!"[53]

This presented a difficult situation for Joseph Goebbels, who as propaganda minister was charged with keeping the streets of Berlin free from civil unrest. Having several hundred Aryan women in the street protesting represented a major threat to stability in Berlin. The Nazis were in the midst of initiating the final solution and maintaining the appearance of stability and civic harmony was central to the successful completion of the "Final Solution." These considerations led Goebbels to order the Gestapo to release the Jews married to Aryans being held at Rosenstrasse 2-4. This protest also affected Nazi policy of deportation; for the rest of the war the Nazis only deported those Berlin Jews whose Aryan spouses were either dead or had voluntarily divorced. For the rest of the war the Rosenstrasse Jews remained in Germany with special exemption from the "Final Solution." However, it should be noted that Goebbles intended to deport the intermarried couples given exemption at Rosenstrasse, but never had the chance because the war ended. This policy only existed in Germany; in all the occupied areas all Jews, their children and their spouses, Aryan or not, were arrested and deported to concentration camps or ghettos.[54] As mentioned above there were very few Aryan Germans who actively engaged in resistance efforts, however, there are a few examples of young German students participating in acts of non-violent protest and resistance. The most well-documented example of this type of Aryan resistance to Nazi tyranny is found in the story of the White Rose.

White Rose Resistance

The story of the White Rose unfolded in Germany between the summer of 1942 and February 1943. During that time a handful of dedicated students led by Hans and Sophie Scholl printed and distributed eight leaflets condemning Hitler and the Third Reich and calling for the passive resistance of all the students and citizens of Munich. To understand this moment of resistance we must outline the development of this small group of students and their intellectual roots.

During the early years of the Third Reich most young Germans were enamored with Hitler and his vision of economic recovery and a resurgence of pride in the Fatherland. However, as the iron grip of the Nazis began to tighten around the citizens of Germany, university students began to see their rights restricted or completely taken away. Increasing restrictions and a heightened state of crisis caused the emergence of a group of students who shared the same ideals and interests in philosophy and politics, which lead to a feeling of disgust with the Third Reich, the Gestapo and Hitler. Awareness of the truth about the Nazis was facilitated by two leading members of the group Hans Scholl and Alex Schmorell and their experiences on the Eastern Front during their mandatory two years of service in the military. While Hans was on the front, his sister Sophie organized other likeminded students to join their small group. This group consisted of Hans, Alex, Jurgen Wittenstein, Christoph Probst, Willi Graf and Kurt Hubert. Between the beginning of June and the end of July, the White Rose wrote and distributed four leaflets around Munich and other parts of southern Germany.[55]

The Gestapo became aware of the White Rose and the danger they represented to maintaining unquestioned order and control over the civilian population of Germany. By this time the "Final Solution to the Jewish Question" was in full swing and the Nazis could not afford any civilian resistance or questioning of Nazis' policies. The Gestapo made it a priority to bring down the White Rose and its leaders. This increased considerably the already dangerous position that Hans, Sophie, and their fellow resisters were in. After arranging to secretly purchase a new, quieter printing press, the group, between December of 1942 and January of 1943, began work on three more leaflets, each more daring and provocative than the last. To distribute the leaflets the members of White Rose risked life and limb, clandestinely delivering the leaflets to the Munich University and other locations around southern Germany. The leaflets exposed the corruption and atrocities against the Jews and others of the German government by printing such statements as,

> It is certain that today every honest German is ashamed of his government. Who among us has any conception of the dimensions of shame that will befall us and our children when one day the veil has fallen from our eyes and the most horrible of crimes—crimes that infinitely outdistance every human measure—reach the light of day?[56]

Following these successes, they decided to print another leaflet at the beginning of February, without knowing that this would be their final statement of resistance. On February 18 of that year, Hans and Sophie decided to take a huge risk and distribute the eighth leaflet at the University of Munich, but it was the middle of the day rather than the middle of the night. Unfortunately, Sophie was spotted flinging 80—100 leaflets from the third floor of the University hall by Jakob Schimdt, a University handyman and Nazi party member. Schimdt called the police and Sophie and Hans were arrested.[57]

During the following four days Sophie and Hans were interrogated intensively at the Gestapo Headquarters. However, because Hans and Sophie were non-Jewish German citizens they were not tortured during this period of interrogation. Remarkably, Hans and Sophie were not broken during their interrogation and never revealed who their collaborators were. Their trial was set for February 22, 1943. For the trial the Gestapo had Roland Freisler, Hitler's hanging judge flown in from Berlin to preside, which was a clear indication of the importance the Nazi leadership considered the White Rose to have. Along with Sophie and Hans, Christoph Probst was convicted of treason and they were all put to death that same evening. Although Sophie, Hans, and

Christoph never divulged the names of their comrades, the Nazis, through a system of informants, discovered the names of Kurt Hubert, Willi Graf and Alexander Schmorell, and arrested and executed them on April 19. After these executions graffiti began to appear on walls around Munich stating: "Their spirit lives!" (http://www.holocaustresearchproject.org/revolt/whiterose.html)

In Chapter 5 we focus on the Armenian and Rwandan genocides, and the resistance and rescue that occurred during those times of tragedy.

Chapter 5

Preconditions of Resistance during the Armenian and Rwandan Genocides

An Armenian survivor named Vartan Misserian of Sivas who was rescued by a Turkish man recalls him saying, "'Do not be afraid, we will protect you'...his mother continued to look after me like my own mother."[1]

From the first hours of the genocide, Senegalese Captain Mbaye Diagne had ignored orders from U.N. to remain neutral and worked to save the lives of hundreds of Rwandans. A friend, BBC journalist Mark Doyle recalls a Senegalese soldier telling him, "You're a journalist; I'm a soldier. Now you've got to tell the world what Mbaye did. You've got to tell the people that he saved lots of lives, even while the U.N. was shamefully pulling out its troops, he was saving people's lives. Please tell the world."[2]

JUST AS IN THE CASE OF THE HOLOCAUST, the Armenian and Rwandan genocides were perpetrated by government authorization and dehumanization of the victims who were numerical and oppressed minorities. These and other similarities in the three cases can be seen in Appendix 1, in which we describe similar preconditions that led to atrocities.

PRECONDITIONS OF RESISTANCE TO THE ARMENIAN GENOCIDE

The Ottoman Empire, as it was once known, developed outward from Constantinople (modern-day Istanbul) extending throughout the Balkans and occupying territories now known as Syria, Lebanon and Palestine. This Empire lasted until World War I, at which time various regions started to rebel in an effort to seek independence. The fast disintegration of the Empire led the Turkish people to fear the fall of the Ottoman Empire completely. After the reign of Sultan Abdul Hamid II in 1908 the "Young Turks," also known as the Committee of Union and Progress (CUP), took over in an effort to rebuild the Ottoman Empire.[3] When it proved unfeasible they resorted to a Pan-Turkish nationalistic view in order to unify the Turkish people, making them the authority of the new monolithic nation. "Talaat the minister of interior...became intent on creating a new empire... in which minorities would be excluded or relegated to having nominal rights."[4]

This made the Armenians a prime target for the Turks since they were Christians in a primarily Muslim empire. They were also seen as a threat since the late nineteenth century cultural reformation often referred to as the Armenian Renaissance. This led to an awakening of the Armenian people to take a stance against the Muslim superiority and demand equal rights.[5]

During the reign of Sultan Abdul Hamid II, the Armenians were treated as second-class citizens in the Ottoman Empire. They were subject to discriminatory taxes on the basis of their Christian belief and they were barred from participating in politics.[6] Resistance was not uncommon to the Armenians who often protested and resisted these unequal practices. Prior to the Armenian genocide, the Armenian population were victims of a series of massacres, most notably the Hamidian Massacres of 1894-1896. These massacres were committed in reprisal to their demand for equal rights and protection by the Ottoman Empire from the Kurds. During what is referred to as the Sasun Revolution, Armenian revolutionaries encouraged the men in the region to defend themselves against Kurdish extortion. They were more than willing to pay taxes if the Ottoman Empire would protect them against the Kurds, but when they were denied protection they took arms against the Kurds. They defended themselves against extortion, unequal treatment, and constant harassment from the Ottoman officials and *zaptitye* (military police). Their self-defense was interpreted by the Sultan as an armed rebellion, so to punish them, Ottoman officials, the *zaptitye*, and Kurds led the Hamidian Massacres where they killed the Armenian men and raped and killed the women. This was a lesson by Sultan Abdul Hamid II to teach the Armenians that infidels were considered inferior in the empire.[7] The massacres were a precursor to the genocide that started in 1915.

The Armenian demand for equal rights and political autonomy instilled fear in the Turkish powers, so they had to come up with a solution to the "Armenian problem." The solution coincided with the onset of World War I, which allowed the Turks to utilize propaganda as a means of scapegoating the Armenians by referring to them as disloyal traitors. The Armenians lived in communities along the border of Turkey and Russia. Because Russia was an Allied power, Turkey was able to justify the genocide by claiming that they feared

> that the Armenians would fight for independence from the Ottoman Empire (with the backing of their Russian Orthodox neighbors to the East), the Empire began to strategize the systematic annihilation of the Ottoman Armenian population. The perfect opportunity arose in the fall of 1914 (August 1, 1914) when Germany declared war on Russia.[8]

But Armenians always recognized themselves as Ottomans—on the same side as the Turks—and never intended to side with Russia.[9] They "never favored separatism or Russian occupation, but pursued a policy of waiting and applying pressure for reforms and autonomy."[10] The Armenians were looking for reform within the Empire, not separatism, but the Islamic Turkish powers did not believe in equality because the Armenians were considered to be Infidels. The Empire still favored an ideology that supported Muslim superiority and by treating Armenians as equal they would be contradicting their view of the relationship between Christianity and Islam. Instead of allowing the Armenians autonomy and equality within the nation, they wanted to annihilate Armenians from the new pan-Turkish Empire.

At the start of World War I the Young Turks, in a burst of confrontational nationalism, appointed ex-criminals, Kurds, and Turkish soldiers to destroy

Armenian communities. The special organization appointed by the Turkish government forced Armenian residents to leave their homes and pursue death marches through the deserts of Syria where most were massacred, raped, robbed, or died of dehydration and starvation.

The atrocities were witnessed by foreigners. U.S. Ambassador to the Ottoman Empire, Henry Morgenthau[11] received telegrams about the massacres and deportations from the staff in the interior of Turkey, and he relayed the stories to the rest of the world.[12] He heard of tortures and spoke to officials who admitted that the government instigated the treatment of the Armenians. Turkish officials also admitted to researching historical records for suggestions of torture.[13] Morgenthau made every effort to expose the atrocities that were occurring in Turkey to the rest of the world, urging President Woodrow Wilson at the time to intervene. Despite Morgenthau's request for intervention, the U.S. refused to intervene stating that the affairs in Turkey did not directly affect American lives or interests.

After persistent urging by Morgenthau and American missionaries in Turkey, the Committee on Armenian Atrocities was established.[14] The committee raised funds for relief of the Armenian people. It started out small, but lasted about fourteen years and ended up being "one of the most remarkable international philanthropic agencies in American history."[15] This relief effort brought a nation together with the focus being charity and relief to the Armenians.

Ambassador Henry Morgenthau is one example of foreign intervention who contributed to the resistance of the Armenian genocide despite it not directly affecting his life. He stated in 1919,

> When the Turkish authorities gave the orders for these deportations, they were merely giving the death warrant to a whole race; they understood this well, and, in their conversations with me, they made no particular attempt to conceal the fact... I am confident that the whole history of the human race contains no such horrible episode as this. The great massacres and persecutions of the past seem almost insignificant when compared to the sufferings of the Armenian race in 1915.[16]

Henry Morgenthau brought the genocide to the consciousness of the rest of the world by not remaining silent about what he had witnessed. There are other remarkable stories of individuals and groups of people that came together to resist the destruction of a race. The modes of resistance ranged from violent to non-violent measures by Armenians as well as Turks.

ARMED RESISTANCE

There is evidence of resistance by the Armenian people and Turkish citizens in response to the genocidal intentions of the Young Turks. One fully-articulated resistance organization known as the Armenian Revolutionary Federation (ARF), founded in 1890 by Simon Zavairan, Kristapor Mikaelian, and Stephan Zoian acted as both the political voice of the Armenian people and organizer of many resistance efforts during the genocide, most notably in the cities Van and Musa Dagh. These resistance efforts were organized and coordinated by the ARF commander, Aram Manougian.

The events that transpired at Musa Dagh were brought to the world's attention in Franz Werfel's historical novel, *Forty Days of Musa Dagh,* which depicts the heroic battle that took place in 1915 and became an international best seller. Prior to Musa Dagh, Armenians were becoming more suspicious of the state's intentions and chose, through the encouragement of the ARF, to leave their villages and retreat into the mountains near the city of Alexandretta. The Armenians of Musa Dagh only had a few hundred rifles and provisions they gathered from the surrounding villages. In spite of their limited resources, the Armenian resisters put up a heroic fight against the Turkish army. They remained in the mountains for fifty-three days, starting on July 21, 1915. On September 12, 1915, a French warship spotted two banners that the Armenians of Musa Dagh had raised in an attempt to flag down help. The French warships, as well as other Allied ships, gathered the remaining 4,000 men, women and children of Musa Dagh and transported them to Port Said, Egypt, where they stayed in refugee camps until the end of the war.[17] Another important resistance battle took place in the city of Van.

Van was a city known for its call for revolutionary reform and for equal treatment of the Armenians within the Ottoman Empire. Its placement near the Russian border allowed for "progressive Russian Armenians [to bring] political ideas across the border."[18] The progressive nature of Van made it a prime target for the Turkish government. The Turkish government sent instructions throughout the province that stated:

> The Armenians must be exterminated. If any Moslem protect a Christian, first, his house shall be burned, then the Christian killed before his eyes, and then his [the Moslem's] family and himself.[19]

In response to these instructions, the Armenians, in the spring of 1915, gathered approximately 1,300 men and boys armed with weapons to protect the thousands of people within the city walls of Van, while the Turks were massacring and destroying Armenian people as well as possessions outside the city.[20] On May 18, 1915, the Russian army occupied the city of Van to assist the Armenians. When the Russian army evacuated, the Armenians were encouraged to leave the city. Upon their retreat the Armenians were massacred. However, thousands were able to find refuge across the Russian border.[21] Despite claims of the Turkish government saying that they went into Van because the people were rebelling against the Ottoman Empire,; missionaries, diplomats, and scholars maintain that Van was a heroic attempt to resist the genocide and save the Armenian culture from annihilation.[22]

Musa Dagh and Van were important symbols for other Armenian resisters throughout the Ottoman Empire and represented the symbolic possibility of success in resisting the Young Turks genocidal campaign.

RESCUE AND NON-VIOLENT RESISTANCE

In addition to examples of armed resistance, we also find those who chose to resist by heroically rescuing Armenian individuals and entire families from death and/or deportation. Rescue occurred in a number of different settings ranging from adoption, marriage, hiding, or warning Armenians of impending danger. These heroic acts were motivated in a variety of forms; some were selfless, some had ulterior motives, and some were motivated due to prior acquaintanceship.

Although some Turkish Muslims participated in the killing of Armenians, there still remained some individuals and provinces as a whole who did not agree with the systematic killing of Armenian women and children. "In his report of August 5, 1915, Scheubner-Richter (German vice-consul serving in the Ottoman Empire) repeated this view, 'those blessed with common sense and reason…do not support the annihilation policy,' and he reported that many local figures condemned the crimes and distanced themselves from them, denouncing them as a Unionist policy."[23] The Turkish people were not the primary perpetrators of the genocide, but many saw it as a government-issued campaign. Even though many resisted, the Ottoman government did not have difficulty finding executioners. These were mainly comprised of the *chettis* (brigands of ex-criminals released to be in the path of the Armenian deportation routes) and Turkish volunteers.[24]

There is a good amount of evidence presented in *Armenians: From Genocide to Resistance* about the mass murder of the Armenians in the Ottoman Empire.[25] One could say that not the whole Turkish population took part in the genocide, many Turkish families hid Armenian children, Turkish villages wanted to give water and food to the columns of the deportees, and several high officials refused to carry out their participation orders.

To address whether all of the Turkish population was bystanders, a careful examination, of interviews by survivors is needed.[26] Survivors frequently mention Turks who helped them and showed them kindness.

> Survivors also told us about Arabs who had treated them kindly during the deportations. A survivor who ended up in Der-Zor said that she had gone blind from starvation. When she was adopted, she was unable to even see the sun: 'These Arabs turned out to be very nice. With home type 'medication,' or actually 'cures,' they treated my eyes. They dug a ditch in the ground, stuck my head in it, and made me sweat. And when I was thoroughly wet, they took me out. Then I saw the sun.' She was treated like a daughter during the year she stayed with them.[27]

In addition, Armenian children were adopted by sympathetic Turkish Muslims. As one survivor named Nazar Nazarian recounts, "Mustafa was a good man. My mother sent me to him because my father knew him. He kept me with him until the end of the war and did not tell anyone in the village that I was an Armenian."[28] But the adoption of a child was not always a selfless act. Turkish families and couples were motivated to adopt Armenian children, some out of the good of their heart, but others were inclined to do so based on positive religious factors. The Armenians were considered Infidels by Muslim standards, but "in the Muslim faith whoever frees a person and converts them will receive great rewards in heaven."[29] Many Turkish Muslims adopted children to convert them and receive a spiritual reward.

Armenian women, specifically, were adopted and converted, so they could be married off to Turkish men. Most women were forced to marry, but this became a beneficial way for them to continue rescuing fellow Armenians. Although women were forced to marry, there are accounts in which the women speak highly of their husbands and the kindness they experienced. In one particular instance a converted Armenian woman named Sirvart Chadirjian was forced to marry a Turkish soldier and after she did so he assisted her in rescuing her fellow Armenians:

> When a caravan of Armenians passed through our village, I was able to save a woman. I took her to my *agha's* (Mr. or a title of respect) house and there she stayed with us as a servant for a year and a half. On another occasion, I found an Armenian boy.... I got him and brought him to our house and gave him my bed. I was now able to free whomever I could. I was all of fourteen years old at the time.[30]

Prior acquaintanceship was a motivating factor for many Turks. However, it is important to note that approximately "three-quarters of the interventions were by individuals previously unknown to the survivors."[31] One such example of prior acquaintanceship can be found in the story of a Turkish man named Ali Effendi who operated a mill with an Armenian man. Henry Vartanian, son of the Armenian man Ali worked with, speaks of his father's friend Ali Effendi who rescued him and his family during the genocide:

> Ali Effendi...he is a Turk, but a beautiful man...Ali Effendi said that he has to bring us to Zara because it is too dangerous there. One of his wives was vacationing and her house was empty. So, he said, 'I will take you to that house.' We were six children and my mother... He used to lock the door and go to his work. He would bring us food and then lock up and go. He kept us there for three months.[32]

Survivors indicated that they were on very friendly terms with neighboring Turks during their deportation times. Typical comments we came across were such as the one below:

> Our Turkish neighbors were very good people. They cried so much at our departure. We had no problem getting along with them. We were peaceful and friendly with each other. We had no fear of Turks. We visited each other and played with their children. When the orders came for us to leave, our Turkish neighbors could not face us. They felt so ashamed. And they did try to keep some of us. They warned us not to leave. They especially wanted to keep us girls. But would my mom leave us behind?[33]

There were many Turks that resisted the genocide by hiding friends and neighbors, but also many intervened indirectly by giving Armenian neighbors and friends forewarning, so they would have time to evacuate their homes and go into hiding before they were subject to death marches or massacres.[34]

There are various cases in which Armenians were rescued for personal reasons, whether selfless or not, but another motivating factor for rescue was economic motivation. Many Armenians bribed Turkish soldiers in order to receive exemption from deportation, or to just postpone their deportation. Bribery was only a short-term solution because it saved them from one Turkish official, soldier, or gendarme, but not the next. Because of this only a minimal portion of the people who were initially saved due to bribery actually survived the genocide.[35]

Skilled Armenians and their families were also spared for economic reasons in order to work for the Turkish military. Many Armenians were deemed useful by the military and Turkish *effendis* (master or lord) and due to this they were saved in order to work. An Armenian woman, Beatrice Kitabdjan recalls her survival due to her father's skill:

> He was highly literate. The Turkish effendis told him to stay and to inventory all the houses, properties, and lands of the Armenians. For that reason my father remained. The effendi liked him very much. They told him to stay in their village, a half-hour from Aintab. And it happened that way. He stayed there, and we remained in our home in Aintab.[36]

Armenians were rescued for a number of reasons, and the unfortunate aspect of the history of the rescue during the Armenian genocide is that we will never truly know all the underlying motivations for which people rescued. The reason for this is because survivors are dwindling in numbers as the years pass, and the Armenian rescuers are no longer with us. The average age of an Armenian genocide rescuer was between 40-60 years of age. This means that most of them have passed away.

The failure of the Turkish government to recognize the Armenian geno-cide as a part of the history of the Ottoman Empire hinders many Turkish relatives of rescuers to speak of the stories that they were told, or may have encountered. The only stories that are with us are those of the Armenians who were rescued and during that time they were just children.[37]

The anger among Armenians for the continuous denial of the genocide and injustice by the Turkish authorities resulted in assassinations of Turkish diplomats in different parts of the world as late as the 1980s. Only when rec-ognition takes place, say most Armenian leaders, will there be a possibility for some sort of reconciliation, as it was between Israel and Germany after World War II and the establishment of the state of Israel. It is the explanation on the part of Turkish leaders at the time of the genocide that the Armenians were killing Turks, and providing supplies to their allies. These are unproven accu-sations and it appears to be, by many scholars, a Turkish ploy to discount the atrocities of 1915 as a genocide.

After the war, the Allies and the surviving Armenians demanded justice. The Allies set up an international trial to prosecute the leaders of the geno-cide but these trials were never fully realized. Instead, a tribunal was set to investigate the claims of genocide. It was titled "The Turkish Court Martial" and it gathered documentation and information about the criminals for the trial. However, due to the very slow bureaucratic nature of these efforts, most of the seven highest-ranking Young Turks who were responsible escaped to Germany. The Armenian Dashnak Party continued to seek retribution for the massacres of 1915 and these efforts have continued into the present day. As recently as the 1970s and 1980s, the Dashnak leaders took part in assassina-tions of forty-one Turkish leaders. Among those who escaped to Germany and the Soviet Union were Namık Kemal, Mehmed Javid Bey, Talaat, Enver

Pasha, Djemal, Nazin, Behaeddin Shakir, Bedri, and Jemal Azmi. Two well-documented examples of this assassination policy occurred in April and July of 1922, when Behaeddin Shakir in Berlin and Djemal in Tiflis (now Tbilisi, capital of Georgia) were gunned down. The Dashnak party continues to oppose any relations with Turkey until it receives a formal apology for the killings and a formal recognition of its claims that eastern Turkey is legitimately part of greater Armenia.[38]

To this day there is a struggle between the Armenians who consider themselves victims of genocide and the Turkish government who claim that genocide never took place.[39] This refusal of recognition of the mass killing of Armenians and attempt to explain that it was a war against disloyal rebels, not only does not give justice to the Armenian people, but it does not give justice to the heroic individuals who tried to resist and inform the world about this tragedy. As a result of the Turkish denial, people are reluctant to speak of the horror and good deeds that others have encountered during such dark times. While it is important to recognize the injustice, history should know about resistance and the ways in which some people can prevail in a destructive setting.

PRECONDITIONS OF RESISTANCE TO THE RWANDAN GENOCIDE

Let us now turn our attention to the last major genocide of the twentieth century, the crisis that engulfed the African nation of Rwanda in the spring of 1994. As with the Holocaust and the Armenian genocide, the case in Rwanda is one of some individuals and groups choosing to fight against certain death in the name of their fellow citizens, no matter their race or religion. What motivated them to do good in the face of such atrocity?

To understand the roots of this conflict one needs to look back at the impact of German and Belgian colonial rule on the relationship between Hutu and Tutsi segments of Rwanda's population. German colonial rule began in 1897, and formally institutionalized unequal power differentials between the Tutsi and Hutu. German rule lasted until the end of WWI in 1918, after which the League of Nations reallocated the territories that make up modern-day Rwanda to the control of the Belgians. It was the Belgians who placed the Tutsi at the top of the hierarchy, which ensured preferential treatment for the Tutsi population, essentially cementing the Tutsi as Rwanda's native ruling class. The Tutsi were selected over the Hutu population by the Belgians because they participated in the colonial government. During 1918–1962, the bitter conflict between the Tutsi and Hutu became deeply entrenched in the psyche of these two ethnic communities. The Belgian administrators instituted a brutal policy of divide and rule designed to heighten the ethnic tensions between the Tutsi and Hutu. They created a political, economically powerful, and educated elite Tutsi population that was dependent of Belgian favor and an uneducated, brutalized, and marginalized Hutu population. One such policy that had a direct impact on the future genocide was the institutionalization of ethnic identification cards for all distinguishing who was Hutu and who was Tutsi. These identification cards were used during 1994 to target Tutsis for massacre.[40]

After the Belgians granted independence to Rwanda in July of 1962, Rwanda's Tutsi and Hutu populations began a bloody civil conflict that resulted in hundreds of thousands of deaths. Between 1962 and 1963, the Hutu population killed 100,000 Tutsis in civil conflicts and from 1972–1973. The Tutsi population retaliated by killing between 80,000–200,000 Hutu civilians and paramilitary militia members, because of ongoing ethnic tension created by real or perceived oppressive policies towards the Hutu by the Tutsi. This conflict spilled over to neighboring Burundi and Uganda with Tutsi militias setting up camps in Uganda and Hutu militias organizing in Burundi. During the next twenty years, there was sporadic violence between these ethnic groups, which further solidified deeply-held ethnic tensions—creating an environment that could support genocide. From 1990–1993 these tensions erupted into a full-blown civil war between the new democratically-elected government run by a Hutu president and the rebel army known as the Rwandan Patriotic Front (RPF), which was organized from bases in Uganda. One of the central elements of this conflict was the right of Tutsi refugees displaced in civil conflict between 1959–1961, 1963–1964 and 1973 to return to their homeland from neighboring Uganda.[41] In 1990 the RPF invaded Rwanda, signaling the beginning of the civil war that would eventually lead to genocide. This event was evidence to the ruling Habyarimana regime that, for the first time since colonial rule, there was a real chance for the Tutsi population to regain significant political power.

Once the government forces fought off the initial invasion, they portrayed the RPF as representing the potential to return to oppressive colonial-style Tutsi rule. From this fear emerged a resurgence of "Hutu Powa!", which was once the battle cry of the first Rwandan republic revolution, characterizing the Tutsi as an alien non-native population. This change in the political environment played a central role in the forthcoming genocide by dehumanizing the Tutsi minority. This effort was intensified by the Habyarimana regime through the use of two central propaganda instruments designed to preach a radical vision of "Hutu Powa!": the radio RTLM (Radio et Television Libres des Mille Collines) and the Rwandan newspaper, *Kangura*. Simultaneously, radical elements of the Rwandan military prepared for what was to become the first genocide of the 1990s.[42]

The final event that initiated the genocide was the assassination of President Habyarimana. The President was returning from a round of diplomatic negotiations in Burundi on the subject of regional stability and the Tutsi refugee situation when his plane was shot down just outside of the Kigali airport. This crash was the final "evidence" needed by radical elements of the military to spring into action and begin a systematic campaign of killing. Government militias (known as *Interahamwe*) under direct command of the military, began setting up roadblocks all over Kigali and surrounding areas and rounding up and killing all Tutsis stopped at those road blocks. The military also targeted political figures beginning with Prime Minister Agathe Uwilingiyimana and expanding to all Tutsi political figures and Hutu moderates opposed to the genocide. The role of RTLM radio in the coordination of the genocide cannot be overstated in that it allowed the military to instruct the Interahamwe and roving mobs where to focus their actions. Between April and June of 1994, 500,000 to 800,0000 Tutsis and Hutu moderates were killed.[43]

Due to the speed of this genocide there was not time for a sophisticated resistance infrastructure to develop, other than the preexisting RPF forces, which were a traditional military force rather than an underground resistance organization. This is not to say that there was no resistance to the genocide. Rather, this points to the individual nature of resistance efforts. As such, we will examine several examples of individuals resisting the genocide through heroic efforts to save individuals from certain death. These acts of heroism occurred in a number of settings. For example, low-level church officials and other individuals made efforts to hide school children and families targeted for killing. In at least one instance, whole groups of orphans were hidden and saved. The efforts of Paul Rusesabagina at the Hotel des Mille Collines provides an important example of heroic rescue of Tutsis and Hutu moderates. Another figure that stands out as an individual with extraordinary bravery and compassion and who is responsible for saving hundreds of victims targeted for killing, is Carl Wilkins, the director of Adventist Development and Relief Agency (ADRA).

Additionally, in Rwanda we are presented with a form of post-genocide resistance, as expressed in the *gacaca* courts, an indigenous judicial effort developed in the aftermath of the Rwandan genocide, which is a uniquely African-modeled effort at truth and reconciliation.[44]

NETWORKS AND CONTEXT OF RESISTANCE

Canadian General Roméo Dallaire was Commander of the United Nations peacekeeping force deployed to Rwanda in 1993. He notified the U.N. in New York that violence was brewing months before the killings began, because the Interahamwe was purchasing machetes, guns, and other weapons, but he was ignored by his superiors.

General Dallaire tried endlessly to orchestrate a meeting between the Crisis Committee of the U.N. and the RPF. His main goal in doing so was to come to a resolution before violence ensued. Eventually, he collaborated with NGOs under his conditions that they help but do not interfere with ceasefire negotiations. General Dallaire created safe areas for people but, more importantly, he wanted to resolve the conflict between the rebels and extremists government. He met with Prime Minister Kambanda in order to discuss the killings, and was able to come to a truce in regards to the humanitarian effort of the secure transfer of people across lines, but Kambanda was not compliant with the ceasefire.

If General Dallaire could not reconcile the situation he would make sure that the world would know of the atrocities occurring in Rwanda. He encouraged a journalist for BBC, Mark Doyle, to stay in Rwanda under the U.N. force's protection and cover the events. The general saved thousands with his truce with Prime Minister Kambanda by securing the transfer of people across lines, and made sure the rest of the world knew what was happening. He eventually documented his stories in *Shaking Hands with the Devil* in order to provide an accurate eyewitness account of those bloody days in April.[45] When other nations pulled troops from Rwanda because it was too dangerous, General Dallaire stayed and refused to abandon his mission. He saw no other option and in an interview he stated, "No way. I would not be able to live with the moral[ly] corrupt decision of packing up and leaving."[46]

Mbaye Diagne, a Muslim-born Senegalese member of the United Nations observation team ignored the U.N.'s orders not to intervene and saved the lives of potential genocide victims by conducting independent rescue missions. On one occasion Mbaye Diagne rescued the children of the moderate Prime Minster Agathe Uwilingiyimana by hiding them in the closet after Uwilingiyimana was killed. On May 31, 1994, Captain Diagne was driving alone back to the U.N. headquarters in Kigali when a mortar shell shot off by the RPF, which was directed to an extremist checkpoint, accidently hit his jeep, and killed him.

One of the many tragic realities of this genocidal campaign was that both adults and children of Tutsis and Hutu moderates were targeted. Many children were killed and orphaned between April and June. These orphans were rescued by individuals when they were found wandering through the bush by the advancing RPF forces. Heroic resistance occurred through the actions of two Spanish nuns who refused to abandon their young children and hid them from the Interahamwe while fending off daily interrogations.

Ultimately, the RPF pushed back the Hutu military and militia, forcing them to retreat without finding the children. Another individual connected to the rescue of orphans was a young woman named Rose Kayitesi, who abandoned her military role with the RPF to gather together children whose parents and relatives had been killed in the massacres and save them from potential death and suffering. Kayitesi, with the help of RPF troops, turned a luxury hotel outside of Byumba into a makeshift orphanage and was able to save several hundred children from a fate of certain death.[47] Another individual who used the security of a hotel to hide hundreds of innocent victims of the genocide is Paul Rusesabagina, whose story is depicted in a major motion picture, *Hotel Rwanda*.

Rusesabagina was born to a farming family on June 15, 1954, in Murama-Gitarama in the central-south region of Rwanda. In 1981 he graduated from a management training program at the Utalii College in Nairobi, Kenya, which included an intensive course in Switzerland. At the end of this program he became employed as the assistant general manager of Hotel des Mille Collines. He held this position from 1984–1992 and in November of 1992 he was promoted to the company's general manager of Diplomate Hotel in Kigali. In 1987, he met his future wife, who happened to be a Tutsi. Fearing increased ethnic tensions and discrimination, he arranged for his future wife to move closer to him, so he could get to know her better. Together they had one daughter (who died as an infant) and a son. In March of 1994 as the civil war between the government forces and the RPF reached a boiling point, Rusesabagina was temporarily made managing director of the Hotel des Mille Collines. Seeing that the situation in the streets was rapidly deteriorating he brought his family to the hotel so that he could ensure their safety.[48]

As the massacres began to unfold on April 7, hundreds of people, most of them Tutsi or Hutu moderates who were being targeted for assassination, began streaming into the hotel in search of refuge. Although the hotel was not in the heart of the city where most of the killing was occurring, the grounds provided very little protection other than its status as a business that had connections in the international community. Hoping to build support and protection for the hotel and its occupants, Rusesabagina pleaded his case to a Belgian newspaper while officials and Sabena (the company who owned the hotel) made the case on Belgian television. As a result of these efforts, the hotel became a powerful symbol of Rwandan suffering. During the following weeks there were many instances where the military attempted to extract those survivors hiding in the hotel. However, through his extensive contacts Rusesabagina was able to keep the soldiers at bay. Finally, on May 13, Rusesabagina was able to successfully send a fax to the director general of the French Foreign Ministry saying that Rwandan government troops planned to massacre all the occupants of the hotel within the next few hours. Reacting to this fax, the French Foreign Ministry contacted their representatives at the U.N. informing the secretariat of the situation, which helped to put pressure on the authorities in Kigali and stopped the impending attack. None of the survivors hiding in the hotel were killed; in total, because of the incredible heroism of Paul Rusesabagina, 1,268 individuals were saved from otherwise certain death. Although Rusesabagina, his wife, and children survived the ordeal, his wife's family sustained heavy losses. Rusesabagina's wife Tatiana lost her mother, brother, sister-in-law, and six nieces/nephews, in the genocide.

Rusesabagina was morally opposed to the senseless killings. Prior to going to the hotel, he was asked by a captain from the Hutu army to kill a Tutsi family that was sitting in a car. He was aware that he could have been killed on the spot, but when he was holding the rifle he calmly said to the captain, "'Listen, my friend, I do not know how to handle a gun,' I told him. 'And even if I did, I do not see what would be accomplished by killing these people.'"[49]

Another compelling example of a righteous individual who risked almost certain death to save hundreds of innocent lives is that of Adventist Development and Relief Agency (ADRA) Rwandan country director Carl Wilkins. Unlike nearly every other expatriate living in Rwanda at the time of the genocide, Wilkins chose to stay and risk his life to bring desperately needed supplies to hundreds of Tutsi and Hutu moderates hiding throughout the country.

Carl Wilkins first came to Africa in 1978 working as a volunteer at a mission school in South Africa. After returning to the U.S. to finish his bachelor's degree in industrial education Wilkins returned to Africa with his new wife, Theresa, settling in Zimbabwe. In 1987 Wilkins brought his family back to the U.S. so that he could complete his Master of Business Administration (MBA) at the University of Baltimore. Once he finished his MBA in 1990, he accepted the post of Rwandan country director for the international relief organization ADRA, which worked primarily to build schools and operate health centers around the country. During the next four years of civil war, because of Wilkins' devotion and determined personality he was able to develop deep relationships with both his staff and the many communities that the ADRA assisted.[50] Because of this in October 1990, during the outset of the civil war, ADRA was one of the only relief organizations allowed access to both rebel- and government-controlled areas of the country.

At the outset of the genocide in April of 1994 Wilkins and his family spent several sleepless nights barricaded in their home thinking that the intense violence and fighting would end quickly as it had done on many other occasions during the preceding four years. Once it had became clear that the fighting would not stop anytime in the near future, Wilkins was forced to decide what to do. Concerned for the safety of his family Wilkins and his wife decided that she should take the children and flee the country to neighboring Burundi. However, Wilkins refused to turn his back on the communities that he cared so much for and decided to remain in Rwanda trying to do whatever he could to save innocent lives. After the first three weeks of the genocide, some travel restrictions were lifted and, due to ADRA's unique status, Wilkins was allowed to travel around the country delivering humanitarian assistance to growing Internally Displaced Persons (IDP) camps. This also allowed Wilkins to bring lifesaving supplies to hundreds of Tutsi and moderate Hutu survivors hiding throughout the country.[51]

Often when the Interahamwe was going to kill people, especially in and around the orphanages, Wilkins would go to the authorities in Kigali to protest and ask for help. He saw the prefect [governor] of Kigali, Colonel Tharcisse Renzaho, who had the power to issue orders to change the policy of roadblocks around the city. On other occasions he was able to meet with the Rwandan Prime Minister Jean Kambanda who initially ordered the massacre, and ask him to intervene in order to stop the killings in the orphanages.[52] In a tribute to "A True Humanitarian," many would-be victims have expressed their gratitude to Carl Wilkens for his bravery and courage.[53]

Wilkins had a background filled with community service, which contributed to his decision to stay. More importantly, similar to General Dallaire, he felt there was no question as to if he should stay or not. When asked by Laura Lane, the political security officer at the American Embassy to evacuate from Rwanda for safety in neighboring Burundi he said, "Laura, as a private citizen, I think I can make that choice, and I have to [stay]."[54] He made the decision to stay despite the danger. Some of the people Wilkens saved cannot even explain his decision. Thomas Kayumba, a survivor who was rescued by Wilkens said, "All the foreigners left, but not Wilkens. He was still young. To take leave of his little children and his wife, to give himself to the Rwandan people, I don't know how to explain it."[55] His overwhelming bravery contributed to the rescue of hundreds of innocent victims.

One example of his heroic effort is found in the story of the Gisimba orphanage. Before the genocide, the Gisimba Memorial Centre, an orphanage located in Nyakabanda and run by Damas Mutezintare, housed around 60 children. However, after April 6, the center took in nearly 300 Tutsi children, women and men. Some were concealed within the ceiling; others hid in the bedrooms. All feared discovery by Interahamwe militiamen who repeatedly came to search the orphanage. Given the limited resources of the orphanage, supplies began to dwindle, rapidly approaching completely running out of water, first aid supplies, and food. When hope was nearly lost, Wilkins arrived with life-giving supplies to meet the immediate needs of those hiding inside. In addition to providing necessary supplies, the visits from Wilkins helped to keep up the morale of both the workers at the orphanage and the survivors hiding throughout the grounds of the orphanage.[56]

Another heroic aid worker is Philippe Gaillard from Switzerland who headed the Red Cross mission in Rwanda during the genocide. He was threatened by armed militias, but still provided safe havens and medical support for sick and wounded Rwandans regardless of ethnicity. On April 14, Gaillard was informed by Red Cross workers that their ambulance was stopped at a checkpoint and the six injured Tutsis in the back were dragged out and killed on the side of the road. Gaillard contacted his headquarters in Geneva and asked them to publicize the incident. This resulted in a promise that was broadcasted on RTLM that the Red Cross ambulances would not be harassed any longer. He is credited to have helped the Red Cross save an estimated 65,000 lives.

There are also cases of whole villages fighting the Hutu militia. Simeon Karamaga, a survivor of the genocide, spoke about his experience fighting the Interahamwe in the village of Bisesero. The village of Bisesero was a congregation of Tutsis who had defended themselves in the past against Hutu militia and other forces that were coming to attack them. In 1994 at the beginning of the genocide, Tutsis from various regions fled to the Bisesero region because the Tutsis there had a reputation of being warriors. When Bisesero was attacked by the Hutu militia, the Tutsis did not succumb. Instead they fought back with clubs, machetes, and spears, which was no match against the Interahamwe's machine guns. The militia finally retreated and when they did Karamaga recalls, "We decided that we should seek protection in numbers, so we barricaded ourselves in with our children, our goods, and our cows to fight from one hill known as Muyira."[57] When the Hutu returned, the Tutsi were prepared to fight on the hill and Karamaga says, "There was nowhere to escape, so we decided to fight and to kill them as they were trying to kill us."[58] A majority of the Tutsi population of the region ended up becoming victims of the genocide, but they resisted bravely. The hill Muyira is recognized as the "Hill of Resistance," and a memorial has been built there in order to commemorate those brave individuals who attempted to save themselves, their friends, their families, and the Tutsi population from savage murder and genocide.

TRUTH AND RECONCILIATION

Reconciliation is very difficult under these conditions. Some people feel as though the mass murderers should face trial, and yet there are not enough resources to implement such a legal system. What has been introduced instead is a community court called a *gacaca* court, whereby offenders meet locally to confess and discuss what transpired during those dark days. In this type of system, communities as a whole judge what their families and neighbors did during the terrible months of violence. To represent the offenders, each community elects nineteen people who are respected in the community. They sit in a general assembly to hear accusations and confessions. Each assembly is empanelled for a certain amount of time. Their job is to establish who was there during the genocide, who was killed, who lost their property, and who was responsible. Offenders who are seen as having committed less heinous crimes during the genocide are able to be tried in the gacaca courts, but conventional courts still exist for people being tried for rape or heinous murder. However, gacaca offers an effective healing tool for society as the guilty confess their faults and ask the victims to forgive them.

Jande Dieu Cyiza confessed to the gacaca court that he killed five Tutsi children because government soldiers told him to do so. He argued that he had to commit murder to save his life, so he hacked the children to death with a machete. The perpetrator in this case confessed and apologized for his actions, and he was forgiven by the community and presently resides in the same neighborhood as the families of the children he murdered. This is an important aspect of the gacaca courts, because many people were put in the same situation as Jande Dieu Cyiza. They were given the choice to either kill or be killed, or kill or have a loved one be killed. Although people such as Cyiza killed, it is important to note that if they themselves were not threatened, would they have killed? The gacaca courts allow for forgiveness and in some cases pity on the killers during the genocide.

Though many acts of apology and forgiveness have been recorded in Rwanda, widespread reconciliation is not discernable. This process takes time and counseling and requires sincere confessions and open discussion by perpetrators and leaders. One complication toward resolution in this case is that the Hutus were not the sole perpetrators of atrocities. The Hutus claim that Tutsis also committed horrible crimes, including mass murder, torture, and rape. Some say that the situation requires all parties to start by admitting to the killings.

Psychology Professor Erwin Staub of the University of Massachusetts, and his associate Dr. Laurie Anne Pearlman of the Trauma Research Education Institute are trying to understand the depth of trauma in Rwanda and have enlisted some indigenous and international non-governmental organizations (NGOs) to conduct research into methods most likely to succeed in reducing resentment and trauma.[59] They have found that many victims with traumatic experiences are less inclined to partake in forgiveness. Some NGOs are trying reconciliation with the young in the hope of achieving success.

The government supports the gacaca courts to encourage voluntary confessions and discussion that may lead to reconciliation at the community level. Studies have found truth-telling often leads to remorse in the offenders and to forgiveness on the part of the victims.[60] In villages where people experienced the terror, the killers often express deep sorrow and guilt.

Although even critics admit that the gacaca system does offer some opportunities for apology and forgiveness, many claim that the system cannot bring precise justice. For true justice, perpetrators of these atrocities must go through a more traditional justice process involving prosecution and a trial. Some supporters of the gacaca system refer to retributive-style justice as "white man's standards." There is concern with finding a balance "between justice and reconciliation, or between retribution and forgiveness."[61] Critics of a retributive justice fear it may stimulate violence. At least 200 Rwandan genocide survivors have been murdered in order to prevent their damning testimony in criminal trials.[62] A Tutsi genocide survivor is afraid that she will be called to testify against her neighbors. The only one of six siblings to survive a slaughter of 40,000 local Tutsis, she says, "They know I could testify against them. That is why I'm scared they will kill me or poison my daughter."[63] This not only prevents any sort of reconciliation from the trials and their verdicts, but may also start a new cycle of violence.

Recently, there has been interesting new research that sheds light on this tragedy. Administering questionnaires forty-five days before the gacaca trial and forty-five days after, Patrick Kanyangara, Bernard Rime, Pieree Philippot, and Vincent Yzerbyt found that the gacaca tribunals have positive potential for future reconciliation.[64] Their data indicates that gacaca ritual has a profound impact both on social psychological and emotional levels. "Our results open the possibility that when contained within social rituals of gacaca, expression and reactivation of the intense negative emotions linked to the genocide provided an opportunity to (re)process these traumatic emotions and to transform them in such a way that they can participate in a reconstructive process both at the individual and collective levels rather than being strictly problematic."[65] At the social psychological level, gacaca fosters an increase in social cohesion and a decrease in social prejudicial attitudes. The authors suggest further research with a larger sample would help to understand the consequences of the emotional reaction of both the killers and victims. In the future the authors would like to see if the emotional reactivation of gacaca leads to positive consequences for the social and emotional processing of genocide trauma. Although it may be too early to judge the efficacy of the gacaca system, it seems to offer a local, more reconciliatory approach that may prove to be a hopeful model for the future.

In our final analysis of this genocide we need to briefly review what networks were in place to support the third genocide of the twentieth century. The ability of extremist elements of the Habyarimana government to initiate, organize, and facilitate the genocide hinged on their use of two powerful propaganda tools. The RTLM (Radio et Television Libres des Mille Collines) and the newspaper *Kangura*, received direct support from the government, providing electrical power to the radio station directly from the presidential palace.

Through these instruments Rwanda's Hutu population was constantly warned that the "Tutsi invaders" were plotting to destroy the country and overthrow the government. The broadcasters for the radio station identified individuals to be targeted for assassination and encouraged Hutus to "kill the rats" (a term referring to the Tutsi population). Additionally, the newspaper *Kangura* published the infamous "Hutu Ten Commandments" calling on Hutus to end all contact with the Tutsi population and stop "showing them mercy." These commandments went as far as encouraging the systematic rape and killing of Tutsi women. RTLM and *Kangura* acted as both a mouthpiece for the organizers of the genocide and the fuel to fan the flames of "Hutu Powa!" extremist ideology and successfully promoted the systematic killing of all Tutsis.[66]

The genocide does not end when the killings end. The imminent goal is to restore this country to a harmonious coexistence. Especially in Rwanda, survivors of the genocide, offenders, and victims may still have animosity, anger, and hatred against the other ethnic group, but the goal is to make sure that hatred is not passed on to the future generations. A country of unity is essential to the future of Rwanda in order to make sure that another atrocity does not occur. A system which allows justice for those harmed is important, because it leads to reconciliation.

A central concern of many resisters in the Ottoman Empire and Rwanda was the desire to save innocent lives; this determination manifested itself in different ways depending on the context, ranging from simple acts of heroism to sophisticated resistance movements. During each of these genocides, government-supported and sponsored mechanisms were put in place to eliminate a particular ethnic group. In both cases, resisters were not only fighting evil in its worst form, but they were fighting a government they had always thought would protect them.

Chapter 6

The Nature of Goodness

"All that I'm saying is that the energy of hate will take you nowhere, but the energy of pardon, which manifests itself through love will manage to change your life in a positive sense."—Paulo Coelho

"There is no trust more sacred than the one the world holds with children. There is no duty more important than ensuring that their rights are respected, that their welfare is protected, that their lives are free from fear and want and that they grow up in peace."—Kofi A. Annan, Former Secretary General of the United Nations

"If we practice an eye for an eye and a tooth for a tooth, soon the whole world will be blind and toothless."—Mahatma Gandhi

WHAT IS GOODNESS? How does one define the attributes or qualities of doing good? The quotations above express important aspects of goodness, such as equanimity, respect for your fellow men and women, leading by example, forgiveness, love, and caring for others in need. Trying to discern these components may be a daunting task, but without a doubt, they make our lives better, happier, and all around more enjoyable. In this chapter we seek to pinpoint some of the qualities of goodness. We know it when we see it, but what are its characteristics? We find that some of these qualities can be visceral experiences that are best revealed through the stories of our lives. Others are common to the human experience and are highlighted through discussion or through principles we can all subscribe to. Most of all, we want to show how a caring society made up of many acts of kindness can lead to a more fulfilled, healthy, and happy human experience. Countries such as Denmark and Bulgaria showed the world that intervening on behalf of innocent people is possible in the face of tyranny; these two countries rescued the bulk of their Jewish citizens from the Nazis during the Holocaust.

Scholars have tried to answer the question of "what is goodness?" Some say that to perform an act of goodness one has to have a selfish motive,[1] that altruism is motivated by an internal reward. We disagree, and believe instead that goodness is an act of caring for others and it is not dependent on an internal reward for egoistic satisfaction. What is important is the positive outcomes for the general welfare of others and the community. We will not be debating the motivation for goodness because there is no doubt that it exists, is measurable, and has a profound effect on society.

Recently published literature by scholars indicates that we are capable of goodness, and some would argue that it is in our nature. "Evil and wrong are aberrations. If wrong was a norm, it wouldn't be news. Our newscasts wouldn't lead with the latest acts of murder or mayhem, because they would be ordinary."[2] Reflecting a similar sentiment is the recently titled book, *The Compassionate Instinct,* edited by Dacher Keltner, Jason Marsh, and Jeremy Adam Smith.[3] Some articles included in their volume deal with the instinct for compassionate behavior. Frans de Waal's chapter, "The Evolution of Empathy" and Sapolsky's "Peace among Primates" have shown convincingly that empathy is evident among primates. McCullough maintains that there is such a thing as a forgiveness instinct. Jonathan Haidt offers another aspect of goodness, which he titles elevation. It consists of inspiring someone with kind words, approval, and expressions of respect and love. Catherine Price speaks about the important human instinct of gratitude. Aaron Lazare sees the importance of apology in maintaining harmonious human relations. Zeno Franco and Philip Zimbardo emphasize the importance of heroism in that many human beings can and do act heroically on the behalf of others.

Post and Neimark identify ten ways of giving that contribute to mental and physical health, including celebration, generativity, forgiveness, courage, humor, respect, compassion, loyalty, listening, and creativity.[4] Stanford philosopher and educator Nel Noddings maintains that caring "is that condition toward which we long and strive, and it is our longing for caring—to be in that special relationship—that provides the motivation for us to be moral. We want to be moral in order to remain in the caring relationship and to enhance the ideal of ourselves as one who cares."[5] President Tito's granddaughter, Svetlana Broz, compiled a book of heroic stories during the tragedy in Yugoslavia.[6] Most of the stories show the humanity of individuals who risked their lives to help members of another ethnic group. Pumla Godobo-Madikizela and Chris Van Der Merwe edited a volume of stories of forgiveness and its role in healing traumas people experienced during apartheid and other times of distress.[7]

Goodness can be defined as the state or quality of being good, specifically, virtuous, kind, generous, and benevolent. Philosophers, numerous writers, scholars, poets, and social scientists have written about this positive aspect of humanity for centuries. The word goodness can sometimes be used interchangeably with loving kindness, agape, empathy, ethical care for others, and social responsibility. However, these are merely descriptive words. This chapter also seeks to define the action that signifies this sort of positive behavior and thought.

Just as in the case of evil, goodness can be seen as a continuum (see figure 1 on the next page) ranging from everyday acts of goodness, such as helping a person carry a heavy load or giving directions, to heroic behavior which consists of risking one's life and family in order to save others from injustice and persecution. In this chapter we will discuss examples and varieties of ways of helping others. These will include both everyday acts of kindness, which may involve a variety of helping behaviors ranging from hospice volunteers to rescuing people from genocide and certain death.

A man who was awarded a Carnegie Heroes medal saw a woman in a wheelchair trying to cross railroad tracks. Unfortunately, she got stuck there while the train was rapidly approaching. The forty-nine year old man was in his car, and he witnessed the woman struggling. He jumped out of his car, and saved the woman:

> The train was about twenty yards away, and I just grabbed her by the collar in the front and pulled her out onto me, and then she kind of fell on top of me because she was paralyzed from the waist down. The train was there and hit her wheelchair and drove it into my leg. And what I thought, the train had caught my leg and cut my leg off, but it was the wheelchair just hitting my leg.[8]

These moral virtues are not merely abstractions, but real acts that help others and enable them to flourish. What we call a continuum of goodness, below, shows a few examples of the variety and types of helping others.

Figure 1: GOODNESS CONTINUUM

Heroic ◄————————————————————————► Conventional

Risking one's life for a stranger	Intervene on behalf of oppressed people	Actions which benefit the environment and all living things	Volunteering on a regular basis	Typical Acts of Kindness
• Hugh Thompson (US officer who saved lives during My Lai Massacre 1968) • Rick Rescorla (saved 2,700 Morgan Stanley employees during 9/11) • Wilhelm Bachner (saved more than 50 Jews while working for a Nazi firm) • Rescuing of Jews and others during World War II. • Carnegie Heroes (Individuals who risk their lives to save strangers in various life-threatening situations)	• John Rabe (saved approx. 200,000 Chinese victims from Japanese massacre -Nanking 1937) • Rigoberta Menchú Tum (A Guatemalan Nobel peace prize winner and indigenous rights promoter.) • Muhammad Yunus (Bangladeshi banker and economist, Nobel peace prize winner for micro-loans aimed at specifically helping poor women.)	• Chico Mendes (He fought to stop the burning and logging of the Amazon Rainforest to clear land for cattle ranching.) • John Muir (His direct activism helped to save the Yosemite Valley and other national parks. His writings and philosophy strongly influenced the formation of the modern environmental movement.)	• Habitat for Humanity has built more than 250,000 houses around the world, founded in 1976 by Millard Fuller and his wife, Linda. • The American Red Cross organized by Clara Barton in 1881 provides disaster relief in the U.S. and has more than 97 million volunteers worldwide.	• Partnersin-kindness.org (An organization founded for the purposes of inspiring and encouraging acts of kindness. More than 30,000 people have submitted their story about giving or receiving kindness.)

The founder of Taoism, Lao Tzu, maintained that kindness in words creates confidence. Kindness in thinking creates profoundness. Kindness in giving creates love. This profound concept is brought to life by those who have emphasized the great importance of love and caring for society.

Mother Teresa said, "Spread love everywhere you go: first of all, in your own house. Give love to your children, wife, husband, to a next-door neighbor. Let no one ever come to you without leaving better and happier. Be the living expression of God's kindness, kindness in your face, kindness in your eyes, kindness in your smile, kindness in your warm greetings."[9]

This chapter is organized into sections that include interpretations of influential scientists, philosophers, and public figures and attributes of goodness from interviews and stories of everyday kindness. We will look at the many facets of goodness, including *love, trust, friendship, forgiveness, peace, empathy, social responsibility, volunteerism,* and *spirituality*. Love in particular is of paramount importance in any act of goodness and is undoubtedly the most universal act which helps goodness to flourish.

LOVE AND FORGIVENESS

Closely connected with forgiveness is the power of love, which is associated with caring and kindness. In his recent book *Unlimited Love: Altruism, Compassion and Service*, Stephen Post examines an important process called unlimited love.[10] Citing Vladimir Solovyov (1853-1900), he states that,

> The meaning and worth of love, as a feeling, is that it really forces us, with all of our being, to acknowledge for another the same absolute central significance, which because of the power of our egoism, we are conscious of only our own selves. Love is important not as one of our feelings, but as the transfer of all our interest in life from ourselves to another, as the shifting of the very center of our personal lives.

Post maintains it has been well established that when processes such as love, compassion, empathy, and other-regarding (valuing others) lead to apology by those who have done harm to victims. This leads to forgiveness, which then leads to unloading one's burden and feeling of hurt, and finally reconciliation for both the victim and the offender. Forgiveness is a powerful emotional release and is a clear acceptance of compassion for the offender and, if genuine, it helps to extinguish the rage and the feeling for revenge, as well as the cycle of violence. A Polish rescuer who saved many lives during the Nazi era said, "Without love, what have you got, a world without a heart."[11]

Oliner has personally experienced an act of loving care during WWII when a simple peasant woman in Poland risked her life and that of her family to protect him from the Nazis. We feel along with the writers below that love is the bond that holds society together and ultimately, what heals emotional wounds.

Viktor Frankl focuses on similar social processes, namely that love is the healing power in human relations.[12] Frankl states that the highest goal to which humanity can aspire is love, which is associated with helping others to flourish. Similarly, Dean Ornish in *Love and Survival: The Scientific Basis for the Healing Power of Intimacy* writes that our knowledge of the nature of love remains primitive, because until recently it was not considered scientifically respectable to investigate love phenomena as it relates to kindness.[13] Furthermore he tells us:

> Love is the fundamental attractive process. It is the process through which you receive information. Therefore, love exists in all systems at all levels from the micro to the macro. For example, take water. You have hydrogen and oxygen, two separate molecules. They come together and create this unbelievable, amazing liquid called water. What [Linda] and I are finally seeing is that what hydrogen and oxygen do, is bring out the best of each other. Through their relationship, they create something bigger than themselves, which is called water. The idea of love is not uniquely human. Love becomes, ultimately, very spiritual. There are levels of love from the micro to the macro.[14]

Ornish concludes that after an analysis of dozens of studies in medical literature, those who are in loving relationships with close ties to family and community are three to five times more likely to live longer, which also affirms Emile Durkheim's classical sociological work on suicide, in which he found that when people are alone or feel like they do not belong to any social group they are more likely to commit suicide.[15]

Sociologist Pitirim A. Sorokin has written extensively on altruism and love. In *The Ways and Power of Love* he writes about different kinds of love, most importantly "agape," or divinel- inspired unconditional love.[16] For Sorokin, love is literally a life-giving force and by its very nature love is goodness incarnate; it brings nobility to human relations.

Rabindranath Tagore, the Nobel Prize-winning Bengali poet, Brahmin religionist, visual artist, playwright, novelist, and composer stated, "Whatever name our logic may give to the truth of human unity, the facts can never be ignored that we have our greatest delight when we realize ourselves and others, and this is the definition of love. This love gives us the testimony of the great whole, which is the complete and final truth of man."[17] Tagore expressed that love is exactly the emotion and feeling through which the potential of humanity can be reached. Only through the affectionate experiences of compassion and love are people truly free to appreciate the bonds of human solidarity.

Christopher Marlowe sees goodness as beauty in the best estate. Others such as Somerset Maugham express that goodness is the only value that seems in this world of appearances to have any claim to be an end in itself.

There are an impressive number of attributes of goodness, and many observations made by other writers overlap. Trust is yet another attribute of goodness which we now turn to, as a major component of why people choose good over evil.

TRUST

Contemporary world surveys indicate a lack of trust in government and interpersonal relationships.[18] There is a feeling of doubletalk in politics; groups are suspicious of each other and their motives. The famous Berkeley psychologist Paul Ekman says, "If you are not trusted, it makes all intimate relationships impossible."[19] Jeremy Adam Smith, senior editor of *Greater Good,* and Pamela Paxton, Associate Professor of Sociology at Ohio State University, did a study consisting of forty-six countries over the last ten years in which it was proven that democratic countries encourage trust in citizens more than authoritarian countries.[20] Some maintain that trust may be an innate part of human nature and that it is a basis of healthy relationships especially between parents and infants. The authors of the study found that trust is a part of human nature. The hormone oxytocin is associated with trust, which starts at infancy between the child and its caregiver. Trust is a necessity for a healthy relationship and biologically it is the expectation that other people's future actions will safe-guard our interests. Trust is the magic ingredient that makes life possible. Smith and Paxton inform us that Gallup's Annual Governance survey shows that trust in government is lower today than it was during the Watergate era at the time of the Nixon administration. The numbers show that from the 1970s to today, trust had declined in the press (24 to 11 percent), education (36 to 28 percent), banks (35 to 31 percent) corporations (26 to 17 percent) and organized religion (35 to 25 percent). This proves that we must inculcate trust once again in social institutions and family relations so that society will benefit from it. Gordon Anderson suggests that the government has been "infected" through the government's attempt to run the economy or industry in the name of justice, as well as the economy's attempt to shape public policy in the name of economic growth.[21] "Both approaches are viruses that have been introduced into the legal system. Both approaches redirect public funds for narrow interests and weaken the entire system." *Bowling Alone: The Collapse and Revival of American Community* is an appropriate metaphor for individu-alism and distrust of others especially between younger and older generations; trust could be part of the solution that brings people together.[22]

When people trust an institution or another person they are more inclined to want to help that institution or individual. For instance, in the wake of the recent natural disasters, such as the earthquake in Haiti and the floods in Pakistan, people from all over the world donated money and supplies to relief funds. These funds didn't always reach those people in the greatest need. Therefore, donors are reluctant to contribute funds to help.

Researchers such as Michael Kosfeld, et al. finds that trust may be a bio-logically based part of all species.[23] The neuorpeptide oxytocin is known to regulate behavior. In non-human species, "oxytocin receptors are distributed in various brain regions associated with behavior, including pair bonding, maternal care, sexual behavior, and the ability to form normal social attach-ments."[24] From this research, Kosfeld and others have concluded that oxytocin also leads to prosocial behaviors such as trust in humans. An element of trust characterizes almost all human social interaction. When trust is absent we are, in a sense, dehumanized. With betrayal comes a loss of trust that results in unhappiness and makes life difficult for the betrayed. Trust coincides with confidence and when one lacks trust they lack confidence in themselves, in others, and in society. This leads to acting in disrespectful ways towards others such as name-calling, and making false accusations against another because there is no trust. Trust is just one variable that explains altruistic behavior and why people choose to help others. Oliner* found several other salient correlates of altruistic behavior explained below.

RELIGIOSITY AND SPIRITUALITY

"All the major religions of the world have similar ideals of love, the same goal of benefiting humanity through spiritual practice, and the same effect of trying to make their followers into better human beings" says the Dalai Lama. Rabbi Hillel (70 BC) stated, "What is hateful to you, do not do to others. That is the whole law, all else is commentary."

In *Do Unto Others* Oliner used existing literature and actual interviews to try to understand motivating factors for why people do altruistic acts.[25] Many of those interviewed identified themselves as Christians. Of those Christians there were rescuers, bystanders, and survivors of the Holocaust, as well as Carnegie heroes, moral exemplars, hospice and non-hospice volunteers. Respondents who expressed a strong inclination to help others all identified some type of religiosity or spirituality as a motivating factor to help.

One philanthropist interviewed based his spirituality on his positive and generous interaction with others:

> I guess I believe my spirituality is not traditionally religious spirituality. It's more of a belief in the value of the individual. It has to do with a concept of how I live my life, which is to be a person who is generous in all aspects; a sort of generosity of spirit, a positive attitude, an attitude of trusting people, an attitude of respect for myself and others. A feeling that each of us... our lives are in some way influenced by the lives of others. Being a person who distributes a sense of good will and good feelings not only enhances the lives the people around me, but my own as well. (Respondent 033)

---

*   *Do Unto Others* consisted of a non-random sample of 450 students, clergy, and others which correlate with empathy, social responsibility, and altruism.

This psychologist-turned-management-consultant believes in the all-encompassing connection between all humans and other species. He states:

> I have a belief that we are all connected; that there is energy in all
> of us; I think there are beings on other planets. I would say that I
> believe in everything, but I don't have the truth in all things. I try
> to treat even the smallest creatures with great respect. If I catch
> a fly or mouse I will throw it outside or in the garden, not kill it.
> (Respondent 008)

This physician intertwines God and friend, so they are one to him. He says:

> My whole life has been loving people. When I hear faithful people
> speak of their sincerity around their particular God, I hear them
> use the language I use for friends, so I assume my metaphor for
> God is friend. (Respondent 050)

This environmental activist has been involved with old-growth redwood stands in Humboldt County, and has internalized her caring for the earth:

> One day I just felt this immense amount of love beginning to fill
> me up, and I was like, "wow, where is this coming from?" And I
> realized that what I was feeling was the unconditional love of the
> earth. (Respondent 004)

A Humboldt County environmental activist wants to create awareness and change about the watersheds, not only for the community, but also for the ecosystem and the fish that use the watershed. She relates her spiritual connection with the world:

> Spirituality is how you connect to the rest of the world and the
> people and the beings in the world. And then also, how long after
> you're gone, how will your presence here have affected what hap-
> pens a long time from now? What you do here now will somehow
> affect that whole. And if you do really good things, then you are
> going to leave that whole a better thing, and add to that energy,
> rather than detract from it. (Respondent 034)

This long-time activist with the League of Women Voters also addresses the spiritual connectedness with people and nature when she says:

> I believe in the goodness of people. I believe in one's spirit living on. I believe there's a great deal that we don't understand out there that is beneficial to us, and so forth...The most important thing is the connectedness of people, and that we connect one another to the spiritual things we don't understand— to the earth, to nature, to all of those things. I believe that it's all connected together, and I think that's important. If we forget our connectedness, then we miss out and we can go astray. (Respondent 042)

SOCIAL RESPONSIBILITY AND PROSOCIAL ORIENTATION

Individuals who have a high prosocial orientation of concern for others are likely to feel a sense of social responsibility for others. Social responsibility, or the quality of assuming an obligation for helping to see that fairness and justice are doled out equally in positive ways, was the second most recognized motivating factor in Oliner's research.[26] Eighty percent of moral exemplars identified social responsibility as being important in their lives, while 89 percent of clergy reported the same.

In two similar studies, researchers Staub, and Briggs, Piliavin, Lorenson, and Becker found that individuals with high social responsibility scores are more likely to be volunteers.[27] Other scholars report there is something called an imperative to volunteer—a cultural theme which states that Americans have an obligation, even a divine obligation, to contribute to the betterment of their community. For example, a nurse and member of her church congregation states her purpose in helping others:

> Sort of like *Tuesdays with Morrie*, that you're not the wave, you're part of the ocean.[28] (Respondent 012)

One businessman feels a sense of responsibility to help his fellow human beings. He states:

> That's an empowering notion that people do not have to be relegated to be poor; that it's not that God wishes you to be poor and

uneducated, but that there is a possibility that change has to come from people who are willing to take responsibilities in their lives who are affected by issues and distinct possibilities. At the same time, to have the resources to connect inner strength to the reality of empowerment, to participate with strength. It's not a charity of simply the good Samaritan helping someone along the road, but going beyond that; more like liberation theology. And I think the morality is that we have to have responsibility for making sure that we do more than the minimum, so it's not just a crumb of bread, but helping people to move beyond the dependency. Anything less than furthering nurturing the whole independence of individuals is minimal; at its best, maternalistic. (Respondent 018)

Another respondent in the study relates a story of racism in our society and why it drives him to help others:

I feel I'm driven more by a sense of fairness, and justice, and equity. I feel that there is a basic obligation that people have to leave things better than they found them. While I'm not a great optimist about the human future, I can't think of anything more interesting or important to do than work on it, so I'm not depressed by that. I think my life was more of a developmental process. I have certainly had experiences, which informed or reinforced views I had. A couple of weeks ago I was in Beverly Hills in a restaurant with an African American friend who was treated very poorly in that restaurant, and I knew exactly what was going on, and so did he. That just reinforced my own concerns about fairness, and equity, and racism, and all that. (Respondent 023)

This man who heads the largest nonprofit service provider to Native Americans in California, asserts that it is everyone's responsibility to do what can be done for the sake of all children and future generations:

Just that I think that it is our responsibility to make this world a better place for our children. Indians believe in our future generations as well, that you have to live your life in accordance with the

> things you know to be important and stand up for the issues that
> you believe in so you can make it a better world. (Respondent 041)

A doctor who works with AIDS patients in Washington, DC, shares his insight on responsibility and the need for all of us to do something positive in order to establish world peace:

> Establishing world peace, of course it depends on justice—true
> peace, that is, the greatest struggle and battle humanity has ever
> had and it is an achievable goal. Most people would say, "Well it
> is not achievable, people are violent, people are jealous, people are
> selfish." But it is an achievable goal. We just have to get it in our
> heads that this is an achievable goal. We are much closer to it today
> than we were one hundred years ago. (Respondent 060)

This environmentalist feels it is a responsibility and a need to care for society and the world. She says:

> I was always one of those people who thought recycling, attending
> rallies and signing petitions is all we needed to do to make this
> world a better place. (Respondent 004)

A twenty-year volunteer for his community and the surrounding environment in central California sees that our planet is in jeopardy and he wants to create awareness through his activities:

> Common good to me has a much broader reach than just for,
> say, one person or community. It's more for the planet and all the
> inhabitants; the environment as a whole. And I think that pre-
> serving land for the future inhabitants, animals and plants that
> live there for the community of people very much fits in to that.
> On a larger scale we have to be looking at that; the planet is in
> jeopardy, in my mind, through the activities of the human beings.
> (Respondent 009)

A Humboldt County, California, native and environmentalist feels it is her responsibility to protect this earth for the future generations:

> We live on a planet, and this is the only one we've got, and that is
> never going to change. We have an absolute responsibility to pro-
> tect it for the generations to come, and if we don't, no one else is
> going to and every one of us has to do our part, otherwise seven
> generations down the line, or ten or fifteen, this is gonna be gone...
> and what a tragedy. It doesn't matter how much money or how
> much power or how much whatever, there's only one planet, and
> we're not getting off it. (Respondent 034)

This writer/nonprofit organizer/curriculum developer is attempting to start
a charter school that connects the head to the heart, and, acting from the heart,
to help humanity. She states her purpose for getting involved in this activity:

> If we're not working for social justice and the betterment of the
> human condition and the moral growth of the world and elimina-
> tion of prejudice, then we're really ignoring the spiritual responsi-
> bility. We can be spiritual in our actions by seeing the goodness in
> everyone and keeping our emotions in check and matching those
> habits of the heart, and we can be spiritual in our global perspec-
> tive and our careers by being persistent in the world, bringing
> unity and harmony to the world. (Respondent 056)

For the past seventeen years this executive director of a nonprofit organization helped raise funds for her local schools to build a theater, a library, and
a health center. She contrasts people's goodness and acting on behalf of others
to those actions of the 9/11 attackers:

> I have such a profound belief in the goodness of people and
> the strength of the human spirit, and so forth, and I am so sad
> when I see people or know of people acting in some way that is
> so against humanity. I think of these nineteen people on these
> planes [September 11 attacks]. What could possess them to do
> that? Where did we miss the boat, we as human beings, that there
> are people who exist to do such horrible things? They are human
> beings after all, and what would come to that? You know, about
> World War II and the Nazis. (Respondent 020)

This woman from Humboldt County, a volunteer on five boards, including the League of Women Voters and Affordable Housing Boards for the Homeless, shares her insight into when and how one should help:

> I guess I would veer more to the volunteerism and being a productive part of society, and making the world a better place in which to live. And again that involves being able to take care of yourself, and then extending. If you can't take care of yourself, you can't do the other. People who don't have the ability to take care of themselves draw from society. Once you have the ability to take care of yourself, and your own life is stable, then you can look to making others around you better off. (Respondent 62)

She elaborates on her work and bridges our discussion onto the topic of the moral goal of volunteering:

> I suppose trying to improve people's basic living conditions would be considered a moral goal. I think it's pretty disgraceful that we let people live on the streets and children go homeless, so I guess that's moral. (Respondent 036)

A Catholic priest explains his understanding of social responsibility:

> It is caring for my fellow brothers and sisters, especially those less fortunate, and to not be afraid. Just look at everything that happens in life as an opportunity for growth and something that is of the direction of God. (Respondent 065)

Another Priest illustrates how he was taught social responsibility:

> My father...being a doctor, he'd go to someone's home and visit them, and give them a treatment. He would find that they didn't have any heat in their home, and this is Michigan, because they didn't have enough money or somebody was out of work, so he'd buy enough coal or fuel oil for the whole winter. Or he'd get the husband a job, he'd buy food for a couple of months for the family, that kind of thing. He did that all of his life. (Respondent 070)

Social responsibility is an important explanatory variable which helps us understand why people care and contribute to a more harmonious society.

EMPATHY AND SYMPATHY*

Researchers such as Irwin et al., suggest that the emergence of social order revealed that the emotion, sympathy moderates self-interest and enables individuals to act selflessly for the greater good.[29] The empathic person has experienced pain and wants to relieve others of that pain.[30] Lauren Wispe found that "sympathy refers to the heightened awareness of another's plight as something to be alleviated. Empathy refers to the attempt of one self-aware self to understand the subjective experiences of another self."[31] Sympathy is a way of relating. Empathy is a way of knowing. I suggest that these are different psychological processes and that the differences between them should not be obfuscated. In our study *Do Unto Others* we found that 55 percent of moral exemplars and 73 percent of the clergy were motivated to become active in the community on the behalf of others.[32] The desire to help others is generally a strong motivating factor in various other avenues of help, including volunteerism, generally, and particularly volunteerism in the hospice institutions because of the empathic inclination of these volunteers as well as modeling themselves after their moral exemplars. The strong desire for clergy to help others might be expected since they have been socialized to be more empathetic and compassionate in their profession. Empathy was an important variable in other research of volunteers and social workers. Allen and Rushton reviewed nineteen studies of community mental health workers and found them to be more empathic.[33] Omoto and Snyder's study of AIDS volunteers found a correlation between an individual's personal characteristics as the primary motivation for volunteering, and those with value-expressive functions of nurturance and empathy as their main motivation.[34] Dancy and Wynn-Dancy, in a study of the elderly, found that several features were embodied in the act of caring, including a level of knowing, patience, courage, trust, and hope.[35] Intrinsic to the concept of genuine caring is the volunteers' ability to empathize, empower, and engage with the geriatric client. Omoto and Snyder approach the

---

*   Sympathy or empathic concern is the feeling of compassion or concern for another, the wish to see them better off or happier.

psychology of volunteering, and specifically AIDS volunteers within the AIDS community.[36] They found that oftentimes the volunteers feel a sense of humanitarian obligation and concern for those with AIDS. Empathy was found to be an important variable in studies of mental health workers, AIDS volunteers, and volunteers for the elderly. A Lutheran minister and foster father expressed it this way, "Putting yourself in another person's shoes and walking their path brings understanding" (Respondent 022).

Empathic motivation is a major contributor to prosocial action. An example is volunteering. It is important to note that American society benefits greatly from this form of service. Omoto, Snyder and Lindsay inform us that volunteerism is beneficial for everyone: those who receive the services, those providing the services, the volunteer organizations, and society as a whole.[37] They find that volunteering represents one of the good sides of human nature, a powerful agency of will and effort that perform necessary works beneficial to all. Other studies have found that some of the motivating factors for volunteering are empathy for those in need, a need for affiliation, a hope for later reciprocity, and self-enhancement. Oliner found that those who reported empathic motivation also scored high on questions regarding social responsibility, of which volunteering is closely related.[38] A woman who directs a literary project helps people who are trying to understand who they are:

> I try to understand better where they come from and how they
> look at things, and what's reasonable for them, instead of judging
> people according to what's reasonable for me. (Respondent 017)

To volunteer one's time and effort is a form of social action from which the recipient, the volunteer, and society itself benefits. Omoto, Snyder and Lindsay maintain that if there were a greater understanding and appreciation of the benefits and costs of volunteerism it would contribute towards increasing the number and types of prosocial action that people do to create goodness in society.[39]

Strong morals and positive, socialization shows a relationship between empathic responses and prosocial behavior, meaning those who express empathy for others are more likely to take actions such as volunteer. For instance, Eisenberg, Valiente, and Champion write about situational empathy-related responding and prosocial behavior.[40] The authors conducted a twenty-three year study in which they followed preschoolers from the age of four through their adolescence and into adulthood. They examined the relationship of preschoolers to others focusing on other orientation and empathy related responses. They concluded that children have a natural moral reasoning in relation to the other. This was expressed at an early age through spontaneous sharing. The practice of spontaneous sharing predicted prosocial behavior as an adult. This kind of research has been completed by other authors about young children and the relationship between empathizing and sharing. Eisenberg et al maintain that,

> Overall, there are many more significant correlations than would be expected by chance between adults, prosocial disposition, and self-reported prosociality—helping, empathy, sympathy and perspective taking in late childhood and adolescence. Thus, there is strong evidence of intraindividual consistency in prosocial disposition over time, including empathy related responding.[41]

What we can take from this work is that children begin to empathize and sympathize at early ages from their socializers. This study shows that empathy, sharing, and other types of prosocial behavior are innate to humans. These traits, if nurtured, lead to altruistic behavior in adults.

As we mentioned above, there exists a relationship between empathy and moral reasoning, which is defined as the ethical decision. Socialization is another important factor of empathic expressivity of parents as well as warmth and support that affects children. Eisenberg et al argues that socializers should learn optimal ways to promote sympathetic concern for others. This concern for others represents yet another dimension of human goodness. We advocate the cultivation of this concern as a way to divert aggression and promote moral reasoning early in life.

In a chapter titled "Reducing Hostility and Building Compassion: A Lesson From the Jigsaw Classroom" Elliot Aronson offers the classic example of moving from the stage of alienation and bullying in a classroom to that of cooperation and resolving problems through a learning method known as the "jigsaw."[42] This well-known method consists of cooperative collective learning rather than leaving out students who are normally shy or uncooperative. The teacher divides up a topic that is shared among students; each has to study and research a different area of a specific topic. Each student has a topic, each is included and each teaches the others. Attempting to avoid the kind of negative outcomes of such tragedy as the Columbine High School shootings, a preventative approach to bullying was taken in a school in Austin, Texas. The Expect Respect program implemented in schools across Texas provides support groups for teens that are victims of bullying, domestic violence, and/or sexual abuse. It is a school-based program that provides support for youth and educates them on what are healthy and unhealthy relationships, violence, and respect. Increasing positive intergroup relations, according to Aronson, has to do with cooperation and inclusiveness. With the jigsaw method these classes began to successfully integrate an otherwise socially cliqued hierarchy. This is a process that I believe is important in my own experiences in a classroom. It increases empathy, reduces dissonance, and offers success rather than failure to those who might typically be left out. This sort of act provides opportunities for increased dialogue and sharing of knowledge rather than singling out the students and ranking them, which reinforces the existing social order.

We asked Lorey Keele, a former member of the Humboldt County Human Rights Commission with much experience as a supervisor with volunteers, why some people volunteer. She believes that people feel that they have a gift to offer; the gift that comes in giving and forgiving; that they have channeled their compassion, passion, and empathy in a particular way, or they feel that they can do that.

A professor and activist in Marin County helps immigrants with legal problems. He says:

> I think there's a natural empathy for people that needs to be cultivated. (Respondent 007)

A nurse and artist feels that empathy is part of her identity:

> I think one of the things I enjoy so much about my work is being with people who are going through terrible circumstances and being able to try and bring joy to their time spent with me, even if it's just a tiny glimpse. Even if I only see somebody for a minute, if they've had a terrible day, if they go away feeling better, to me that's

a privilege to have been able to do that. I think that that's a big part
of who I am. (Respondent 049)

A social worker and professor helps the community and wants others to
extend their love and help if and when they can. He says:

> I would say my ultimate goal would be to be present to people
> when they are struggling. To help them find in themselves the
> inner strength and in their families, and the systems, which in part
> have the strength to heal and to support them while they do that.
> I hope to let them experience being cared for and loved uncondi-
> tionally and to help them find the ability to extend that love inside
> themselves to others. (Respondent 054)

Empathy can grow as one works with and learns about diverse populations.
This clinical psychologist emphasizes the need for empathy and caring. She says:

> What I have done has certainly shaped and enlightened my aware-
> ness of how people have suffered and how people are in need of
> compassion, response, and real concrete help. (Respondent 024)

A male rabbi states that:

> Empathy is a real attempt to be accepting and to have reverence
> of the others, no matter how different they might be from us.
> (Respondent 078)

A Catholic priest said that he has learned to care for other people and
wants to accommodate people's real needs. Loving your neighbor as yourself is
one of the precepts that he has acquired. (Respondent 070) Another Catholic
priest said that he was greatly influenced by saints:

> ...people like the Pope and Mother Teresa, these people giving of
> their lives. Talk about altruism, right? That's all there is, twenty-
> four hours a day for these people. Can you imagine what it is like
> to live in the slums of Calcutta? Faith and altruism are ultimately
> linked to these people. It's not just humanitarianism; it's more than
> that. (Respondent 080)

Empathy, caring, and social responsibility are positively correlated with altruistic behavior.

Moral Exemplars*

Anne Colby and William Damon give us some empirical insight into the nature of moral heroes such as Mandela, Gandhi, and Wallenberg, the rescuer of Hungarian Jews, as well as an organized approach for looking at their motivations.[43] They have identified a four-step process of reciprocity in the social influence and moral transformation that occurs between the actors and their supporters. This influential development may exist throughout a lifetime, which results in one coming to the aid of their fellow human beings (whether as a volunteer or a rescuer) and a relationship that develops between them. The four steps are: (1) an understanding match of goals between the two parties develops, (2) there is communication and sharing of new information and knowledge, (3) the parties engage in new activities, which (4) results in adopting and broadening new moral goals. For instance, Balwina Piecuch, a Polish peasant woman who helped rescue the author of this book during the Holocaust.

Although personality and motivation play an important role in creating moral change within one person, the primary force is social support and communication, which allows for feedback and development of the whole, thus benefiting the group and ultimately motivates the desire to help. Positivity (including optimism, love, and joy) is also closely linked with morality, because this quality is evident in the lives of most moral exemplars, as shown in Oliner's *The Altruistic Personality* and in Colby and Damon's sample. Moral exemplars do not blame others for their situation in life.

In moral exemplars there is a uniting of self and morality. Among the noteworthy patterns are: (1) the exemplars' disregard for risk and their disavowal of courage, (2) their certainty of response about matters of principle, (3) their unremitting faith and positivity in the face of the most dismal circumstances,

---

*   Moral exemplars—individuals who have a moral commitment to achieve justice, equality, and fairness for those in the community who are in need of loving kindness, compassion and caring. (Oliner 2003 p.22)

(4) their capacity to take direction as well as social support from the followers they inspire, and (5) the dynamic interplay between continuity and change in their personal life histories. These characteristics of moral exemplars lead to the interpretation that it is possible to have an individual personality and also be committed to a moral cause, and that there is no conflict between the two attributes. "Moral exemplars are both highly individuated persons as well as highly committed ones."[44]

APOLOGY AND FORGIVENESS

The ability to apologize and to forgive are important attributes of goodness and caring.

> We must develop and maintain the capacity to forgive. He who is devoid of the power to forgive is devoid of the power to love. There is some good in the worst of us and some evil in the best of us. When we discover this, we are less prone to hate our enemies.
> —*Martin Luther King Jr.*

> Forgiveness is the key that can unshackle us from a past that will not rest in the grave of things over and done with. As long as our minds are captive to the memory of having been wronged, they are not free to wish for reconciliation with the one who wronged us.— *Lewis B. Smedes* (Theologian)

> Forgiveness and reconciliation are not just ethereal, spiritual, other-worldly activities. They have to do with the real world. They are real politick, because in a very real sense without forgiveness, there is no future.—*Bishop Desmond Tutu*

Apology means that the offender feels, acknowledges, and expresses regret for a harm committed and expresses an intention to make reparations to the person harmed, and also makes a genuine promise to change his or her behavior. Forgiveness is the willingness to abandon one's right to resentment, negative judgments, and indifferent behavior to one who has unjustly injured the victim, while fostering the undeserved qualities of compassion, generosity, and even love towards the offender. Forgiveness can occur without apology when the harmed person is motivated to reestablish human contact with the offender. Sometimes an apology is given, but forgiveness was not forthcoming because the harmed individual could not forgive the hurt. Such as in the case of Simon Wiesenthal who was unable to forgive a dying German who asked for forgiveness for killing Jews.[45] On his deathbed he said to Wiesenthal, "I am left here with my guilt. In the last hours of my life you are with me. I do not know who you are, all I only know that you are a Jew and that is enough."[46] Wiesenthal left the room because he could not forgive on behalf of those who were murdered. Rudolf Vrba who suffered imprisonment in Auschwitz for two years, and escaped telling the world about what he witnessed, decided he could not forgive the perpetrators of murder.[47]

The rage that a victimized person carries is debilitating and is in need of being released from the burden this individual carries. Not so long ago, the discussion of forgiveness and apology had been assigned as a weakness or deemed the domain of religion, such as confession in Catholicism, whereas now the culture of apology is much more prevalent. When the relationship between the harm-doer and forgiver is "right again," it may foster self-confidence and a sense of efficacy. In the medical arena, it may actually reduce disease, preventing pathologies that result in hostile feelings, depression, and hopelessness. Forgiveness also may provide a higher level of perceived social and emotional support, which may also include a greater sense of community. Lastly, forgiveness also may encourage self-healing as well as help to refocus on the goodness and altruism that exists in the world. The forgiveness process helps us think in terms of higher values, beyond the pain of the individual (Oliner 2008).

Dr. Andrew Weil, the author of many popular books on healing, summarizes the powerful gift of forgiveness in an article regarding the upcoming New Year. He says:

> As one year ends and another begins, you may wish to take stock
> of your mental health. Are you holding onto any anger and hurt
> from the past that's interfering with your emotional well-being? If
> so, perhaps one of the best gifts you can give yourself is the ability
> to forgive. Long a tenet of many religions, forgiveness is now being
> studied in scientific circles. And there's good evidence that it's a

powerful healing agent for body, mind, and spirit. I've noticed
that people who are able to forgive say it lifts a psychic burden and
offers a profound sense of relief and inner peace.[48]

Apology and forgiveness can be a healing process for all who are involved.
In 2003, Oliner interviewed a sample of individuals who were involved in
apology and asking for forgiveness. The following are some positive results
from genuine apology and forgiveness.

We interviewed members of three convents in Kentucky who apologized
to African Americans for their participation in maintaining slavery. In 2001, as
part of a worldwide effort by Catholics to repent for the mistreatment of others, the Sisters of Charity of Nazareth, Sisters of Loretto, and the Dominicans
of Saint Catherine, wanted to reconcile the past in order to confront past
injustices of slavery and the present-day racism.

Slaves had cleared the land and built the church in the early 1800s, and
these rural Kentucky communities also established the three convents where
sisters resided and inherited the slaves. All these years later, the sisters regret-
ted that their communities did not do more to oppose the system of slavery,
and they struggled to understand the role that slavery played in their past. The
Sisters also acknowledged that racial segregation has existed in their orders.
The apology took place at a church in Bardstown, Kentucky, and was attended
by nearly 400 people. The Dominicans of Saint Catherine also apologized
for the burning of African-American churches in the United States by issuing a statement in 1996 proclaiming: "to promote the dignity of persons...
transform unjust structures...and work against the violence that alienates and
marginalizes."

The African-American community in Kentucky accepted the apology
of the three religious communities. Elaine Riley, an African-American said,
"We hear you, we have listened to your stories, and we humbly accept your
apology." She cautioned that there are steps to be taken in the healing process
and that a close connection must be established with the African-American
community. Deacon James Turner also accepted the apology, stating, "May
God of all understanding forgive you and grant you peace," which ushered in
a commitment to fighting racism in the community. Other members of the
African-American community rejoiced in the power of the apology, offered

forgiveness and commented on how all of their ancestors, black and white, were "crying tears of joy in heaven." The three orders have since established scholarships for minorities in their high schools and colleges, and continue to make efforts to bring racial diversity to their various boards, especially on the local level. For more than a year after the service, racially-mixed groups from the reconciliation service continued to meet regularly. Their primary focus continues to be eradicating racism in all of its forms.

Another example of apology took place in Humboldt Country, California, on May 4, 2001. On this day a group of clergy approached a Native American tribe, the Wiyot, and its council in order to apologize for racism and oppression, but most specifically for a massacre that took place February 25, 1860, on Indian Island. They offered a signed statement of apology, which said,

> Recognizing that the land upon which we gather was once Wiyot tribal land, as was this whole Arcata/Eureka area, we consider it a supreme honor to have you here tonight as Native hosts to this conference. We have become increasingly aware in recent years of the history between our peoples. To say "We are sorry" for the past injustices and atrocities, including the Indian Island Massacre, seems so little to offer, so miniscule when compared with the horrific nature of what your people suffered. But sorry we are indeed. We choose not to hide behind the excuse that "These were sins of prior generations." We recognize that the community and church leaders of our race, though they did not all agree with the wickedness involved, did precious little, if anything, to find the guilty parties or bring them to justice. Little, if anything, was done to make amends or restitution.
>
> Although we cannot represent our entire race, we of the Christian churches in our community acknowledge to you our guilt and humbly ask for your forgiveness. We empathize with you and your desire to own Indian Island again and to build a center of remembrance for the lives of your people that were so brutally destroyed. Tonight we present to you the first fruits of our commitment to partner with you in buying the land and building that center. With hearts full of love for you and desire for your full

restoration as a people, we present this gift of $1,000.00. And we pledge our ongoing intention to pray for you and to work with you in this endeavor until its completion.[49]

Since that date, the churches and others have raised more funds and have donated them to the Wiyot tribe in order to purchase Indian Island. This apology and request for forgiveness is a hopeful example of what we hope is a trend for groups, both religious and political, to attempt to restore relations between people harmed by their forebears. While apologies to native peoples in several countries took place before the dramatic and well-publicized apology by Pope John Paul II to the Muslims for the Crusades, to Jews for 2,000 years of anti-Semitism, burning "witches" and other "heretics," and castrating boy singers so they would preserve their voices. The Pope's apology has given impetus to other faiths to apologize for their past wrongdoings.

COMPASSION AND CARE

With this section we hope to illustrate the concepts related to human goodness. Action is necessary to manifest this goodness and we have selected individuals who represent aspects of helping in both everyday and heroic acts related to dramatic historical events from everyday altruism to heroic altruism.

Chinue Sugihara was a Japanese diplomat serving as Vice Consul for the Japanese Empire in Lithuania during the Holocaust. Soon after the occupation of Lithuania by the Soviet Union in 1939, he helped several thousand Jews leave the country by issuing transit visas to Jewish refugees so that they could travel to Japan. Most of the Jews who escaped were refugees from Poland or residents of Lithuania. Because of his actions in saving Jews from the Nazis, Sugihara was honored by Israel as one of the Righteous Among the Nations in 1985, which is a medal given to non-Jews who risked their lives during the Holocaust. Afterward he said, "I cannot allow these people to die, people who have come to me for help with death staring them in the eyes. Whatever punishment may be imposed on me, I know I should follow my conscience."[50]

Canadian brothers, Craig and Marc Kielburger, then 12 years old, began an anti-child labor group called Free the Children, which has more than 100

chapters around the world. Organizers all are under the age of 18. They educate the public, write letters, and raise funds to create alternatives for children
who are abused and exploited.* Craig Kielburger is also the Co-founder and
Director of Me to We. The goal of Me to We focuses on encouraging ethical
living and social responsibility, while also helping Free the Children achieve
financial sustainability.

The well-known story of the four chaplains further illustrates heroic
altruism. The four chaplains, Alexander D. Goode, Jewish; George L. Fox,
Methodist; Clark V. Poling, Dutch Reformed; and John P. Washington,
Roman Catholic, were on a troop ship by the name of Dorchester, which
was taking American soldiers oversees. The troop ship left Saint John's,
Newfoundland, and headed towards the Atlantic carrying 902 soldiers. At
12:55 A.M., on February 3, 1942, a torpedo from U-boat U-223 slammed
into the starboard side of the Dorchester below the water line. Hundreds
of shocked and panicked men emerged from below deck.[51] The ship rapidly
drifted to starboard, rendering twelve of the thirteen lifeboats inaccessible.
Frightened and despairing soldiers called out for their mothers. All of the
four chaplains tried to locate life jackets and to calm the men. Unfortunately,
the Dorchester started sinking rather quickly and all of the life jackets were
already distributed; there were not enough life jackets for everyone. At this
striking moment, the four chaplains performed what we call the most heroic
act of love and heroism by giving up their own life jackets and handing them
over to frightened soldiers. The witnesses reported that the four chaplains were
holding hands and singing and praying to God in their various ways. Of the
902 soldiers, only 227 survived, and survivors told this heroic story over the
years. The offspring of the victims were dedicated to promoting the memory
of the Dorchester destruction. They attempted to find the perpetrators, that
is, the U-boat shooter who torpedoed the Dorchester. The two shooters, Kurt
Roser and Gerhard Buske, were found alive in Germany and were brought to
Washington to seek reconciliation with the offspring of the four chaplains.
Sax informs us that the widow of Chaplain Goode had problems with the idea
of reconciliation.[52] Soon thereafter, though, when remorse and apology was
expressed by the two German members of the U-boat crew, she was able to

---

*   http://www.freethechildren.com/aboutus/theteam/craigkielburger.php

forgive. Buske's grandson and the grandson of the Rabbi Alexander D. Goode were communicating with each other and they, as well as the elder generation, committed themselves to ensuring that this heroic story of the four chaplains will not be forgotten.

Metropolitan Chrysostomos saved 275 Jews on the island of Zakynthos in Greece.[53] In 1943 during the German occupation, the Nazis demanded a list of all Zakynthian Jews from the mayor, Pavlos Carreris, and Metropolitan Chrysostomos. The two men turned in a list containing only two names, theirs, which prompted the Germans to back down and not pursue their extermination plans in Zakynthos. The Jewish families remained hidden in Christian homes throughout the island until the withdrawal of the German troops.

Rosa Parks became a civil rights icon in 1955. She stood up to the Jim Crow custom for African Americans to sit in the back of buses. With her challenge to institutionalized racism, she effectively set a precedent that desegregated the bus system in Montgomery, Alabama. Parks' act of defiance created the modern Civil Rights Movement and Parks became an international icon of resistance to racial segregation. She organized and collaborated with civil rights leaders, including boycott leader Martin Luther King, Jr., helping to launch him to national prominence in the civil rights movement.

Muhammad Yunus is a Bangladeshi banker and economist. He previously was a professor of economics and is famous for his successful application of microcredit—the extension of small loans. Yunus is the founder of Grameen Bank. In 2006, Yunus and the bank were jointly awarded the Nobel Peace Prize for their efforts to create economic and social development from below. These loans are given to people too poor to qualify for traditional bank loans, mostly women entrepreneurs who experience restricted economic activity due to Bangladeshi cultural and religious customs. Yunus and his colleagues encountered everything from violent radical leftists to the conservative clergy who told women that they would be denied a Muslim burial if they borrowed money from the Grameen Bank. As of July 2007, Grameen Bank has issued US$ 6.38 billion to 7.4 million borrowers. This helped these poor women out of poverty by becoming involved in the production of goods for sale.

Geoff Williams is a plastic surgeon. He is a modest individual who lives his life helping others. He decided to specialize in children's deformities because he found that his efforts could heal disfigured children and their parents. Williams has corrected cleft palates, deformities caused by tumors, and just about any other facial problem one can imagine. Vietnam was the first country he visited on a volunteer training trip; he was surrounded by mothers pleading for help for their children. Since then he has made an effort to help as many children as possible in more than ten different countries, spanning four continents. Williams created the International Children's Surgical Foundation in December 2005 to raise money so his work could continue when his savings ran out. His modest lifestyle and dedication to helping others set him apart from other doctors who chase lavish lifestyles in the highly lucrative American medical business.[54]

Mata Amritanandamayi ("mother of immortal bliss") has been teaching spiritual aspirants all over the world since 1981. She founded a worldwide organization, the Mata Amritanandamayi Mission Trust, which is engaged in many spiritual and charitable activities. She addressed the United Nations General Assembly and was recognized as a universal mother figure. Mata Amritanandamayi is known to the world media as "the hugging saint." She offers a hug to everyone who approaches her and in India she has been known to individually hug over 50,000 people in a day, sitting sometimes for more than twenty hours. Worldwide, Mata Amritanandamayi is said to have hugged at least 30 million people in the past thirty years.

Rigoberta Menchú Tum is an indigenous Guatemalan, of the Quiché-Maya ethnic group. Menchú has dedicated her life to publicizing the plight of Guatemala's indigenous peoples during and after the Guatemalan Civil War (1960-1996), and to promoting indigenous rights in the country. She was the recipient of the 1992 Nobel Peace Prize and Prince of Asturias Award in 1998. Menchú is a UNESCO Goodwill Ambassador. She is the subject of the testimonial biography *I, Rigoberta Menchú* and the author of the autobiographical work, *Crossing Borders*.[55]

The people described above all have at least one thing in common—action. They all acted on their beliefs and created a positive change in their world. We include their stories to give an idea of the types of manifested goodness that exist in the past and present. This potential exists virtually everywhere and we advocate the kind of courage, tenacity, and prosocial behavior exhibited by these people and all the others who act in typical and heroic ways every day. Unsung heroes and heroines of every variety can take confidence in the fact that they are applauded for their positive and beneficial actions.

MILLARD FULLER AND HABITAT FOR HUMANITY

Millard Fuller was the founder and former president of Habitat for Humanity International, a nonprofit organization known globally for building houses for those in need, and the founder and former president of The Fuller Center for Housing. Fuller was widely regarded as the leader of the modern-day movement for affordable housing and had been honored for his work in the United States and abroad.

In early 1984, Millard contacted the man who would become Habitat's most famous volunteer, President Jimmy Carter. A native of Plains, Georgia, just a few miles from Habitat's headquarters in Americus, Georgia, Carter gave not only his name and reputation to the new nonprofit, but his own resources as well. Jimmy and Rosalynn Carter, over time, made financial contributions regularly, but most significantly to Habitat, and they developed the Jimmy Carter Work Project, an annual weeklong effort of building Habitat homes all over the world. The Carters participated the entire week at these events, which later came to attract thousands of volunteers each year.

The Carters' involvement with Habitat for Humanity propelled the organization to even faster growth. By 2003, Habitat affiliates world-wide had built over 150,000 homes and were active in ninety-two nations.

The goal of Habitat for Humanity is to eliminate substandard housing and replace it with simple, decent homes fitting for people who are part of this incredible community. A long-range plan has been developed and implemented to address the growing need for adequate housing, including the generation of all of the essential resources required to accomplish this huge undertaking.

Operation Home Delivery is Habitat for Humanity International's response to the destruction caused by Hurricanes Katrina and Rita. While Habitat for Humanity cannot be the answer to all low-income housing needs created by the hurricanes, Habitat expects to assist thousands of people and to work together in partnership with other organizations to serve as a catalyst in the rebuilding process. More than 1,100 new homes are complete or under construction in partnership with hurricane-affected families, making Habitat the region's largest builder in the wake of the hurricanes. Habitat built 2,219 homes in the five years following hurricane Katrina. With donations totaling nearly $123 million, Operation Home Delivery has expanded its scope to include evacuees who have relocated to other regions.[56]

GIRAFFE PROJECT

The nonprofit Giraffe Heroes Project was founded by Ann Medlock, a freelance editor, publicist, speech writer, and author living in Manhattan. Ann started the Project in 1984 as an antidote to the mind-numbing violence and trivia that pervaded the media, eroding civic energy and hope. People needed to know about the heroes of our times and all that they were accomplishing as courageous, compassionate citizens.*

We would like to tell two stories of *Giraffe Heroes*—people who are commended for "sticking their necks" out for the common good. Their stories inspire others to take on the public challenges they see—speaking out against corruption, building bridges across conflicts, taking a stand against injustice, being a voice for the powerless. Their website, giraffe.org, features inspiring stories of Giraffe Heroes, information on Giraffe programs, and interactive ways of sharing the Giraffe message of courageous compassion. Below are two stories that we share because they represent a type of goodness.

The facts of the story are these: Azim Khamisa's 20-year-old son, Tariq, was making a delivery for a San Diego pizza parlor when he was shot and killed in a failed robbery attempt by a gang. The killer was Ples Felix's 14-year-old grandson and ward, Tony Hicks, who was sentenced as an adult for the murder and is now serving a twenty-five year prison sentence.

Khamisa, a banker whose family had fled violence in East Africa years earlier, was devastated by his son's death, yet he reached out to the killer's family, realizing that they too had lost a boy. Felix, a former Green Beret who is a program manager for San Diego County, was devastated by what his grandson had done—on the first night he had ever defied his grandfather and left the house to meet with the gang. Felix went alone to a gathering of the grieving

---

*   http://www.giraffe.org/aboutus_founder.html

Khamisa family, telling them of his own grief over what his grandson had done. Khamisa established a foundation in his son's memory. Khamisa and Felix formed an alliance that transforms their losses into a resolve to see that other families do not suffer such tragedies. "There were victims on both ends of the gun," says Khamisa. "Ples and I have become like brothers."

Today Khamisa and Felix go again and again into schools—together—to talk to students about Tariq's death and about gangs, to help the kids talk about the awful effects of violence on their own lives, and to affirm that they will avoid violence themselves. Kids who hear the two men's story and seeing them working together also get an unforgettable picture of a response to violence that is not revenge and hatred. Commenting on their work in schools, Khamisa says, "Every time you talk one youngster out of committing homicide, you save two."

Both Felix and Khamisa are speaking out for "restorative justice," a way of dealing with criminals that helps lawbreakers understand what they have done and makes restitution to those they have harmed, rather than just sending them to prisons. "The way we deal now with lawbreakers does nothing for those they have injured, for reforming the criminal or for repairing society," says Ples Felix.*

Wangari Maathai, a professor of biology at Nairobi University in Kenya, could simply enjoy the prestige and security of being a highly educated, well-paid woman in a country where most women lead far different lives. Instead, she founded a movement that has set out to transform those women's lives and the entire economy of her nation. This is clearly a positive mission, but it has put Maathai in great personal danger.[57] Her Green Belt Movement has enlisted more than 80,000 rural women in planting and tending more than 20 million trees. Everywhere that the movement is strong, the villages and the countryside are green with gracious trees that give bananas, mangoes, and papayas to people who remember starvation and malnutrition. The people in these areas see that their own local women have brought about this transformation to health, beauty and economic independence. But to the one-party government of strongman Daniel Arap Moi, such independence is "subversive."

President Moi has blamed Maathai for giving many people the idea that

---

* http://www.giraffe.org/hero_Azim.html

they can take charge of their own lives; he has had her imprisoned repeatedly for defying his dictatorship, but she will not be silenced.

Working in the city as well as in the countryside, she organized demonstrations to stop the building of a skyscraper in Nairobi's only park. Moi put her in jail again, but the people's protest and her letters to the building's financiers caused the financiers to withdraw from the project.

The city of Nairobi still has a people's park. And in the country, the women of the Green Belt tend their trees, feed their families, and walk tall—like Wangari Maathai.

THE WILL TO DO GOOD

It is well known, but not well publicized, that a greater number of people would be willing to help and care for others in different ways if we sensitized them to the great need for trust, forgiveness, and reconciliation with their relatives, friends and neighbors, but the question remains of how to encourage all people to become involved with humanity. We are optimistic that there is a trend toward caring and that political leaders, environmentalists, civil leaders, educators, and clergy will be able to recruit people to help others and teach them the rewards and benefits of helping, apologizing, and forgiving. Schools, communities, the workplace, the family, and all religious institutions can do more to encourage and model the benefits of reconciliation, and provide opportunities for people to help each other reconcile and resolve their painful hurts. Research has shown that people who have been encouraged to help have internalized the ethic of caring for others, and that there are positive benefits of volunteering and caring, not only to society, but also for the caring person, as well as helping with moral development in the forgiver.[58]

As our several examples show, many people care, forgive, and help. Nurturance of humanity can be taught to people of all ages. Goodness, love, and forgiveness are a timely and a necessary area of study, because people in many places around the world are hurt and suffer from humiliation and injustice. It is possible to encourage conflicting groups to heal the pain and recognize each other's need for respect, fairness, justice and love. Doing good is a force that has the ability to overcome evil, and should be taught, cultivated, and valued.

Chapter 7

The World of Heroes: Why We Need Heroes

"We need heroes, people who can inspire us, help shape us morally, spur us on to purposeful action and from time to time we are called on to be those heroes, leaders for others, either in a small, day-to-day way or on the world's larger stage. At this time in America, and in the rest of the world, we seem to need moral leadership especially, but the need for moral inspiration is ever present."—Robert Coles, *Lives of Moral Leadership* (2000)

HEROISM HAS MANY FORMS and nearly always involves the battle between goodness and evil. From a firefighter going into a burning house to rescue the occupants to the individuals who risked their lives to save victims during the Holocaust and the Armenian and Rwandan genocides. Heroism is a unique manifestation of behavior with a far-reaching set of implications. In this chapter, we will review some of the relevant literature pertaining to this social phenomenon. Dictionaries often list three qualities in common for the definition of a hero: extraordinary achievement, courage, and serving as a moral role model. We will reexamine the scope of what is generally referred to as heroic to explain why some groups or individuals are deemed heroes while others are bystanders or defined as anti-heroes or villains. The uniqueness of heroism lies in its varied manifestations within works of literature including sociology, psychology, and other social sciences. There exists what could be defined as sick or "evil" anti-heroes such as mass murderers like Hitler and Idi Amin, as well as moral or "good" heroes such as Nelson Mandela and others, depending on the social-cultural milieu. The essential connection to altruism and prosocial behavior that leads a person to become perceived as a hero is an important piece to this puzzle. Theories in social science are used in conjunction with the literature from several academic fields to give an interdisciplinary view of heroism. Examples and narratives of heroes from various settings are interwoven in the text to enrich the understanding of heroic behavior. A prime example of a hero is Raul Wallenberg, the Swedish diplomat who rescued several thousand Hungarian Jews from certain death. Additional examples will follow as to what makes a person heroic, what motivates them, and the various types of heroic activity.

We begin by discussing what is considered heroic behavior. The Altruistic Personality and Prosocial Behavior Institute at Humboldt State University has been researching and writing about heroic behavior for more than twenty years and has successfully conceptualized heroic altruism. Significant to this work is an examination of the existing theoretical and scholarly literature on heroes and the culture that produces them. Ordinary helpers, such as hospice volunteers, and those who helped during natural disasters such as Hurricane Katrina, the earthquakes in Haiti, and the floods in Pakistan are also revered as conventional altruists. Heroism is unique in that it allows communities and nations to establish a common public good with attainable goals to bring about a more caring society.

Acts considered heroic are at the crux of individual agency, or individual action, and social structure. The duality of structure and agency that Giddens and Sewell espouse helps to clarify how heroic figures are placed within society.[1] "Structures shape people's practices, but it is also people's practices that constitute (and reproduce) structures."[2] Heroic figures, especially moral exemplars, create an image of behavior that can be emulated by society and succeeding generations. Typically, certain people are deemed heroic for deeds that lead to the rescue of innocents or the distinction of bravery in military combat. Often people dubbed as heroes have been involved in the rescue of someone or something from a dangerous or harmful situation, but this is only the beginning of what social groups consider heroic. Heroes often possess a common attribute—altruism.

DEFINITIONS

The word altruism is derived from the Latin root *alter,* which means *other.* To Auguste Comte, the father of sociology, the word altruism meant the discipline and eradication of self-centered desire and a life devoted to the good of others, particularly selfless love and a devotion to society. Vincent Jeffries suggests that there are overlapping attributes found in heroism and altruism—and discusses a variety of definitions of altruism.[3] Among these attributes are courage, social responsibility, empathy, efficacy, and caring. Berkowitz and Macaulay maintain that altruistic behavior benefits another without the helper anticipating external rewards such as payment, medals, etc.[4] Similarly, Rushton explains altruism as a social behavior carried out to achieve positive outcomes for another person rather than benefitting themselves.[5]

To examine heroism sociologically is to examine the perception of what is deemed heroic and the structural conditions that produce heroes. This can be seen in the works of Oliner and Oliner, Oliner et al, Oliner, Goode, and Sorokin. However, when conceptualizing heroism, this chapter seeks to include the perspective of other subjects including history,[6] anthropology,[7] and mythology.[8] Heroism has been examined in various works by scholars such as psychotherapist Miriam Polster,[9] and social psychologists Anne Colby and William Damon as well as Selwyn Becker and Alice Eagley.[10] These works will be discussed briefly along with narratives and examples of heroes in various settings. We hope that readers will have gained an integral perspective of heroism and a clearer picture of the value and expectation placed on heroes.

Oliner and Oliner, in *The Altruistic Personality,* distinguished many facets of this particular subject.[11] Specifically, they present material and offer conclusions on the research related to the rescuing of Jews during Nazi Occupied Europe. They interviewed more than 700 people in Europe, and North America who were living in Nazi-occupied Europe during World War II who were rescuers, rescued survivors, and bystanders. They found several explanatory concepts, such as assuming commitment and responsibility towards diverse groups of people, and the propensity to attach oneself to others in committed interpersonal relationships, and toward inclusiveness with respect to the diversity of individuals and groups to whom one will assume obligations.

A hero is traditionally defined as any human being who saves the life of another, or does some good for the benefit of the other at some cost or risk to himself or herself. This dangerous act on behalf of others we call heroic altruism.[12] These types of heroes exhibit extraordinary bravery, firmness, wisdom, fortitude, and most of all, action. Heroism is considered a universal act of goodness, an act of courageous rescue that involves high risk to the helper. The manifestation of that act varies with the cultural climate of tolerance and acceptance of minorities throughout centuries and decades. For example, the Danish population involved in rescuing their Jewish citizens from the Nazi's attempt to exterminate them contrasts with the French Vichy government, which chose to cooperate with the Nazis. In this chapter, we will show how heroism is perceived over time and across societies. Through comparison of different heroic acts, it is possible to explain the trajectory of heroism in self and society.

Oliner distinguishes two types of altruism: *conventional* and *heroic*.[13] Behavior is *heroically* altruistic when (1) it is directed toward helping another; (2) it involves a high degree of risk or sacrifice to the person involved; (3) it is accompanied by no external reward; and (4) it is voluntary.[14] The risk involved in heroic behavior may even lead to death for the helper. Therefore, Carnegie Heroes, named for rescuing strangers in dangerous situations, rescuers of Jews in Nazi-occupied Europe, receivers of Britain's Victoria Cross or the Congressional Medal of Honor, and various other awards that involve high risk to one's life would fall into this category. Conventional altruism, on the other hand, involves acts of helping others for which we do not expect external rewards, nor do we expect to risk our lives in order to do so. These can be everyday acts such as helping a stranger carry their groceries, or giving change to a homeless person.

William Goode attributes the influence of prestige as a contributing factor to the formation of heroes.

> Devotion to group goals, as against self-interest may be common enough to be of practical importance in many groups or organizations. Heroism in either military actions or civilian life, however, has too small a practical effect to explain the great respect it arouses. One therefore looks for its symbolic meaning: It represents an extreme conformity with the ideal of putting group

> interests ahead of one's own, and asserts dramatically that the ideal
> is not mere rhetoric but lies within human capacities.[15]

Goode is attempting to explain the great importance prestige has in the formation of the hero in collective consciousness. People engage in cost/reward
calculations of prestige exchange between themselves and their communities,
meaning that some may gain self-benefit from helping. While this view takes
an egoistic and internal reward system for granted, it still offers a process by
which people evaluate themselves in relation to another. The human capacity for putting group interests ahead of one's own can be seen cross culturally in many different nations. In the United States, Habitat for Humanity
builds homes for homeless around the world, and The Alliance of European
Voluntary Service Organization, an international non-governmental organization, promotes volunteer services in various countries around the world.

In his many studies on altruism, Pitirim Sorokin maintains that altruistic behavior keeps communities cohesive and it is the glue that bonds society together. He states, "The very fact that individuals interested in the same
creative task tend to and do establish a society for realization of their common purpose well demonstrates the fruitfulness of free cooperation in creative
work."[16] Collective projects where the individuals involved have a common
goal of helping others, such as the Red Cross, help bond societies together.
Sorokin's analysis had begun, in part, with Auguste Comte, who is credited
with coining the terms *altruism* and *egoism*. Furthermore, he viewed altruism
as an experience of concern for others' well being by overcoming self-interest.
He wrote that human nature was driven by egoism, and that altruism must
eclipse egoism if society is to survive. Sorokin's views would later mirror those
of Comte. Heroism is the manifestation of overcoming self-interest in a measurable form of behavior.

Sorokin expanded on the egoism/altruism dichotomy. He wrote of altruism as existing on a continuum, with egoism and genuine altruism as its opposing points. Behaviors falling along intermediate points on the continuum were
defined as *nonaltruistic* or *pseudoaltruistic* acts. Philosopher Moses Maimonides
(1135-1204) illustrated a spectrum of helping in *Eight Levels of Giving*. A *pseudoaltruistic* act would be, "giving *tzedakah* (charity) publicly to an unknown
recipient."[17] This would be an act motivated by egoistic factors, which would

enhance the public image of the giver. A *nonaltruistic* act is when an individual is asked to help someone in need, but refuses even though they are in a position to help. Sorokin states that altruistic action can be thought of as an individual sacrificing his rightful interest in favor of the well being of another.

According to Sorokin, the solution to this endless cyclical dichotomy of self vs. well-being of another was the pursuit of integral truth. Through integralism, which is the idea that social sciences contain the three elements; empirical-sensory, rational-mindful, and superrational-supersensory, Sorokin united the religious, scientific, and rational aspects of human experience. Ultimately, based on years of scientific research, he proposed that the resolution of societal crisis must be the development of an integral culture and that in order to do this Sorokin states that we must transform integral knowledge and values into personal and collective action.[18] Through a similar lens this chapter seeks an integral understanding of heroism, one that is more comprehensive and expansive.

In Oliner and Oliner, a rescuer maintains, among other things, that without love, what does one have, a world without a heart?[19] Thus, it appears that love for the other, or caring for the other is an important attribute of altruism and heroism. Iris Murdock strongly supports the idea that caring for the other is an important aspect of altruism, as well as heroism.[20] Paul Tillich maintains that love and justice are indispensable to caring and compassion.[21] "The roots of justice and love seem to be a kind of emotional state, which, like all emotions, cannot be defined, but which must be described as qualities and expressions and not a matter of intention or demand, but of happening or gift."[22] Love without justice does not exist. Neither does justice without regarding the other as part of self. Love, then, is elevated as emotion into the ontological realm. It is well known that from Empedocles and Plato, to Augustine and Pico, to Hegel and Schelling, to existentialism and depth psychology, as a central, ontological role. In other words, without love development, healthy compassionate development is not possible.[23]

GENDER AND HEROISM

Heroism has a unique place within culture. While heroes and the hero's saga have traditionally been associated with masculinity, this association is being expanded into the realm of femininity as well. Kathleen Noble says that the word heroine "does not begin to describe the many women who pursued lives of courage, strength, initiative, and independence. Most heroic myths celebrate the qualities only in men and, as a result, many people believe that women are not heroic, or are unique or deviant if they strive to be so."[24]

In this section we highlight the many scholars who identify this courage, strength, and initiative in a myriad of settings so that heroism can be seen as a phenomenon of humanity rather than a single gender.

In an article titled "The Heroism of Women and Men," Becker and Eagly address some of the same issues as Kathleen Noble.[25] These two psychologists make the case that heroic behavior should be culturally shifted to a more androgynous (shared) perspective, that women are consistently just as empathic and risk-taking as men, despite the somewhat outdated traditional position that men are more suited for heroic deeds. The purpose of their study was intended to show representations of women and men in five different settings—two of which were dangerous or life-threatening. The authors used baseline population data in order to compare the percentages of women and men in heroism and prosocial actions. Becker and Eagly maintain that in western culture heroism and masculinity are directly linked and males are expected to be the rescuers. This cultural expectation could account for a greater percentage of males recognized as heroes in the Carnegie Commission. However, when we focus on rescuers of Jews in Nazi-occupied Europe, Anderson found that after qualitatively analyzing the interview transcripts from Oliner and Oliner, female rescuers were more likely to exhibit a caring and heroic orientation than were males.[26] Carol Gilligan offers an explanation for this difference by citing Nancy Chodorow, "In any given society, the feminine personality comes to define itself in relation and connection to other people more often than the masculine personality does."[27]

Donna Rosenberg, in *World Mythology*, says that heroes in mythologies are largely male and this masculine representation still continues.[28] Women have been largely ignored throughout history and very few have become recognized as heroines. Males dominate history in Greek times, as well as in Hindu and Buddhist times. However, in the *Iliad*, which is dominated by men, more Homeric heroes placed a high value upon women, especially aristocratic women. Besides instances throughout history of an occasional priestess, such as Miriam in the Jewish Bible, or Joan of Arc, there are few women that are celebrated or commemorated in history and literature. When war heroes appear on the pages of history books they are often in the Apollonian form of masculinity, exhibiting strength. This proves true even as the first American woman began service in the military. In 1778, a woman from Plympton, Massachusetts, Deborah Sampson, felt the need to do her part during the Revolutionary War, so she enlisted in the military. Women were not allowed to enlist, so she disguised herself as a man by the name of Robert Shurtleff. She had little trouble doing this, since she was tall and just as strong as most of the men. Even her own mother failed to recognize her while she was disguised.[29] She fought in several skirmishes and was wounded multiple times. After her honorable discharge by Washington, she fought hard to receive benefits due to veterans and eventually won them.

Sampson plays a unique role as the forerunner of female heroism in the United States military. Her long and ultimately successful public campaign for the American Revolutionary War pension bridged gender differences in asserting the sense of entitlement felt by all of the veterans who had fought for their country. She stood up to gender inequality by asserting herself and proving her capability as a soldier. According to the U.S. Census, the total number of active duty women in the military, as of September 30, 2008 was 197,900.* Those 197,900 female soldiers were preceded by a courageous woman who began breaking down gender barriers more than two hundred years ago.

Displaying courage does not have to occur on the battlefield. Every day women in this country struggle for equality in the home and at work. Ruth Sidel in her book *Unsung Heroines* connects the values of courage, determination, commitment to others, and independence of spirit with that of single mothers attempting to make a living in an American capitalist society.[30] Sidel contends that these hard-working women deserve positive coverage and celebration rather than stigmatization and hardship. Sidel interviewed fifty single mothers to present a picture of women who struggle against the odds, raising children without comprehensive health care, a living wage, or child care during working hours. The determination of these single mothers puts them in a

---

* U.S. Department of Defense, as cited in the Statistical Abstract of the United States: 2010, Table 498. <http://www.census.gov/compendia/statab/>

heroic category, which should not be overlooked. How many people cite their mother as their personal hero? Who amongst us has the strength to survive life's challenges as a single parent in a single breadwinner household facing inequality and stigma?

> Battered and bruised, emotionally and sometimes physically, many of these women have lived and are living their lives with uncommon courage, determination, and creativity. Soledad Martinez obtained the education she dreamed of, left an abusive marriage, and went on to fashion a rewarding career and form a loving compassionate marriage; Linda Powell's pregnancy at 14 left her impoverished and virtually alone, but she nonetheless has a rewarding life with her daughter and has managed somehow to hold on to her dreams for the future.[31]

These women were able to overcome the odds and bring up their children in a safe and loving environment so that they could become responsible citizens. These are only some examples of ordinary heroes.

Perhaps the will of these women is inherent in their genes, but this only paints a partial picture. As sociologists, we contend that there is much more to their dedication than pure biology. The women described by Sidel have ridden the social roller coaster with its ups and downs; they have learned to survive the hardship of socialization into poverty as well as find the tools which assisted in their eventual success. The dedication it takes to emerge from a stacked deck of inequality with children by your side exhibits social skills and a predisposition for selfless behavior, something that cannot be learned from a book. In the case of single mothers, their altruistic behavior makes them everyday heroines leading lives of importance and dignity. While they may not have run into a burning building to save a stranger, they still deserve respect for their efforts to survive and flourish under difficult social and economic conditions. The moral duty of these women to their selves and families is evidenced in hard-fought struggles. Morality is an important aspect of understanding both everyday heroism and life saving feats and it is the next topic which we turn to.

Moral Heroes

In all cultures and ethnic groups, heroism is important because it promotes pride in the culture. Moral heroes are often leaders and exemplars of charity, goodwill, and peace. Mahatma Gandhi was the proponent of nonviolent revolution in India and is a moral hero who had a profound effect on the world as a man of peace and compassion. A moral hero must be sincere and have the function of creating some ideology or idea in history which moves forwards, not backwards, and is for the betterment of human beings. In her book about African American heroes and heroines, Kathryn Bel Monte documents the various faces of African-American heroism in our time.[32] She profiles a number of African Americans who have made a difference throughout United States history. Martin Luther King Jr., Soujourner Truth, and Harriet Tubman fought for black emancipation and equal rights. A conscious effort must be made to make known those contributions that benefit all and those that exemplify what is loftiest in the spirit of humankind in order to end feelings of alienation and oppression.

Moral Leaders

The position to act in accordance with one's moral ideals or principles implies a consistency between one's actions and intentions. The work of social psychologists Anne Colby and William Damon is especially helpful in understanding what makes a moral leader and what spurs such people to action.[33] These researchers find that such people often share the following characteristics: A sustained commitment to moral ideals or principles that include a generalized respect for humanity or a sustained evidence of moral virtue. They possess a willingness to risk one's self interest for the sake of one's moral values. Moral exemplars have a tendency to be inspiring to others and thereby move them to moral action. These people use a sense of realistic humility about one's own importance relative to the world at large, implying a relative lack of concern for one's own ego.

Although Colby and Damon have found that a leader's individual personality and charisma play an important role in effecting broader moral change, the primary force for such action is social support and communication, allowing feedback and development of the whole person, and thus benefiting the group and ultimately the cause. As we have seen in history, for example, the Danish King Christian X and the Danish Lutheran church created a climate which enabled the rescue of Danish Jews in 1943 from the Nazis. Where such a climate did not exist, many more perished.

Colby and Damon mention *positivity*, an attitude which includes optimism, love, and joy, as closely linked with morality and a positive quality evident in the lives of most moral exemplars. The relationship between a positive approach and absence of focus on self is known as *learned optimism*. Moral leaders often share this quality; they would not blame others for their lot in life, instead, they focus on how best to tackle the task at hand. Learned optimism, as the name suggests, can be *learned*. It offers an understanding as to why exemplars have positive attitudes. Colby and Damon maintain, "The key to understanding optimism lies in people's habitual styles of explaining to themselves the causes of good and bad events."[34] Optimists tend to attribute a good event to something about themselves, and they view a bad event as temporary and able to be overcome.

Moral exemplars need not be perfect people, but they must have an accurate moral compass, fortitude, and a fervent wish to serve their fellow human being. They must provide a moral example to those who follow them. Educators assert that it is important for children to have positive moral role models to emulate. It is vital that we read and hear about moral exemplars as role models, and it is particularly crucial for our children to know such models. Since moral exemplars achieve different degrees of recognition, it is especially vital that we understand and teach our children that there are exemplars all around us who live their daily lives performing service to their communities and who never become famous.

TYPOLOGY OF HEROISM

There are four types of heroism with circumstances that facilitate rescue.[35] Saving others' lives is both a matter of opportunity and character, which include a comprehension of need, risk, material resources, and a precipitating occasion. The first types of heroes are *trained* and *professional* rescuers. These include firefighters, police officers, coast guard, etc. Although these people are paid and trained professionals, they are expected to save lives, and they often go beyond the call of duty risking their own lives, especially in precipitating circumstances (such as the 9/11 tragedy). Another example would be military heroes who are expected to honor the code of courage and bravery, and protect their comrades. These acts of bravery are heroic, but are in short duration, and it is expected of them even though it is not expected they should lose their lives in the process. No Western army demands that its people go beyond the call of duty.

The second type of heroism is *not paid*, and also in short duration involving a risk to one's life. These heroes voluntarily put themselves in harm's way in order to save lives and are not professionally trained. These kinds of heroes include Carnegie heroes. These rescuers are involved in a short duration precipitating circumstance, such as the case of Wesley Autrey.[36] Mr. Autrey is a New York construction worker and Navy veteran, who in 2007 achieved international recognition after he saved Cameron Hollopeter, a 19-year-old film student who had suffered a seizure and fallen onto the train tracks, from being struck by a New York City subway train.

The third type of heroic altruism is also *unpaid* and *voluntary*, but it is over a long duration. Rescuers of Jews in Nazi-occupied Europe fit this category. There are thousands of stories regarding these events. One such story which exemplifies this propensity for long-term rescue is that of Magda and Andre Trocme. They were residents of the village of Le Chambon-sur-Lignon in southern France. They risked their lives to feed, clothe, hide, and protect those who would have died in concentration camps without their help. Magda and Andre Trocme have been credited by Yad Vashem with saving some 5,000 refugees, about 3,500 of them Jewish, many of them children, over a four-year period from 1941–1945.[37]

The fourth type of heroism is *conventional altruism*. This is voluntary and over a long duration, but it does not involve high risk to the helper/hero. These are volunteers of various kinds who on a regular basis help and aid other individuals, including hospice volunteers. These are conventional heroes who comfort people as they are dying. These acts require dedication, compassion, and courage. But conventional altruists are relatively safe from pain in their own life for the act of helping. Becker and Eagley focus on living kidney donors,

Peace Corps volunteers, and Doctors without Borders,[38] which would fall under what we consider conventional altruism.[39] Interestingly enough, Becker and Eagly found that of the 60,259 live kidney donations, 57 percent were women. Volunteerism on a regular basis to help others in need is prevalent in this country. Some estimate that if these volunteers were paid a minimum hourly wage that the volunteers would earn good salaries. This behavior is an indication that a large percent of the American population cares for others.

Motivating Factors of Heroism: What Makes a Hero Heroic?

There is no single reason why some people leap forward to rescue others, while others look the other way. There are, however, patterns of behavior which can be examined. What continues to surprise many is that some characteristics widely assumed to correlate with altruistic behavior do not, including self-esteem. Individuals of both high and low self-esteem are nearly equally apt to become rescuers. It may be that some with high self-esteem rescue others because they already feel good about themselves, while their lower self-esteem counterparts rescue others to bolster their sense of self. Almost uniformly, heroic rescuers exhibit courage, moral conviction, and behavior that they had acquired from moral exemplars as they were growing up. Values of caring and prosocial behavior were instilled in them, and a belief that the mistreating of others for ideological or any other reason was never justified and could not be tolerated. Rescuers, by and large, exhibit a commonality with all human beings and did not distinguish between themselves and the other. Although these motivating characteristics were found in all rescuers, some were triggered to action by their empathic predisposition, some by their normocentric values meaning that the values of leaders as well as society dictate that helping is a moral imperative, and a small part by principled motivation, which consist of a person's moral stance that injustice must be combated whenever one finds it.

Characteristics which correlate with propensity to rescue include some of the following motivations. Some rescuers had a lesser focus on the world at large, in favor of a focus on an individual's own immediate domain. Rescuers thus see themselves less as victims of outside events, and more as in charge of their own lives, thus maximizing their own private personal power. Rescuers are more likely to act when they can join with others in a network, either underground or in the open, enhancing their chances of success. In Nazi Europe, defying the Nazis by saving their fellow victimized countrymen became a reassertion of nationalistic pride. Rescuers are much more likely to come from families in which reason, rather than physical punishment, is used for discipline. As they become adults, they are more likely to develop a nuanced sense of right and wrong, as opposed to a more traditional deference to authority. Rescuers are more likely to have grown up in multicultural neighborhoods, surrounded by rich and poor, as well as those of different religions and races. There they were more likely to develop friendships with different ethnic groups. They thus tend to identify less with their own ethnic or national group, and more often view themselves as part of a larger universe. Rather than seeing the world through an "us vs. them" prism, rescuers often have the feeling that "we're all in this together."

Having sheltered others for prolonged periods of time, rescuers become incensed at any talk of suicide by desperate victims, which would render nil the time and effort they had expended. Rescuers often negotiate a labyrinth of clues as to whom they could and could not trust, especially when to trust the wrong individual could lead betrayal and death. To safeguard their charges, rescuers sometimes had to be creative, including having to lie to authorities. With white lies, they might also turn away family members who might want to visit, for fear of what they might inadvertently discover. And yet, under other than during exceptional times, they believe in the value of telling the truth. Being a rescuer, then, means having the ability, to see the grey area and maintain a balance. They tend to have a more developed imagination. This was true of the strategy a Polish woman reportedly used to get rid of a suitor who appeared in her apartment at unexpected times. The woman acquired the photograph of a handsome Nazi officer stationed in the vicinity, and hung it over her bed. After that, her would-be "boyfriend" bothered her no more.

People see heroes in nearly every aspect of culture. The embodiment of heroism in different settings changes according to what behaviors are valued. In the next few paragraphs we would like to give a few examples of what some people consider heroic.

Rescuers in Nazi-occupied Europe

In 1953, the Israeli parliament established the Yad Vashem Remembrance Authority whose mission was to establish a memorial to the Righteous Among the Nations, those who risked their lives to save Jews in Nazi-occupied Europe. Since the establishment of Yad Vashem, more than 25,000 non-Jews have been recognized for their acts of valor and heroism. Despite the miserable failure of the major world powers, such as the United States and England, to save Jews, there were individuals, groups, and countries who did. Among those individuals recognized by Yad Vashem were Aristides de Sousa Mendes, general-consul of Portugal located in Bordeaux, France, who issued visas to refugees; Swiss border police commander Paul Grueninger, who allowed hundreds of fleeing Jews to enter Switzerland even though his own government was against it; and Raoul Wallenberg, who saved tens of thousands of people by issuing protective passports and housing several thousand Jews in Hungary.

Examining the stories of famous rescuers during the Holocaust who have been recognized by Yad Vashem as Righteous Among Nations, one is led to the conclusion that these rescuers exhibited altruistic behavior by: (a) what they thought; (b) what they did; and (c) what motivated them. All the aforementioned people were rescuers of Jews, Roma, and others who were labeled undesirable by Nazi authorities. Combined, they rescued thousands and represent a stalwart symbol of liberation and safety. They rescued others because they were empathic towards victims' pain, they couldn't stand by and see moral principles of justice, fairness, and equity violated, and they acquired and obeyed moral authority and the moral precepts of their communities.

As a young woman in the early days of the German occupation of Poland, Irena Sendler (who was nominated for a Nobel Peace Prize a year before she died in 2008 at the age of 97) was affected by the suffering of her Jewish friends and acquaintances.* She was employed at the social welfare department of the Warsaw municipality and obtained a special permit allowing her to visit ghetto areas for the purpose of combating contagious diseases. But unbeknownst to the occupiers, Sendler was also a member of a Polish underground organization in Warsaw called *Zegota*—the Council for Aid to Jews. Her job

---

*   Israel Gutman, (ed.), 1990b. *Encyclopedia of the Holocaust.* Volume 4, New York: MacMillan Publishing, pp. 1339-1340.

with the municipality gave her unique access and enabled her to supply many Jews with clothing, medicine, and money. She wore an armband with the Star of David when going about in the ghetto as a sign of solidarity with the Jewish people and as a ploy to divert attention away from herself. She recruited a large number of people to *Zegota*, and become a valuable asset to the movement. The sheltering of families in the ghetto was supported by funds from *Zegota*, and each of her recruits was responsible for several blocks of apartments. She oversaw approximately ten apartments where Jews were hiding. She also had a companion, Irena Schulz, with a network of contacts both in the ghetto and on the Aryan side, so Sendler was able to smuggle children out of the ghetto and place them with non-Jewish families around the region.

In October of 1943, Irena Sendler was arrested by the Gestapo and taken to the infamous Pawiak prison in Warsaw where she was questioned and tortured. Because the police were unable to secure information from her, Irena's interrogators told her she was doomed. However, on her execution day, one of her underground companions bribed a Gestapo agent and she was freed. Since she was still listed on public bulletin boards as being among the executed, she was compelled to stay in hiding for the remainder of the German occupation. Even so, she continued working secretly for *Zegota*. In 1965 she received the Righteous Among the Nations medal on which is written a line from the Talmud, "She who saves one life is as if she saved the entire universe." When we interviewed her in Warsaw, she exuded confidence and courage, and said, "I wish I could have done more to help during these dark years."

Military Heroes

Heroes in military service have a long recorded history. There are centuries of men and women who risk their lives or even perish in war to do some good for another such as saving them from enemies or some harm. Military heroes who have achieved their distinction in violent situations often carry with them some dilemma and ambiguity because often military heroism involves killing the enemy as a necessary element of the courageous deed. This is very much the opposite of the rescuers who were heroes precisely because they preserved life while risking their own lives. Societies tend to remember the military heroes who preserve their liberty or defend their homeland. William Wallace is remembered for his defense of Scotland against British invasion. George Washington is an American icon known for his military brilliance and might. Joan of Arc is revered as a national heroine of France for her role during the Hundred Years' War. Former emperor of Ethiopia, Haile Selassie, is more than a heroic leader of his nation, to many Rastafarians he is the embodiment of Christ. While all these figures served as military leaders, they are also part of the social fabric of their respective nations. They are memorialized with honor and integrity; more than flesh and bone, they represent ideas and a standard of excellence.[40]

Carnegie Heroes

Carnegie Heroes are civilians who rescue others, most often strangers with no relation to the rescued. Carnegie's definition of a hero is "a civilian who has willingly risked his or her own life to an extraordinary degree while saving or attempting to save the life of another person." The Carnegie Hero Fund Commission was established following a massive explosion in a Pittsburgh area coal mine on January 25, 1904, which claimed the lives of 181 people. While emotionally distraught over the incredible loss of life in what remains one of the worst U.S. mining disasters of the last century, Andrew Carnegie was inspired by the heroic action of two individuals who lost their lives attempting to rescue those trapped underground. Carnegie praised these two men as heroes and soon put $5 million under the care of a commission for civilian heroism. Since that time, the commission has awarded 8,500 medals—10 percent posthumously—and more than $25 million in grants of scholarship aid or continuing assistance to people who risked their lives for the benefit of others.[41] With these funds, the commission also offers financial support to people who have been injured as a result of their heroic activity and to the families of individuals who died as a result of their attempts to rescue others. Carnegie did not expect to motivate future acts of heroism with this fund; rather, it was his desire that if a hero is killed or injured attempting to save another, he and those dependent upon him should not suffer monetarily. Ten hero funds in Europe, including Carnegie's native Scotland, carry out similar missions.

Local Heroes

Berkowitz, in discussing what motivates local heroes, says that it is possible to call forth a new type of hero that does exist, if rarely: those whose role is self defined; whose actions transform the community; whose personal qualities move us; who serve as inspiration; whose social achievement can be imitated and deserves to be.[42] This is the local hero and here is what one looks like. Generally the behavior of local heroes can be considered as conventionally altruistic although symbolically no less important than saving a life.

In *Local Heroes*, Berkowitz illustrates a variety of different local heroes who we call "conventional" heroes.[43] Their kindness and acts of altruism are exemplified by individuals such as Curtis Sliva, who is founder of the Guardian Angels and was concerned with safety in subways, and other public transportation venues of various cities, including New York. He has reported that when he initially founded this organization and trained individuals to protect innocent passengers, and others, he was considered an outcast. Later on, he was accepted as a welcome part of the community. Lois Gibbs is another example of altruistic behavior. She was concerned with dumping of hazardous waste, therefore founded Citizens Clearinghouse of Hazardous Wastes, whose aim was to protect communities from hazardous waste dumped by factories. Haroldine Trower was upset about garbage, especially in the vacant lots where trash piled up, and drug users hung out, and the cleanliness of the neighborhoods where she lived. She formed the Point Breeze Beautification Committee, which prompted city halls in various communities to try to clean up these rat-infested places and where drug users hung out.

Community heroes are central to the collective history that Bellah et al. describes in *Habits of the Heart*.[44] Communities of memory are involved in the retelling of stories, ones that "offers examples of men and women who have embodied and exemplified the meaning of the community."[45] The stories embody the characteristics of a good person, especially the virtues on which people model their behavior.

Human capacity for good and evil has been the subject of written and verbal thought since biblical times. The dualistic spectrum between the two is often represented by both moral and immoral subjects. A comparison is one way that humans cognitively establish right and wrong, through a dialectic relationship where one concept informs the other. Many concepts can be treated similarly.

Heroes can be historic figures or fictional ones. Allan Pasco has examined three centuries of heroism in French literature, and maintains that art and literature expose a society consciously or unconsciously to the reality in all its glory and in its shame.[46] Historians, such as Eugene Weber, have demonstrated that literature constitutes and copies reality.[47] The variety of romantic or violent anti-heroes who did evil to others are replete in literature and have committed various crimes against society or against self. The "sick heroes," by definition, are egoistic and indulge in vices. What is especially important in this study of "sick" heroic figures or icons is that they are regarded as virtuous by some group and have redeeming and perhaps virtuous qualities in the eyes of their admirers. Good and evil are not mutually exclusive labels, especially in the complex global societies of today. There are figures in history that have been glorified in the moment but in modern days seem less than deserving of praise.

Evil Heroes

There are individuals who are perceived as heroes by those they control, and have negative consequences because they are mentally deranged and destructive to themselves and their followers. For example, David Koresh and Jim Jones are two cultist heroes who have lead people down the path of annihilation. Those that some regard as heroes because of their obsession, ideology, and supportive following are divorced from moral codes and can cause numerous people to suffer and die. Often these people are leaders of small groups or even entire nations, such as former Ugandan President Idi Amin or the recently prosecuted leaders of the Khmer Rouge Regime in Cambodia. These leaders took power with a military coup and proceeded to persecute and destroy ethnic and rival groups within their own borders. This is perceived by some scholars as *auto-genocide*, which is execution of its own people, such as in the case of Pol Pot in Cambodia. Time is an important element in the conception of a sick hero; historical and conditional factors pave the way for leaders who engage in these destructive actions, often in times of political strife, destabilization, famine, or war. They are engaged in the heroic ideal of access to power that becomes perverted into extreme acts of violence. One of the common attributes of most anti-heroes is that the community or society recognizes them as having some sort of superiority and because of that people serve or follow them and promise allegiance.[48] These people are egoistic, indulge in vices, and certainly do not put the welfare of diverse others before their own or involve themselves in high risk rescue behavior as do conventional and altruistic heroes. Nevertheless, these people are considered heroes by their followers who will often go to the most extreme lengths to prove their devotion.

Heroism and altruism as concepts are socially constructed. That is, some behavior can be regarded as altruistic, heroic, and just in some societies. In others it is regarded as evil, non-heroic and destructive. For example, while overall mainstream Western culture views the donation of blood as an altruistic act, Jehovah's Witnesses consider it a sin. To give another example, some groups consider capital punishment to be just while others oppose it. Perception is a key factor in the transmission of ideas. Nazis executed Jews because they perceived Jews as evil and destroyers of German culture. White settlers perceived Native Americans as uncivilized savages who were occupying "empty land." In all these cases, "heroes," including military leaders and generals, have led soldiers in perceived heroic attempts to cleanse the world of people who were perceived as evil destroyers and traitors to culture. There exists a fine line between behavior that is revered and behavior that is widely condemned. The dialectic between these two types of behavior helps to shape collective consciousness. While consensus is hard to reach in a diverse society, there are certain exemplars of both virtuous behavior and behavior considered to be amoral.

The hero in history is especially important to the formation of narratives to exemplify. Historian Peter Gibbon in *A Call to Heroism* suggests that the linguistic construction of a hero in modern times associates other words like role model, legend, idol, icon, or mentor that "conceals bravery and diminishes heroism."[49] According to Gibbon, heroism was more influential in the past, such as with the Greek notion of hero as a demigod and imitation of the admirable was the norm. More recently, perfection from heroes is less expected because heroes can also have flaws. For example, Gandhi was a man of peace, but did not treat his wife well. The concept of hero has become democratized to include everyday local heroes. Distinction between celebrity, legend, icon, idol, and hero, creates a climate of cynicism about heroism—a climate of indifference in his view. Gibbon explains the hero worship and admiration of self-reliance from Emerson and Carlyle.

Thomas Carlyle held a belief in the importance of heroic leadership which found form in his book *On Heroes, Hero-Worship, and the Heroic in History*, in which he compared different types of heroes.[50] Carlyle made an attempt to draw a picture of the development of human intellect by using historical people as coordinates. A similar statement was made by Sidney Hook:,

> Great men and women in history are those that we can say on the basis of available evidence, that if they had not lived when they did or acted as they did, history of their countries and of the world to the extent that they are intertwined would have been profoundly different. Their presence, in other words must have made a substantial difference in the world and its betterment.[51]

Moral behavior defines humanity through the important acts of figures such as Nelson Mandela, Cesar Chavez, and Minerva award winner Betty Chinn.* Both Hook and Carlyle are trying to show that the acts of individuals are a primary indicator about the potential caring qualities of the world.

Mythic Heroes

The myths of a hero as a savior of the tribal nation is older than written history. The symbolism that myths provide translates in sociological and psychological realities. Joseph Campbell in his book *Hero with a Thousand Faces* delves into the symbolic expression that are given to heroes and emanated within societies.[52] Until 200 years ago, the hero functioned as not merely a myth or cult, but as a principle of moral explanation. Campbell attributes sophisticated wisdom to the shaman as skilled in communication and analogy. Tribal leaders and priests have used metaphors for millennia that have served societies as mainstays of thought and life. Also important to the study of mythic heroes

---

*   A Chinese American in Humboldt County, CA who devoted her life to nurturing the homeless. She won the Minerva award 2010, which recognizes people's altruistic devotion to those in need.

are inherited symbols from religious prophets, such as Buddha, who embody spiritual principles.

SELF, CULTURE, AND HEROISM

Self and society have long been a staple in the social sciences. In order to reconcile some of the contradictions between cultural meaning and physical objects, Ernest Becker wrote *The Birth and Death of Meaning*.[53] Opportunities to bolster self-esteem in society help stave off anxiety. Becker describes the role of culture and personality in constructing what he called "Hero Systems." "Culture is a structure of rules, customs, and ideas which serve as a vehicle for heroism."[54]

Becker eloquently balances the often paradoxical elements of culture and personality. Becker maintains that people, when asking themselves, "Who am I, what is the value of my life?" are essentially asking to be recognized as an object of primary value in the universe. This simple question is important in recognizing the transformation from ordinary citizen to glorified hero. The following quote helps fully grasp Becker's conceptualization.

> This is the uniquely human need, what man everywhere is really all about, each person's need to be an object of primary value, a heroic contributor to world-life, *the* heroic contributor to the destiny of man. This seems to be the logical and inevitable result of the symbolic constitution of self-worth in an unbelievably complex animal with exquisitely sensitive and effusive emotions.[55]

With this statement Becker has laid out the central theme of *The Birth and Death of Meaning*. While it assumes humanity has an enlightened self interest, a need to be of primary value, Becker's work also offers a way of analyzing heroic behavior—as a constant push and pull between the needs of the self and the expectations of society. We are all captives of our cultural systems, whether that cultural system dictates the stoning of one's sister for tarnishing family honor or a system that finds cosmic heroism through a process that maximizes the rate at which we preserve our planet. Becker may not have been directly addressing heroic rescues as behavior, but he sets the pattern for understanding how the self and society dovetail. Hero systems are put in place by cultural means so that people may strive to socially valued goals and feel an inherent self worth. When the self and society are out of balance, hero systems get thrown into a tailspin and meaning is lost. This does not have to be, as a society we can uphold standards of caring, a positive hero system that provides primary value to everyone who seeks it. By shifting our hero system from sports and movie stars to upstanding citizens who work for positive change, our society can bring about a more attainable and focused future for the next generation.

Conclusion

What can be learned from heroes and their behavior? We find that heroes exist everywhere, from our own neighborhood to the farthest reaches of mythology and religion. A hero can be a rescuer from the 9/11 tragedy, a community organizer that takes action to alleviate poverty, or a single mother who successfully raises a family while working two jobs and putting her children through school. The comparative aspect of this chapter is meant to bring to our attention the many ways that altruistic individuals manifest in society and how society can shift to manifest altruism. Comparing a war hero such as Hugh Thompson* to a local activist fighting hunger highlights the underlying selflessness that exists virtually everywhere. We find that goodness knows no bounds in our world. In fact even when examining the tragedy of an event such as genocide there are resistors who make a profound positive difference in people's lives. This is at the heart of what it means to be a hero—making a difference through our thoughts and deeds. The picture of heroes that we have attempted to portray includes a whole spectrum of people and behavior. Broadening the scope of heroes beyond pop culture is important for an informed and healthy society. The tendency to be enthralled by sports heroes, movie and rock stars are limiting for social good.

Why do societies need heroes? They set the benchmark for positive relations, whether it be a local hero or an international figure such as Nelson Mandela. They serve as an object of primary value in society. Heroes help

---

*   Hugh Thompson, a Warrant officer in the U.S. Army who served in Vietnam during the My Lai massacre in 1968. He and his colleagues tried to stop it. For this act he became a pariah. Years later he was honored by the military and received a soldiers medal.

to bridge divides over troubled social problems. The potential positive outcome of altruistic behavior is nearly limitless in the daily life of ordinary (and extraordinary) people. Societies need figures like Martin Luther King Jr. to hold a standard of potential change and a positive hero system. People need to know about Carnegie heroes, rescuers during WWII, and other caring organizations so that standards of morality are upheld. Moral heroes, local heroes, military heroes, just about any hero can perform positive functions for larger societies. They serve a need in our hearts and minds that we may rise above our individual material lives and further the wellbeing of others even in small ways. Heroes help to restore a balance. When people see injustice, heroic people see potential for positive social change, such as racial harmony, or equal pay for equal work. Mutual reinforcement of caring and empathy are in demand in a competitive and individualistic society. Heroes are an integral part of moving toward a more just and burden-free world; we hope to stimulate the motivation for positive change through our portrait of righteous humanity. A society without heroic behavior is greatly impoverished.

Chapter 8

Summary and Conclusion

"Hatred and bitterness can never cure the disease of fear; only love can do that."—Martin Luther King Jr.

MANY TIMES I HAVE HEARD STATEMENTS, "enough talk about evil." Throughout the book, we have heard many stories about genocide and destruction of human beings: stories of mayhem, murder, mistreatment, oppression and other such harmful acts. But it is my belief that not enough is said about evil. Even though we continue talking and writing on evil, it still persists throughout the world in different forms; whether it is mass murder in Darfur, assassinations by drug cartels in Mexico, or the dispute over our border, whether it is terrorism and killing of the innocent, or such things as abuse by the rich and powerful. The Wall Street tycoons, even though we cannot say all of them, are taking an unfair advantage of the current economic conditions. Greed, a particularly insidious form of evil, exists and has to be addressed and exposed again and again.

As we discussed in Chapter 2, there are a variety of different evil acts. Radical evil, such as the Holocaust, is destruction of a human population. Ordinary evil, everything from rumor-mongering to stealing, is not destructive to total populations, but is still harmful. Philosopher Martin Buber maintains that humankind may possess both natures: that is the nature of evil and evil inclinations as well as the nature of goodness and loving-kindness.[1] Sadly, modern society guides people into a dizzy whirl where some cannot discern between good and evil; competitiveness, inability to think critically and evaluate the environment in which they live, the daily economic, emotional, psychological and personal troubles that people face do not give them a chance to distinguish between the two. Media bombardment from different political perspectives confuses people's realities as to what the real issues are, and who is to blame for their plight. Humanity seems to be enticed with the temptation that many people experience chaos and spiritual bankruptcy as well as uncertainty.

Gandhi addressed the notion of hatred and vengeance when he said, "If we believe in an eye for an eye, that would make the whole world blind."

We addressed specific examples of where and when evil took place. We focused on the Holocaust and other genocides to illustrate how leaders, as well as institutions by their indifference, can bring about mass destruction.

As we've seen, the role of bystanders is very important in society. Many of us may have experienced being bystanders. Frequently, we see accidents on the road, and many of us drive by and adopt the attitude, "Well, let George do it," "Let the cops do it," "I am in a hurry," "Besides, what can I do?" These sorts of excuses are pervasive throughout the world and frequently when it comes to mass destruction of human beings, bystanders often adopt the attitude, "these are not my groups and, besides, I am not so sure I like those people." In some cases people unfortunately say, "I'm glad they cleared out these people from our country because they were not doing much good for our culture and our society. Besides they are not like us—they are different and foreigners."

We continued our discussion of bystanders in Chapter 3, "Silently Standing By." In the Yiddish language there is a song which says, "Our poor small town is burning and you men are standing by with your folded arms doing nothing. Please we appeal to you take pails of water and try to extinguish the fires." (This is a rough translation).

Elie Wiesel, Nobel Peace Prize winner, urges us not to be bystanders, but instead get involved with humanity. Upon winning the Nobel Prize, Wiesel (1986) said, "Sometimes we must interfere. When human lives are in danger, and human dignity is in jeopardy, national borders and sensitivity become irrelevant. Whenever men or women are persecuted because of their race, religion or political views, that place must become the center of the universe."

Willingness to forgive those who harmed us, as well as ask for forgiveness from those who we have harmed can have a positive outcome for human relations.

We have used several narratives throughout the book to show individuals who have taken the moral road and have tried to help. Turkish diplomat Behic Erkin rescued 20,000 Turkish Jews.[2] Behic Erkin fought in World War I and in the Turkish War of Independence. He was an army expert during World War I. Turkey was an ally of Germany at that time and Erkin won five Iron Cross medals First Class. This helped to influence Nazi diplomats to free Jews of Turkish origin in both occupied France and Vichy France. France was occupied in June 15, 1940 and in July Marshall Philippe Petain became President of what became known as the Vichy Republic. He pledged his support and collaboration with the Germans occupying Northern France.

The Vichy authorities ignored the Turks letter requesting that Turkish Jews be exempt from anti-Semitic legislation, Erkin took it up with German consul general Krug von Nidda in Paris, who ordered the French to comply with every request from the Turkish consulate concerning the Jews. In order to avoid an incident with Turkey, the French agreed to release all of the Turkish citizens. The end result was that 10,000 other Jews who somehow or other who may have had some type of Turkish origin or affiliation with Turkey were also "granted" these Turkey citizenship certificates and Erkin managed to get them to Turkey. Erkin was able to convince the Nazis and the French authorities to save 20,000 innocent souls during Europe's darkest moment.

The process of love and caring for others is a major factor in helping. Pitirim Sorokin said it best: "Love is literally a life-giving force by its very nature. Love is goodness itself. Therefore, it makes our life noble and good."

We believe there is never enough goodness in the world. There is also way too much evil in the world, hence this volume has simply revisited these two forms of human behavior. We suggest that processes of love, respect, dignity and security for us and others are vitally important. The question remains: "How do we move humanity from the position or place of doing harm to others to that of intervening on behalf of good, and thereby helping humans and society to unite?" There have been a number of studies, including our own past publications, that show that people who help others feel better about themselves, and their children feel proud of their parents who have made a profound difference in the human condition. Peter Singer in *The Life You Can*

Save maintains that most Americans can give to the poor without much sacrifice to their lifestyle.

> A survey of 30,000 American households found that those who gave to charity were 43 percent more likely to say they were 'very happy' about their lives than those who did not give. The survey does not show whether giving made people happy, or happy people were more likely to give, but the anecdotal evidence is strong that many people find that when they begin to give, they free themselves from the acquisitive treadmill and find new meaning and fulfillment in their lives.[3]

Journalist Sharon Begly addresses the important question about the nature of good and evil.[4] One of her major conclusions is that people who are emotionally secure and view life's problems as manageable show a greater empathy for strangers. On the other hand, people who are anxious and doubt their own worth and competence and who avoid close relationships with others tend to be less altruistic as well as less generous.

So the question remains: "How do we diminish the nature of evil and its inclination?" We know that evil will always be around, but we must try to reduce its intensity and prevent and stop its destructive deeds before they get started. We believe that education that spends time addressing consequences of indifference to others is vitally important. Besides reading, writing, and arithmetic, which are essential in every school, more time needs to be devoted to moral and immoral behavior and the nature of goodness and evil. It is a very complex subject. There is no single solution, just as there is no single explanation of what causes evil to triumph. We know quite a bit about how it comes into being. We see this from history, when societies are in trouble they look for scapegoats. Staub, discussing the nature and roots of evil, maintains evil is seen in a number of different sources of mistreatment of groups and causes them to perceive grievances, real or imagined.[5] He points to economic problems that threaten people's livelihood. Hence, they retaliate against the outsider. Cultural factors and troubling personal preconditions cause the group to regard the out-group as enemy. Political factors such as authoritarian or totalitarian governments, may foster hatred and encourage genocide, as do evil leaders for their benefit. Staub believes that humankind is capable of goodness and morality as well as selfishness and destructiveness towards others. As we have previously stated, Kelman who examines several genocides and mass murders, addressed a profound question of how it is possible for ordinary mothers and fathers to perform extraordinary acts of violence without moral restraint.[6] He concluded that three processes have to be present for mass killing to take place: a) dehumanization of victims; b) authorization by the government or other individuals in power; c) routinization, which makes it easier to commit and carry out genocide. Psychiatrist Robert Lifton addresses the issues of Nazi doctors committing mass murder and focuses on the process of "doubling."[7] Doubling means "the division of the self into two functioning wholes, so that a part-self acts as an entire self. An Auschwitz doctor could kill Jews, and then go home and hug his wife and children that same evening.

Religious traditions often contribute to moral human behavior, while at the same time they can contribute to hatred and separation of people by claiming, "My religion is best, through my religion alone can one obtain salvation. Other religions, at best should only be tolerated and at worst should be ignored and considered as an infidel religion." Philosopher Rollo May sees a relationship between love and caring.[8] He says, "Care is a state in which something does matter; care is opposite of apathy. Care is a necessary source of eros, a source of human tenderness."[9] Further, emphasizing the notion of loving relationships, he maintains it is, "when the other's existence matters to you; a relationship of dedication, taking the ultimate form of being willing to get delight in ultimate terms, to suffer for another."[10]

One of the major aims of education is to be able to resist malevolent persuasions and propaganda and to function more justly in society. This is one of the major roles of education and other forms of socialization, which have been charged to look for effects and seeing both sides of the situation. Philip Zimbardo in his book, *Lucifer Effect: Understanding How Good People Turn Evil,* suggests useful steps to help resist unwanted influences as well as distorted images of the other.[11] Among these ideas is to come to the conclusion that the person has made a mistake by following destructive ideologies. That specifically means, not only does one apologize, but also one asks for forgiveness for having made mistakes and followed along with ideologies. An example that he gives is Secretary of Defense, Robert McNamara, who knew that the Vietnam War was a terrible mistake and that he followed distorted misinformation. Another aim is mindfulness. This is that people should become mindful and get off the auto-pilot of believing in harmful ideologies. That is to say, you transform yourself from mindless thinking and following other people's ideas and orders. It is a wake-up call that one has followed wrong thinking and need to add critical thinking to resist malevolent authority or ideology in the future. The third aim is social responsibility. This is taking personal responsibility and trying to be accountable for actions which will hopefully lead to less obedience to vicious authority and following orders. Another one is to not allow others to deindividuate you. That means letting oneself to be put into a category or a slot and turn you into an object. This frequently leads to following orders like Eichmann, who was in charge of shipping people to their death in World War II. Another one is to respect moral authority, but to strongly rebel against unjust authority. To resist pseudo experts is to question these experts and look for evidence. Be willing to cooperate with society, but value one's independence. One has to live within one's own mind and not give up ones independence regardless of social pressure and social rejection. We need to reframe ideas that have been framed a certain way. Frequently these come from sound bytes, visual images, slogans and so forth. They seem to influence people without the public and/or the individual being conscious of it. The next aim is not going with the flow, that is to say, being aware of the fact that "50 million Frenchmen could be wrong." Another one is to be cooperative, but not sacrifice your individuality or your civic freedom for some sort of promise for security. Unjust systems have a powerful and pervasive presence everywhere and it's tough to fight systems, but it is up to us not to give in.

Learning about moral examples is important so we can emulate their behavior. Buddha advocated a strong pacifist element and nonviolent orientation, which has been significant in the political history of Buddhist countries. Jesus Christ preached love to all. Moses improved the life of people by advocating, "Rest on the seventh day." Mother Teresa visited the terminally ill and gave them comfort daily. When asked how, she replied, "It's not hard because in each one, I see the face of Christ in one of His more distressing disguises." Martin Luther King Jr. was a clergyman and Nobel Prize winner. He was a leader of the civil rights movement who advocated change through peaceful protest. Mohandas Gandhi advocated India's freedom through a peaceful revolution. There are also thousands of lesser luminaries who care for others in different settings. Education, moral role-modeling, love, caring for diverse others, respect, and social and economic justice for all may be the antidote for a divided world.

Appendix

	Holocaust	Armenian Genocide	Rwandan Genocide
Genocide committed on powerless minority group that was treated as second class citizens	Jews as a minority, for the last 2,000 years, have held a pariah status in the European world. Nazis have taken from various teachings of contempt of Jews and added their own racist ideology.	"Armenians were exempt from serving in the military, but forced to pay an exemption tax; were not allowed to bear arms; Armenian testimonies against Muslim's were prohibited in Islamic courts." (Attallah 40)	In the 1980s Habayarimana issued quotas to all Rwandans, but most officials used them as a means of restricting Tutsi from employment and higher education. (Des Forges 46)
Genocide committed during time of war or political and economic unrest (other nations would not intervene)	Hitler started World War II with a maniacal ideology of racial superiority in the midst of an economic depression and political unrest. He needed scapegoats around which to unify his people.	The rest of the world was preoccupied with World War I. The war also allowed the Turks to justify the genocide by referring to them as disloyal, traitors, and not true Ottomans.	Post Civil War racial tensions and still high economic distress due to collapse in coffee prices, which was their major export overpopulation famine. (Latham)
Victims perceived as enemies and disloyal	Jews were perceived as dominating German society including the economy, science, and general scholarship. One German scholar said, "The Jews are our misfortune."	The Turks used the war as a way to issue propaganda and scapegoat the Armenians calling them disloyal and accusing them of planning an uprising against the CUP. (Balakian 181)	Tutsi were identified as feudal class associated with the colonial occupation that was oppressing the Hutu. (Verwimp 3)
Dehumanization/ Demonization/ Xenophobia	Jews along with gypsies were regarded by German "anthropologists" as inferior by nature, culture, and genetics.		Tutsi were referred to as "cockroaches." The killing was referred to as "bush clearing" or "weeding." (Latham 115)

	Holocaust	Armenian Genocide	Rwandan Genocide
Authorization (Overt/Covert)	Using euphemisms such as "resettlement", "final solution," and "special treatment" clearly implied orders to destruction of all the Jewish people.	The Young Turks set up "special organizations" of ex-criminals and soldiers, and gave them orders to kill Armenians. (Balakian 182)	Propaganda, radio stations, and the mass media, which the Hutu government monopolized, gave the orders to kill.
Routinization (methods of effective mass killing)	Bureaucratization, which is interchangeable with routinization, implies efficient methods of mass destruction of a people, such as gas chambers, starvation, and mobile killing units.	The Turkish government issued edicts for the Armenian communities to be deported or massacred. They were sent on death marches into the desert, robbed, and shot.	Hutu were ordered to kill Tutsi by the Rwandan government over the radio. Tutsi were identified by their ethnic identity cards that were started by the Belgians. Tutsi were mass slaughtered with machetes and guns. Tutsi women were subject to rape.
Racism/ Antisemitism (historic trends of dehumanization of the out-group)	Nazi filmmakers produced over a thousand films using clever propaganda to show the German people that the Jews are destroyers of German culture and are a kind of vermin.	The Ottomans referred to the Armenians as "infidels" in a negative connotation because they were Christian.	Perceptions of the Tutsi being taller with lighter skin, so more closely related to the European colonizers. Elitist minority imposed by Belgium during times of colonialization, so they were seen as oppressors.
Nationalism (desire for monolithic state)	Desire for a monolithic Aryan race and state without inferior minorities. They wanted Germany to be Judenrein.	Favored a pan-Turkish ideology where the Turks would have one language and one religion. The pan-Turkish empire would be free of all minority groups.	The Hutu had a desire for agriculture while the Tutsi were perceived as the minority elite, involved in government and cattle raising.

	Holocaust	Armenian Genocide	Rwandan Genocide
Cultural/ Religious differences	Jews perceived as parasites who have infested business and professions, culturally considered inferior and cowardly.	The Armenians were Christian before the Muslim empire came upon the scene.	Classist cultural differences where the Hutu were deemed peasants and the Tutsi bourgeoisie.
Factor of genocide is to reinforce power and intimidate other minority groups who might be perceived as threatening	By destruction of Jews, gypsies, homosexuals, and educated classes, the Nazis were able to instill terror in others who might resist them.	The Turks wanted a monolithic empire with one religion and language. The Armenians were used as an example to other minority groups to show the power of the Turks.	Retaliation against Tutsi and frightening foreigners as well as the Tutsi forces (Rwandan Patriotic Front) from coming back to liberate Rwanda from the Hutus in power.
Major purpose of genocide is acquisition of land/ property	Needed property and land for Germans called Lebensraum. Depriving Jews of their property and all other assets in Nazi-occupied Europe.	The land, livestock, houses, and any valuables of the Armenians was either kept or sold for profit. Any loans by Armenian's were declared void. (Latham 31)	Population growth led to scarce land resources. The perceived solution to the scarcity of land was to annihilate the Tutsi and take their land because the less people that survived, the more land the Hutu could acquire.

Notes

PROLOGUE

1. *Southern Poverty Law Center.* Spring 2009, 39: 1.

2. Mark Potok (February 28, 2009), "SPLC's Intelligence Report: Hate Group Numbers Rise Again," *Southern Poverty Law Center.*

3. Samuel Oliner and Pearl Oliner (1988), *The Altruistic Personality: Rescuers of Jews in Nazi Europe* (New York: The Free Press); Samuel Oliner (2008), *Altruism, Intergroup Apology, Forgiveness and Reconciliation* (St. Paul: Paragon House); Samuel Oliner (2003), *Do Unto Others: Extraordinary Acts of Ordinary People* (Boulder: Westview Press) and Pearl Oliner and Samuel Oliner (1995), *Toward A Caring Society: Ideas into Action* (Westport: Praeger).

4. Manny Fernandez, "Lessons on Love, From a Rabbi Who Knows Hate and Forgiveness," *New York Times,* January 4, 2009.

5. Jewish Learning Institute (2010), *Beyond Never Again: How the Holocaust Speaks to Us Today* (Brooklyn, NY: Rorh Jewish Learning Institute).

6. Robert G. Waite (1977), *The Psychopathic God: Adolf Hitler* (New York: New American Library), p. 302.

7. (2010) "Top Ten Evil People of All Time" (Retrieved from http://www.bahrainonline.org/showthread.php?p=856833 on September 27, 2010).

8. Retrieved from http://staffwww.dcs.shef.ac.uk/people/R.Gaizauskas/other/quot_by_a.html#Genghis%20Khan, July 19, 2011.

9. Morton Hunt (1990), *The Compassionate Beast* (New York: William Morrow and Company).

CHAPTER 1: FOLLOW THE LEADER

1. Kevin Hogan and James Speakman (2006), *Covert Persuasion: Psychological Tactics and Tricks to Win the Game* (New Jersey: John Wiley and Sons).

2.   *Alternative Considerations of Jonestown and the People's Temple,* The Jonestown Institute, San Diego State University (retrieved at: http://jonestown.sdsu.edu/ on July 15, 2010).

3.   "Propaganda Techniques" (Retrieved at http://library.thinkquest.org/ C0111500/proptech.htm on July 15, 2010).

4.   Southern Poverty Law Center, "The Rough Guide," *Intelligence Report,* Summer 2010, 25.

5.   Staub, Ervin (1989), *The Roots of Evil: The Origin of Genocide and Other Group Violence* (New York: Cambridge University Press).

6.   John Toland (1977), *Adolph Hitler* (New York: Ballantine Books) p. 116.

7.   Alice Miller (1984), *For Your Own Good: Hidden Cruelty in Child-Rearing and the Roots of Violence* (New York: Farrar, Straus and Giroux), p. viii.

8.   James A. Aho (1994), *This Thing of Darkness: A Sociology of the Enemy* (Seattle: University of Washington Press).

9.   S. Opotow (1990), "Deterring Moral Exclusion," *Journal of Social Issues,* 46: 173-182.

10.   Raul Hilberg (1961), *The Destruction of European Jews* (New York: Quadrangle).

11.   Christopher Browning (1992), *Ordinary Men* (New York: Harper Collins).

12.   Daniel Goldhagen (1996), *Hitler's Willing Executioners* (London: Abacus).

13.   Renzo De Felice (1976), *Fascism: An Informal Introduction to its Theory and Practice* (New Jersey: Transaction Books).

14.   M. Gilbert (1985), *The Holocaust: A History of the Jews of Europe During the Second World War* (New York: Holt, Rinehart & Winston).

15.   Y. Bauer (1982), *A History of the Holocaust* (New York: Franklin Watts).

16.   D.S. Wyman (1984), *The Abandonment of the Jews: America and the Holocaust, 1941-1945* (New York: Pantheon Books).

17.   Elie Wiesel (1960), *Night* (New York: Hill and Wang).

18.   Deborah Lipstadt (1994), *Denying the Holocaust: The Growing Assault on Truth and Memory* (New York: Plume).

19.   Lucy Dawidowicz (1975), *The War Against the Jews: 1933-1945* (New York: Hole, Rinehart and Winston).

20.   Malcolm Hay (1951), *The Foot of Pride: The Pressure of Christendom on the People of Israel for 1900 Years* (Boston: Beacon Press); Anthony Julius (2010), *Trials of the*

Diaspora: A History of Anti-Semitism in England (USA: Oxford University Press) and Robert E. Wistrich (2010), *A Lethal Obsession: Anti-Semitism from Antiquity to the Global Jihad* (New York: Random House).

21.   Lawrence Baron (1988), "The Historical Context of Rescue" in *The Altruistic Personality,* Eds. Samuel P. Oliner and Pearl M. Oliner (New York: Free Press: 13-48).

22.   Samuel Oliner (2003), *Do Unto Others: Extraordinary Acts of Ordinary People* (Boulder: Westview Press).

CHAPTER 2: HOW COULD THEY DO THAT?

1.   Philip Zimbardo (2007), *The Lucifer Effect: Understanding How Good People Turn Evil* (New York: The Random House), p. 5.

2.   James Waller (2007), *Becoming Evil: How Ordinary People Commit Genocide and Mass Killing* (Oxford: Oxford University Press).

3.   Mia Pia Lara, ed. (2001), *Rethinking Evil* (New Jersey: University of California Press).

4.   Svetlana Broz (2004), *Good People in an Evil Time* (New York: Other Press).

5.   Lionel Tiger (1987), *The Manufacture of Evil: Ethics, Evolution, and the Industrial System* (New York: Harper & Row Publishers).

6.   Hannah Arendt (1963), *Eichmann in Jerusalem: A Report on the Banality of Evil* (New York: The Viking Press).

7.   http://www1.yadvashem.org/education/conference2006/Naveh,%20 Sippy%20.pdf.

8.   Jeffrey C. Alexander (2003), *The Meanings of Social Life: A Cultural Sociology* (New York: Oxford University Press).

9.   Plato (1999), *Timaeus.* Translated by Benjamin Jowett (Hazelton: Pennsylvania State University Electronic Classics Series) (retrieved on January 10, 2006 at http://www2.hn.psu.edu/faculty/jmanis/plato/timaeus.pdf).

10.   Robert Bellah (1971), "Evil and American Ethos," in *Sanctions for Evil.* eds. Nevitt Sanford and Craig Comstock (San Francisco: Jossey-Bass), pp.177-191.

11.   Roy Baumeister(1997), *Evil: Inside Human Violence and Cruelty* (New York: Freeman).

12.   Adorno, Theodor W. Else Frenkel-Brunswik, Daniel Levinson and Nevitt Sanford (1950), *The Authoritarian Personality* (New York: Harper and Row) and

Nevitt Sanford (1971), "Authoritarianism and Social Destructiveness." In *Sanctions for Evil*, eds. Nevitt Sanford and Craig Comstock (San Francisco: Jossey-Bass).

13. Richard Rubenstein (1975), *The Cunning of History: The Holocaust and the American Future* (New York: Harper & Row).

14. Herbert Kelman (1973), "Violence Without Moral Restraint: Reflections on the Dehumanization of Victims and Victimizers." *Journal of Social Issues* 29, 4: 25-62.

15. James A. Aho (1994), *This Thing of Darkness: A Sociology of the Enemy* (Seattle: University of Washington Press).

16. Malcolm Hay (1951), *The Foot of Pride: The Pressure of Christendom on the People of Israel for 1900 Years* (Boston: Beacon Press).

17. Milton Leitenberg (1997) "Rwanda and Burundi Genocide: A Case Study of Neglect and Indifference" in *Race, Ethnicity, and Gender*, eds. Samuel P. Oliner and Phillip T. Gay. (Dubuque: Kendall-Hunt Publishing Company), pp. 253-279.

18. Frontline. *Valentina's Nightmare*. Produced by BBC Television, aired on April 1, 1997. (Transcript retrieved on March 2, 2006 at http://www.pbs.org/wgbh/pages/frontline/shows/rwanda/etc/script.html).

19. Erich Fromm (1973), *The Anatomy of Human Destructiveness* (London: Macmillan Press), A. Freud, 1936. *Ego and the Mechanisms of Defense* (London: Hogarth) and Konrad Lorenz (1963), *On Aggression* (Florida: Harcourt Brace).

20. Philip Zimbardo (2004), "A Situationist Perspective on the Psychology of Evil: Understanding How Good People are Transformed into Perpetrators," in *The Social Psychology of Good and Evil: Understanding Our Capacity for Kindness and Cruelty*, ed Arthur Miller (New York: Guilford Publishers), pp. 21-50.

21. Zimbardo, *The Lucifer Effect*, p. 295.

22. Philip G. Zimbardo (1991), *Quiet Rage: The Stanford Prison Study*. (Videotape). Stanford: Leland Stanford Junior University: Academic distribution, Stanford University, 1992.

23. Zimbardo, "A Situationist Perspective on the Psychology of Evil."

24. Christopher Browning (1992), *Ordinary Men: Reserve Police Battalion 101 and the Final Solution in Poland* (New York: Harper Collins).

25. Wikipedia, "Heinrich von Treitschke," (Retrieved from http://en.wikipedia.org/wiki/Heinrich_von_Treitschke on July 27, 2010).

26. Marshall Rosenberg (1999), *Nonviolent Communication: A Language on Compassion* (Encinitas: Puddle Dancer Press).

27. Zygmunt Bauman (1989), *Modernity and the Holocaust* (New York: Cornell University Press).

28. Leonard Doob (1978), *Panoramas of Evil* (Connecticut: Greenwood Press).

29. Paul Vincent (2005), "The Genocidal Mind: In Search of a Definition." in *The Genocidal Mind: Selected Papers from the 32nd Annual Scholar's Conference on the Holocaust and the Churches* eds. Dennis B. Klein, Richard Libowitz, et al. (St. Paul: Paragon House), pp. 39-59.

30. Ibid, p. 41.

31. Samuel Oliner (1968), *Narrow Escapes: A Boy's Holocaust Memories and Their Legacy.* (St. Paul: Paragon House).

32. Plato, *Timaeus.*

33. Aristotle (n.d.), *Nicomachean Ethics (retrieved on February 16, 2006 at* http://plato.stanford.edu/entries/aristotle-ethics).

34. Benedict Carey, "For the Worst of Us, the Diagnosis May be Evil." *New York Times*, February 8, 2005, D1.

35. Ibid.

36. David Patterson (2005), "The Complicity of Modern Philosophy in the Extermination of the Jews," in *The Genocidal Mind: Selected Papers from the 32nd Annual Scholars' Conference on the Holocaust and the Churches.* eds. Dennis B. Klein, Richard Libowitz, et al. (St. Paul: Paragon House), pp. 105-123.

37. John Toland (1977), *Adolf Hitler* (London: Book Club Associates).

38. Lucy S. Dawidowicz (1975), *The War Against the Jews 1933-1945* (New York: Holt, Rinehart and Winston).

39. Alice Miller (n.d.), *Interview with Natural Child Project* (retrieved on February 15, 2006 at http://www.naturalchild.com/alice_miller/rootsviolence.html).

40. Adolf Hitler cited in Hannah Vogt (1965), *The Burden of Guilt: A Short History of Germany 1914-1945* (New York: Oxford University Press), p. 163.

41. Ibid., p. 146.

42. Julian Lieb (2006), "Hatred Often Lurks in the Shadows of Mania," (retrieved on March 1, 2006 at http://www.codoh.com/newrevoices/nrandom/nrandomania.html).

43. Ibid.

44. Ibid. and Alice Miller (1983), *For Your Own Good: Hidden Cruelty in Child-Rearing and the Roots of Violence* (New York: Farrar Strauss Giroux).

45. Theodore R. Sarbin (1986), "The Narrative as Root Metaphor for Psychology," in *Narrative Psychology: The Storied Nature of Human Conduct*, ed. Theodore R. Sarbin (New York: Praeger), pp. 3-21, Paul C. Vitz (1990), "The Use of Stories in Moral Development: New Psychological Reasons for an Old Education Method." *American Psychologist* 45, 6: 709-720 and Endel Tulving (1983), *Elements of Episodic Memory* (New York: Oxford University Press).

46. Tulving, *Elements of Episodic Memory*.

47. Iris Chang (1997), *The Rape of Nanking: The Forgotten Holocaust of World War II*, (New York: Penguin Groups).

48. Robert Coles (1989), *The Call of Stories: Teaching and the Moral Imagination* (Boston: Houghton Mifflin Co).

49. Alex Haley (1976), *Roots* (New York: Doubleday).

50. Elie Wiesel (1969). *Night* (New York: A Discuss Book/Avon Books).

51. Ibid., p. 32.

52. Frontline, *Valentina's Nightmare*.

53. Robert Gellately cited in Victoria J Barnett (1999), *Bystanders: Conscience and Complicity during the Holocaust* (Westport: Greenwood Press), p. 36.

54. Ervin Staub (1989), *The Roots of Evil: The Origins of Genocide and Other Group Violence* (Cambridge: Cambridge University Press).

55. Richard Taylor (2000), *Good and Evil* (New York: Prometheus).

56. Aho, *This Thing of Darkness*.

57. Jan Gross (2002), *Neighbors: The Destruction of the Jewish Community in Jedwabne, Poland* (New York: Penguin Books).

58. Frontline (1985), "A Class Divided." WGBH Educational Foundation video presentation of the 1968 Jane Elliott experiment produced by Yale University Films, aired on March 26, 1985.

59. Solomon E. Asch (1951), "Effects of Group Pressure upon the Modification and Distortion of Judgment" in *Groups, Leadership and Men*, ed. Harold S. Guetzkow (Pittsburgh: Carnegie Press).

60. Irving Janis (1971), "Groupthink Among Policy Makers." in *Sanctions for Evil*. eds. Nevitt Sanford and Craig Comstock (San Francisco: Jossey-Bass), pp. 71-89.

61. Irving Janis (1982), *Victims of Groupthink* (Boston: Houghton Mifflin).

62. Arthur Miller, ed. (2004), *The Social Psychology of Good and Evil* (New York: Guilford).

63. Arendt, *Eichmann in Jerusalem,* p. 64.

64. Ibid., p. 32.

65. Ibid., p. 26.

66. Ibid., p. 27.

67. Ibid., p. 103.

68. Ibid., p. 103.

69. Ibid., p. 161.

70. Ibid., p. 163.

71. Ibid., p. 166.

72. Daniel Jonah Goldhagen (1996), *Hitler's Willing Executioners: Ordinary Germans and the Holocaust* (New York: Alfred A. Knopf).

73. Kelman, "Violence Without Moral Restraint."

74. Yale Law School (1998), "Nuremberg Trial Page" *The Avalon Project* (retrieved on February 10, 2006 at http://www.yale.edu/lawweb/avalon/imt/proc/naeve.htm).

75. Philip G. Zimbardo (2000), "The Psychology of Evil," *Eye on Psi Chi,* Fall: 16-19.

76. William L. Shirer (1941), *Berlin Diary: The Journal of a Foreign Correspondent* (New York: Alfred A. Knopf), p. 270.

77. Stanley Milgram (1969), *Obedience to Authority: An Experimental View* (New York: Harper Colophon Books).

78. Ibid., 145.

79. Elie A. Cohen (1953), *Human Behavior in the Concentration Camp* (New York: Grosset and Dunlap), p. 270.

80. Milgram, *Obedience to Authority*, pp. 145-146.

81. Ibid., 54.

82. Ibid., 54.

83. Kelman, "Violence Without Moral Restraint," p. 46.

84. Benedict Carey, "When Death Is on the Docket, The Moral Compass Wavers." *New York Times*, February 7, 2006 D1.

85. Frontline, *Valentina's Nightmare.*

86. Kelman, "Violence Without Moral Restraint," p. 48.

87. Ludwig Rosenthal (1979), *The Final Solution to the Jewish Question* (Berkeley: Western Jewish History Center: Judah L. Magnes Memorial Museum), p. 25.

88. Frontline, *Valentina's Nightmare.*

89. Arendt, *Eichmann in Jerusalem.*

90. Rosenthal, *The Final Solution to the Jewish Question,* pp. 66-70.

91. Cohen, *Human Behavior in the Concentration Camp,* p. 255.

92. Gerard Prunier (n.d.), "Interview with Fergal Keane." *Frontline.* (retrieved on March 9, 2006 at http://www.pbs.org/wgbh/pages/frontline/shows/rwanda/etc/interview.html).

93. R.J. Lifton (1986), *The Nazi Doctors: Medical Killing and The Psychology of Genocide* (New York: Basic Books).

94. Albert Bandura (1990), "Selective Activation and Disengagement of Moral Control," *Journal of Social Issues* 46, 27: 46.

95. Carey, "When Death Is on the Docket."

96. University of Arkansas (2004), "'But is it Really Cheating?' UA Researcher Examines Moral Judgment vs. Behavior in College Classrooms," (retrieved on February 20, 2006 at http://listserv.uark.edu/scripts/wa.exe?A2=ind0409&L=daily_headlines&P=906).

97. Vincent, "The Genocidal Mind," p. 49.

98. Ibid., 50.

99. Cohen, *Human Behavior in the Concentration Camp,* p. 276.

100. Staub, *The Roots of Evil,* p. 10.

CHAPTER 3: SILENTLY STANDING BY

1. Samuel Oliner and Pearl Oliner (1988), *The Altruistic Personality: Rescuers of Jews in Nazi Europe* (New York: The Free Press), p. 4.

2. Ibid.

3. Victoria J. Barnett (1999), *Bystanders: Conscious and Complicity during the Holocaust* (Westport: Greenwood Press).

4. Svetlana Broz (2006), "Courage Under Fire," *Greater Good,* Fall/Winter: 10-13, p. 11.

5.   Gregory A. Gahm, Barbara A. Lucenko, Paul D. Retzlaff, and Seiya Fukuda (2007), "Relative Impact of Adverse Events and Screened Symptoms of Posttraumatic Stress Disorder and Depression Among Active Duty Soldiers Seeking Mental Health Care," *Journal of Clinical Psychology* 63, 3: 199-211; Tiffany M. Greene-Shortridge, Thomas W. Britt, and Carl A. Castro (2007) "The Stigma of Mental Health Problems in the Military," *Military Medicine* 172, 2: 157-161 and Charles W. Hodge, Artin Terhakopian, Carl A. Castro, Stephen C. Messer, and Charles C. Engel (2007), "Association of Posttraumatic Stress Disorder with Somatic Symptoms, Health Care Visits, and Absenteeism Among Iraq War Veterans," *American Journal of Psychiatry* 164,1: 150-153.

6.   Lois W. Morton (2003), "Rural Health Policy," in *Challenges for Rural America in the Twenty-First Century*, ed. David L. Brown and Louis E. Swanson (University Park: The Pennsylvania State University), pp. 290-302; Michel Van Herp, Veronique Parqué, Edward Rackley, and Nathan Ford (2003), "Mortality, Violence and Lack of Access to Healthcare in the Democratic Republic of Congo," *Disasters* 27, 2: 141–153 and Ahmed M. Syed, Jeanne P. Lemkau, Nichol Nealeigh, Barbara Mann (2001), "Barriers to Healthcare Access In a Non-Elderly Urban Poor American Population." *Health & Social Care In the Community* 9, 6: 445–453.

7.   Thomas A. Lyson (2004), *Civic Agriculture: Reconnecting Farm, Food, and Community* (Lebanon: Tufts University Press); Sing Chew (2001), *World Ecological Degradation: Accumulation, Urbanization, and Deforestation 3000 B.C.– A.D. 2000* (New York: Rowman & Littlefield Publishers, Inc.) and Wendell Berry (1977), *The Unsettling of America: Culture and Agriculture* (San Francisco: Sierra Club Books).

8.   David D. Cesarani and Paul A. Levine (2002), *Bystanders to the Holocaust: A Re-evaluation* (Portland: Frank Cass); Irena Steinfeldt (2002), *How Was it Humanly Possible?: A Study of Perpetrators and Bystanders During the Holocaust: Pedagogical Guidebook* (Jerusalem: International School for Holocaust Studies Beth Shalom Holocaust Memorial Centre), Arne Johan Vetlesen (2000) "Genocide: A Case for the Responsibility of the Bystander," *Journal of Peace Research* 37, 4: 519-532; Barnett, *Bystanders*; Ervin Staub (1989), *The Roots of Evil: The Origins of Genocide and other Group Violence* (New York: Cambridge University Press); Oliner and Oliner, *The Altruistic Personality*; Fred Grünfeld and Anke Huijboom (2007), *The Failure to Prevent Genocide in Rwanda: the Role of Bystanders* (Boston: Martinus Nijhoff); Adam LeBor (2006), *"Complicity with Evil": The United Nations in the Age of Modern Genocide* (New Haven: Yale University Press); Robert Lyons and Scott Straus (2006), *Intimate Enemy: Images and Voices of the Rwandan Genocide* (Cambridge: Zone Books); Power, *A Problem from Hell*; Michael N. Barnett (2002), *Eyewitness to A Genocide: The United Nations and Rwanda* (Ithaca: Cornell University Press); Broz,

"Courage Under Fire";Thomas Cushman and Stjepan Gabriel Meštrović (1996), *This Time We Knew: Western Responses to Genocide in Bosnia* (New York: New York University Press) and B. Latané and J. Darley (1970), *The Unresponsive Bystander: Why Doesn't He Help?* (New York: Appleton- Century-Crofts).

9.   Samuel Oliner (2003), *Do Unto Others: Extraordinary Acts of Ordinary People* (Boulder: Westview Press).

10.   Oliner and Oliner, *The Altruistic Personality*.

11.   Staub, *The Roots of Evil*.

12.   Dianne M. Tice and Roy F. Baumeister (1985), "Masculinity Inhibits Helping in Emergencies: Personality Does Predict the Bystander Effect," *Journal of Personality and Social Psychology* 49, 2: 420-428; Mary Douglas (1986), *How Institutions Think* (Syracuse: Syracuse University Press) and Cecilia L. Ridgeway (1993), "Gender, Status, and the Social Psychology of Expectations" in *Theory on Gender/Feminism on Theory*, ed. Paula England (New York: Aldine de Gruyter), pp. 175-197.

13.   Barnett, *Bystanders*.

14.   Zygmunt Bauman (1989), *Modernity and the Holocaust* (Ithaca: Cornell University Press).

15.   Daniel Jonah Goldhagen (1996), *Hitler's Willing Executioners: Ordinary Germans and the Holocaust* (New York: Alfred A. Knopf); Power, *A Problem from Hell*, Barnett, *Bystanders* and Staub, *The Roots of Evil*.

16.   Staub, *The Roots of Evil* and S.Reicher, Cassidy, C., Hopkins, N. & Levine, M. (2006), "Saving Bulgaria's Jews: An Analysis of Social Identity and the Mobilisation of Social Solidarity," *European Journal of Social Psychology*, 36: 49-72.

17.   Michael Bar-Zohar (1998), *Beyond Hitler's Grasp: The Heroic Rescue of Bulgaria's Jews* (Massachusetts: Adams Media Corporation).

18.   Samuel Oliner (2008), *Altruism, Intergroup Apology, Forgiveness and Reconciliation* (St. Paul: Paragon House) and John Mueller (2000), "The Banality of 'Ethnic War,'" *International Security*, 25: 42-70.

19.   United States Holocaust Memorial Museum (2010), "Overview: Sudan" (retrieved at http://www.ushmm.org/genocide/take_action/atrisk/region/sudan on August 3, 2010).

20.   Marlise Simons and Neil MacFarquhan (2009), "Court Issues Arrest Warrant for Sudan's Leader," *The New York Times* (retrieved on May 15, 2009 at http://www.nytimes.com/2009/03/05/world/africa/05court.html).

21. J. Darley and B. Latané (1968), "Bystander Intervention in Emergencies: Diffusion of Responsibility," *Journal of Personality and Social Psychology* 8, 4: 377-383; B. Latané and J. Darley (1970), *The Unresponsive Bystander: Why Doesn't He Help?* (New York: Appleton- Century- Crofts) and B. Latané and J. Darley (1975), *Help in a Crisis: Bystander Response to an Emergency* (Morriston: General Learning Press).

22. R.M. Levine (1999), "Rethinking Bystander Non-Intervention: Social Categorisation and the Evidence of Witnesses at the James Bulger Murder Trial," *Human Relations* 52: 1133-1155.

23. B. Latané & S. Nida (1981), "Ten Years of Research on Group Size and Helping," *Psychological Bulletin* 89, 2: 308-324, p. 309.

24. David D. Cesarani and Paul A. Levine, *Bystanders to the Holocaust.*

25. Arne Johan Vetlesen, "Genocide," p. 523.

26. Vishavjit Singh (2002), "A Nation of Bystanders," *Sikh Spectrum* (retrieved on May 15, 2009 at http://www.sikhspectrum.com/102002/nation.htm); D. Bar-On (2001), "The Bystander in Relation to the Victim & the Perpetrator: Today and During the Holocaust," *Social Justice Research* 14, 2: 125-148; Staub, *The Roots of Evil* and Darley and B. Latané, "Bystander Intervention in Emergencies."

27. Darley and B. Latané, "Bystander Intervention in Emergencies."

28. Ibid.

29. B. Latané and J. Darley, *The Unresponsive Bystander.*

30. Darley and B. Latané, "Bystander Intervention in Emergencies."

31. R.M. Levine, "Rethinking Bystander Non-Intervention."

32. Michael Kodas (2008), *High Crimes: The Fate of Everest in an Age of Greed* (New York: Hyperion Books).

33. Arne Johan Vetlesen, "Genocide."

34. Staub, *The Roots of Evil.*

35. Darley and B. Latané, "Bystander Intervention in Emergencies."

36. Staub, *The Roots of Evil,* p., 266.

37. George Kateb quoted in Barnett, *Bystanders*, p. 43.

38. Tamaki Mino (2006), "*Ijime* (Bullying) in Japanese Schools: A Product of Japanese Education Based on Group Conformity." Presented at the Second Annual Rhizomes: Re-Visioning Boundaries Conference of The School of Languages and

Comparative Cultural Studies, February 24-25, Brisbane, Australia; Staub, *The Roots of Evil*, Ervin Staub (1989),"The Evolution of Bystanders, German Psychoanalysts, and Lessons for Today," *Political Psychology* 10: 39-52 and Ervin Staub (1985), "The Psychology of Perpetrators and Bystanders," *Political Psychology* 6, 1: 61-85.

39. Barnett, *Bystanders;* Staub, *The Roots of Evil* and Staub, "The Psychology of Perpetrators and Bystanders."

40. Barnett, *Bystanders* and Staub, *The Roots of Evil.*

41. Oliner, *Altruism, Intergroup Apology, Forgiveness and Reconciliation.*

42. Tice and Baumeister , "Masculinity Inhibits Helping in Emergencies" see also Douglas, *How Institutions Think* and Levine, "Rethinking Bystander Non-Intervention."

43. Ridgeway, "Gender, Status, and the Social Psychology of Expectations."

44. Barnett, *Bystanders.*

45. Ibid., p. 53.

46. Power, *A Problem from Hell.*

47. Oliner, *Altruism, Intergroup Apology, Forgiveness and Reconciliation.*

48. Arne Johan Vetlesen, "Genocide."

49. Barnett, *Bystanders.*

50. United States Holocaust Memorial Museum, "Overview: Sudan."

51. Sarah Glazer (2004), "Stopping Genocide: Should the U.S. and U.N. Take Action in Sudan?," *The CQ Researcher* 14, 29: 685-708.

52. Jim VandeHei (2005), "In Break with U.N., Bush Calls Sudan Killings Genocide," *Washington Post* (retrieved on June 8, 2007 at http://www.washingtonpost.com/wp-dyn/content/article/2005/06/01/AR2005060101725.html).

53. Power, *A Problem from Hell.*

54. Glazer, "Stopping Genocide: Should the U.S. and U.N. Take Action in Sudan?," p. 690.

55. Lance R. Shotland and Charles A. Stebbins (1983), "Emergency and Cost as Determinants of Helping Behavior and the Slow Accumulation of Social Psychological Knowledge," *Social Psychology Quarterly* 46, 1: 36-46.

56. Power, *A Problem from Hell.*

57. Glazer, "Stopping Genocide: Should the U.S. and U.N. Take Action in Sudan?"

58. Pamela Oliver and Gerald Marwell (1993), *The Critical Mass in Collective Action: A Micro-Social Theory* (New York: Cambridge University Press).

59. Ervin Staub (1996), "Responsibility, Helping, Aggression, and Evil," *Psychological Inquiry* 7, 3: 252-254.

60. Alan J. Lambert and Katherine Raichle (2000), "The Role of Political Ideology in Mediating Judgments of Blame in Rape Victims and their Assailants: A Test of the Just World, Personal Responsibility, and Legitimization Hypotheses," *Personality and Social Psychology Bulletin* 26: 853-86 and Naomi J. Freeman (2006), "Socioeconomic Status and Belief in a *Just World*: Sentencing of Criminal Defendants," *Journal of Applied Social Psychology* 36: 2379-2394.

61. Don Forsyth (2004), "Big Ball of Blame," *Style Weekly* (retrieved on August 5, 2009 at http://oursocialworld.blogspot.com/).

62. Mino, "*Ijime* (Bullying) in Japanese Schools: A Product of Japanese Education Based on Group Conformity"; Barnett, *Bystanders*; Staub, *The Roots of Evil*; Staub, "The Evolution of Bystanders, German Psychoanalysts, and Lessons for Today" and Staub, "The Psychology of Perpetrators and Bystanders."

63. Oliner and Oliner, *The Altruistic Personality*.

64. Singh, "A Nation of Bystanders."

65. Ibid.

66. Herbert Blumer (1969), *Symbolic Interactionism: Perspective and Method* (New Jersey: Prentice- Hall).

67. Oliner and Oliner, *The Altruistic Personality*; Oliner, *Do Unto Others* and Oliner, *Altruism, Intergroup Apology, Forgiveness and Reconciliation*.

68. Jack Shaffer and Samuel Oliner (1995), "Disaffiliation from Hate Groups," Presented at Pacific Sociological Association.

69. Emile Durkheim ([1933] 1984), *The Division of Labor in Society* (New York: The Free Press).

70. Glazer, "Stopping Genocide: Should the U.S. and U.N. Take Action in Sudan?"

71. Associated Press (2008), *7 Bosnian Serbs Guilty of Genocide 4 Others Acquitted in Srebrenica Massacre* (retrieved on August 6, 2008 at http://www.sfgate.com/cgi-bin/article.cgi?f=/c/a/2008/07/30/MN7S121D1I.DTL&hw=bosnia+leader+sentenced&sn=002&sc=659).

72. Lynn Stephen (2002), *Zapata Lives!: History and Cultural Politics in Southern Mexico* (Berkeley: University of California Press).

73. Lyson, *Civic Agriculture*; Michael M. Bell (2004), *Farming for Us All: Practical Agriculture and the Cultivation of Sustainability* (University Park: The Pennsylvania State University Press) and Berry, *The Unsettling of America*.

74. Detlef F. Sprinz, and Tapani Vaahtoranta (1994), "The Interest-Based Explanation of International Environmental Policy," *International Organization* 48, 1:77-105.

75. Ibid.

76. Chew, *World Ecological Degradation: Accumulation, Urbanization, and Deforestation 3000 B.C.– A.D. 2000*.

77. A.L. Beaman, P.J. Barnes, B. Klentz & B. McQuirk (1978), "Increasing help-ing rates through information dissemination: teaching pays," *Personality and Social Psychology Bulletin*, 4,3: 406–411.

78. Dennis J. Barr (2005), "Early Adolescents' Reflection on Social Justice: Facing History and Ourselves in Practice and Assessment," *Intercultural Education* 16, 2:145-160.

79. Ibid.

80. Suelan Toye (2005), "Silent Bystanders No More: Movie Inspires Teachers, Students to Act (Teachers, Students Send Stern Message to UN.)" *News@UofT— Social Sciences Business and Law* (retrieved on March 6, 2006 at http://www.news.utoronto.ca/bin6/050429-1307.asp).

81. Amory Starr (2004), "How Can Anti-Imperialism Not Be Anti-Racist? The North American Anti-Globalization Movement," *Journal of World Systems Research* 10, 1: 118-151; Ann Reisner (2003), "Newspaper Construction of a Moral Farmer," *Rural Sociology* 68: 46-63; Anthony Pratkanis and Elliot Aronson (1992), *Age of Propaganda: The Everyday Use and Abuse of Persuasion* (New York: Henry Holt and Co) and Noam Chomsky (1991), *Media Control: The Spectacular Achievements of Propaganda* (New York: Seven Stories Press).

82. Lloyd E. Levine (2007), "One Step Closer to Lights Out for the Incandescent." *California Progress Report*.

83. Ibid.

84. Chew, *World Ecological Degradation: Accumulation, Urbanization, and Deforestation 3000 B.C.– A.D. 2000*.

CHAPTER 4: PAVING THE WAY TO RESISTANCE

1.   J.M. Barbalet (1985), "Power and Resistance," *The British Journal of Sociology* 36: 531-548.

2.   Kristina Thalhammer, Paul L. O'Loughlin, et al. (2007), *Courageous Resistance the Power of the Ordinary People* (New York: Palgrave Macmillan).

3.   Herbert C. Kelman (1973), "Violence Without Moral Restraint: Reflections on the Dehumanization of Victims and Victimizers," *Journal of Social Issues* 29: 25–61.

4.   Raul Hilberg (1961), *The Destruction of European Jews* (New York: Quadrangle Books Inc).

5.   Hilberg, *The Destruction of European Jews.*

6.   Ibid., p. 113.

7.   Yehuda Bauer (2001), *History of the Holocaust* (New York: Holmes and Meier).

8.   Ibid., p. 273.

9.   Nechama Tec (1990), *In the Lion's Den the Life of Oswald Rufeisen* (New York: Oxford University Press); Nechama Tec (1993), *Defiance: The Bielski Partisans* (New York: Oxford University Press); Trudi Alexy (1993), *The Mezuzah in the Madonna's Foot: Marranos and Other Secret Jews* (San Francisco: Harpers); M.R. Marrus and R.O. Paxton (1983), *Vichy France and the Jews* (New York: Schocken Books); E. Kulka ed. (1976), *Collection of Testimonies and Documents on the Participation of Czechoslovak Jews in the Second World War* (Jerusalem: Yad Vashem); Lester Eckman and Chaim Lazar (1977), *The Jewish Resistance: The History of the Jewish Partisans in Lithuania and White Russia under Nazi Occupation, 1940-45* (New York: Shengold); S. Krakowski (1983), *The War of the Doomed: Jewish Armed Resistance in Poland 1942-1944* (New York: Holmes and Meier); Michael Berenbaum (1993), *The World Must Know: The History of the Holocaust as Told in the United States Holocaust Memorial Museum* (Boston: Little, brown); Nora Levin (1968), *The Holocaust: The Destruction of European Jewry 1933-1945* (New York: Schocken Books); Reuben Ainsztein (1974), *Jewish Resistance in Nazi-Occupied Eastern Europe* (New York: Barnes and Nobles Books); T.H. Halivni (1979), "The Birkenau Revolt: the Poles Prevent a Timely Insurrection," *Jewish Social Studies*, 41: 123-154 and Miriam Novitch (1980), *Sobibor* (New York: Holocaust Library).

10.   Alexy, *The Mezuzah in the Madonna's Foot* and Lucien Lazare (1996), *Rescue as Resistance: How Jewish Organizations Fought the Holocaust in France* (New York: Columbia University Press).

11.   L. Poliakov (1979), *Harvest of Hate* (New York: Holocaust Library).

12. Ignaz Maybaum (1965), *The Face of God after Auschwitz* (Amsterdam: Polak and van Gennep).

13. Stephen T. Katz (1983), *Post- Holocaust Dialogues: Critical Studies in Modern Jewish Thought* (New York: New York University Press).

14. "Wilhem Marr," *Wikipedia* (Retrieved on August 5, 2010 from http://en.wikipedia.org/wiki/Wilhelm_Marr#Theories).

15. Hilberg, *The Destruction of European Jews*, H. Arendt (1965), *Eichman in Jerusalem* (New York: Viking Compass); B. Bettelheim (1971), *The Informed Heart: Autonomy in a Mass Age* (New York: Avon) and L. Poliakov, *Harvest of Hate*.

16. B. Bettelheim, *The Informed Heart: Autonomy in a Mass Age*.

17. Ibid.

18. Ainsztein, *Jewish Resistance in Nazi-Occupied Eastern Europe*.

19. Lucy Dawidowicz (1976), *A Holocaust Reader* (New York: Behrman House Inc) and Bauer, *History of the Holocaust*.

20. Helen Fein (1997), "Genocide by Attrition 1939-1993: The Warsaw Ghetto, Cambodia, and Sudan: Links between Human Rights, Health, and Mass Death," *Health and Human Rights*, 2: 10-45.

21. Martin Gilbert (1985), *The Holocaust: A History of the Jews in Europe during the Second World War* (New York: Holt, Rinehart & Winston).

22. Lawrence L Langer (1982), *Versions of Survival: The Holocaust and the Human Spirit* (New York: State University of New York Press), p. 145.

23. Samuel P. Oliner (1998), "Rescuers of Jews During the Holocaust: A Portrait of Moral Courage," in Michael Berenbaum and Abraham Peck eds. *The Holocaust and History: The Known, the Unknown, the Disputed, and the Reexamined* (Indiana: Indiana University Press): 678-690 and Hilberg, *The Destruction of European Jews*.

24. Hilberg, *The Destruction of European Jews*.

25. Bauer, *History of the Holocaust*.

26. Wener Rings (1982), *Life with the Enemy: Collaboration and Resistance in Hitler's Europe, 1939-1945* (New York: Doubleday).

27. Ainsztein, *Jewish Resistance in Nazi-Occupied Eastern Europe*.

28. Samuel P. Oliner (2003), *Do Unto Others Extraordinary Acts of Ordinary People* (Boulder: Westview Press).

29. Jewish Virtual Library (2010), "Witold Pilecki" *The American Israeli Cooperative Enterprise* (Retrieved on August 10, 2010 from http://www.jewishvirtuallibrary.org/jsource/biography/Witold_Pilecki.html).

30. Tec, *Defiance: The Bielski Partisans.*

31. Tec, *Defiance: The Bielski Partisan* and Peter Duffy (2003), *The Bielski Brothers The True Story of Three Men Who Defied The Nazis, Saved 1,200 Jews, and Built a Village in the Forest* (New York: Harper Collins Publishers Inc.).

32. Tec, *Defiance: The Bielski Partisans.*

33. Ibid.

34. Lydia Lee (May 2, 2003), "Warsaw Ghetto survivor recalls hunger, fear and grief" (retrieved August 17, 2010 from http://www.jweekly.com/article/full/19799/warsaw-ghetto-survivor-recalls-hunger-fear-and-grief/).

35. Ronnie S. Landau (1992), *The Nazi Holocaust* (Chicago: Ivan R, Dee) and Rich Cohen (2000), *The Avengers A Jewish War Story* (New York: Borzoi Books).

36. Eric Sterling ed. (2005), *Life in the Ghettos during the Holocaust* (New York: Syracuse University Press).

37. Ibid.

38. Cohen, *The Avengers A Jewish War Story*; Sterling, *Life in the Ghettos during the Holocaust* and Dawidowicz, *A Holocaust Reader.*

39. Sterling, *Life in the Ghettos during the Holocaust*, p. 61.

40. Cohen, *The Avengers A Jewish War Story* and Dawidowicz, *A Holocaust Reader.*

41. Viktor Frankl (2006), *Man's Search for Meaning*, (Boston: Beacon Books), p. 66.

42. Gilbert, *The Holocaust: A History of the Jews in Europe During the Second World War*; Sybil Milton (1979), *The Stroop Report* (New York: Pantheon Books); Yuri Suhl (1967), *They Fought Back: The Story of The Jewish Resistance in Nazi Europe* (New York: Schocken Books); Gunther Deschner (1972), *Warsaw Rising* (New York: Ballantine Books Inc.) and Landau, *The Nazi Holocaust.*

43. Oliner (2003), *Do Unto Others Extraordinary Acts of Ordinary People.*

44. Sara Bender (2008), *The Jews of Bialystok During World War II and the Holocaust* (New Hampshire: University Press of New England).

45. Samuel Rajzman (1945), *Uprising in Treblinka* in U.S. Congress House Committee on Foreign Affairs, *Punishment of War Criminals.* 79th Cong., 1st sess. (Washington D.C.: GPO), 120-125.

46. Samuel Rajzman (1945), *Uprising in Treblinka* in U.S. Congress House Committee on Foreign Affairs, *Punishment of War Criminals*. 79th Cong., 1st sess. (Washington D.C.: GPO), 120-125 and Isaiah Trunk (1979), *Jewish Responses to Nazi Persecution Collective and Individual Behavior in Extremis* (New York: Scarbrough).

47. Alexander Pechersky (1967), "Revolt in Sobibor," in Yuri Suhl ed. *They Fought Back* (New York: Schocken Books), 7-30; Toivi Thomas Blatt (1997), *From the Ashes of Sobibor A Story of Survival* (Illinois: Northwestern University Press); Toivi Thomas Blatt (2004), *Sobibor The Forgotten Revolt: A Survivors Report* (Washington: Fifth paperback printing) and G. Konnilyn Feig (1979), *Hitler's Death Camps: The Sanity of Madness* (New York: Holmes and Meier Publishers).

48. Oliner, *Do Unto Others: Extraordinary Acts of Ordinary People*; Suhl, *They Fought Back*; Feig, *Hitler's Death Camps*; Landau, *The Nazi Holocaust* and Levin, *The Holocaust*.

49. Joseph Hanania (2005), "When Risk-Taking Becomes a Victim," *Forward.com* (Retrieved August 17, 2010 from http://www.aceupoursleeve.com/downloads/ForwardOpEd.pdf).

50. Levin, *The Holocaust: The Destruction of European Jewry 1933-1945*.

51. Feig, *Hitler's Death Camps: The Sanity of Madness*; Rudolf Vrba (1964), *I Cannot Forgive* (Vancouver: Regent College Publishing) and Levin, *The Holocaust: The Destruction of European Jewry 1933-1945*.

52. Monika Scislowska (2010), "Former inmate recalls daring escape from Auschwitz," *SFGate*.com (Retrieved August 17, 2010 from http://articles.sfgate.com/2010-07-20/world/21991462_1_auschwitz-warehouse-gas-chambers).

53. Ruby Rohrlich (1998), *Resisting the Holocaust* (New York: Oxford International Publishers Ltd.), p, 152.

54. Thalhammer, O'Loughlin et al., *Courageous Resistance: The Power of Ordinary People* and Rohrlich, *Resisting the Holocaust*.

55. George W. Wittenstein (1997), *Memories of the White Rose* (retrieved from http://www.historyplace.com/pointsofview/white-rose1.htm).

56. Carmelo Lisciotto (2007), "The White Rose Leaflets: Translations of the 6 Printed Leaflets" *Holocaust Education and Archive Research Team* (Retrieved on August 10, 2010 from http://www.holocaustresearchproject.org/revolt/wrleaflets.html).

57. Wittenstein, *Memories of the White Rose*.

CHAPTER 5: PRECONDITIONS OF RESISTANCE

1.   Richard G. Hovannisian (1992), "The Question of Altruism during the Armenian Genocide of 1915," in *Embracing the Other* eds. Pearl Oliner, Samuel Oliner, et al. (New York: New York University Press): 282-305, p. 294.

2.   Memories of Captain Mbaye Diagne," Interview with Mark Doyle, *Frontline* (retrieved August 17, 2010 at http://www.pbs.org/wgbh/pages/frontline/shows/ghosts/video/capt.html).

3.   Robert Melson (1992), *Revolution and Genocide: On the Origins of the Armenian Genocide and the Holocaust* (Chicago: University of Chicago Press).

4.   Ibid., p. 138.

5.   Ibid.

6.   Rouben Paul Adalian, "Armenian Genocide," *Armenian National Institute* (retrieved August 13, 2009 at http://www.armenian-genocide.org/genocide.html).

7.   Donald Miller, and Lorna Touryan Miller (1993), *Survivors: An Oral History for the Armenian Genocide* (Berkeley: University of California Press) and Maral N. Attallah (2007), *Choosing Silence: The United States, Turkey and the Armenian Genocide* (Unpublished Master's Thesis, Humboldt State University, Arcata).

8.   Attallah, *Choosing Silence* p. 46.

9.   Peter Balakian (2003), *The Burning Tigris: The Armenian Genocide and America's Response* (New York: Harper Collins) and Roderic Davison (1948), "The Armenian Crisis, 1912-1914," *American Historical Review* 53,10: 481-505.

10.   Davison, "The Armenian Crisis," p. 485.

11.   Balakian, *The Burning Tigris*; Melson, *Revolution and Genocide* and David Lampe (1957), The *Danish Resistance: A History of Five Years of Secret Warfare Against The Nazi Occupation* (New York: Ballantine Books).

12.   Balakian, *The Burning Tigris*.

13.   Ibid.

14.   Ibid.

15.   Ibid., p. 280.

16.   Henry Morgenthau, Sr. quoted in "Armenian Genocide Quotes," *Armeniapedia* (retrieved August 17, 2010 at http://www.armeniapedia.org/index.php?title=Armenian_Genocide_Quotes#Henry_Morgenthau_Sr.).

17. Rouben Paul Adalian, "Musa Dagh," *Armenian National Institute* (retrieved August 13, 2009 at http://www.armenian-genocide.org/musa_dagh.html).

18. Balakian, *The Burning Tigris*, p. 198.

19. Ibid., p. 204.

20. Ibid.

21. Ibid.

22. Ibid.

23. Taner Akcam (2006), *A Shameful Act: The Armenian Genocide and the Question of Turkish Responsibility* (New York: Holt Paperback), p. 179.

24. Gerard Chaliand and Yves Ternon (1983), *The Armenians: From Genocide to Resistance* (London: Zed Press), p. 16.

25. Ibid.

26. Miller, and Miller, *Survivors*.

27. Ibid., p. 183.

28. Hovannisian, "The Question of Altruism during the Armenian Genocide of 1915," p. 298.

29. Ibid., p. 296.

30. Ibid., p. 196.

31. Ibid., p. 301.

32. Ibid. p. 300.

33. Miller, and Miller, *Survivors*, p. 183-184.

34. Richard G. Hovannisian (1992), *The Armenian Genocide: History, Politics, Ethics* (New York: St. Martin's Press).

35. Ibid. and Akcam, *A Shameful Act*.

36. Hovannisian, "The Question of Altruism during the Armenian Genocide of 1915," p. 293.

37. Ibid.

38. G.B. Graber (1996), *Caravans to Oblivion: The Armenian Genocide, 1915* (New York: J. Wiley Publishing); Balakian, *The Burning Tigris* and Vahakn Dadrian (1995), *The History of the Armenian Genocide: Ethnic Conflict from the Balkans to Anatolia* (Providence: Berghahn Book).

39. Hovannisian , *The Armenian Genocide*, Yves Ternon (1990), *The Armenians: History of A Genocide* (Delmar: Caravan Books) and Miller, and Miller, *Survivors*.

40. Mahmood Mamdani (2001), *When Victims Become Killers Colonialism, Nativism, and the Genocide in Rwanda* (Princeton: Princeton University Press) and Howard Adelman and Astri Suhrke (2000), *The Path of a Genocide: The Rwanda Crisis from Uganda to Zaire* (London: Transaction Publishers).

41. Fergal Keane (1995), *Season of Blood: A Rwandan Journey* (New York: Penguin Books USA Inc.) and Gerard Prunier (1995), *The Rwandan Crisis: History of A Genocide* (New York: Columbia University Press).

42. Ibid., and Alim Taisier et al. eds. (1999), *Civil Wars in Africa: Roots and Resolution* (Canada: McGill-Queen's University Press).

43. Peter Uvin (1998), *Aiding Violence The Development Enterprise in Rwanda* (West Harford: Kumarian Press) and Arthur Klinghoffer (1998), *The International Dimension of Genocide in Rwanda* (New York: New York University Press).

44. Valerie Rosoux (2006), "The Figure of the Righteous Individual in Rwanda," *International Social Science Journal* 58: 491-499.

45. General Romeo Dallaire (2003), *Shaking Hands with the Devil* (Canada: Random House).

46. Frontline (2004), "Interview General Romeo Dallaire" *Ghosts of Rwanda* (Retrieved on August 12, 2010 from http://www.pbs.org/wgbh/pages/frontline/ shows/ghosts/interviews/dallaire.html).

47. Adelman and Suhrke, *The Path of a Genocide* and Prunier, *The Rwandan Crisis: History of A Genocide*.

48. Rosoux, "The Figure of the Righteous Individual in Rwanda."

49. Paul Rusesabagina (2006), *An Ordinary Man* (New York: Penguin Group), p. 89.

50. African Rights (2002), *A True Humanitarian* (retrieved at http://www.human-rightsblog.org/reports/Wilkens.pdf).

51. Ibid.

52. Ibid.

53. Ibid.

54. Ibid.

55. Ibid.

56.   Ibid.

57.   SURF, *Heroes of Our Time: Rwandan Courage and Survival* (retrieved on May 26, 2010 at http://www.survivors-fund.org.uk/assets/docs/exhibition/surf-hereos-exhibition-web.pdf).

58.   Ibid.

59.   Erwin Staub, Laurie Ann Pearlman, et. al (2005), "Healing, Reconciliation, Forgiving and the Prevention of Violence after Genocide or Mass Killing: An Intervention and its Experimental Evaluation in Rwanda," *Journal of Social and Clinical Psychology* 24: 297-334.

60.   Raymond G. Helmick and Rodney L. Petersen eds. (2001), *Forgiveness and Reconciliation: Religion, Public Policy, and Conflict Transformation* (Pennsylvania: Templeton Foundation Press) and Robert D. Enright, Suzanne Freedman and Julio Rique (1998) "The Psychology of Interpersonal Forgiveness," in Robert Enright and Joanna North eds. *Exploring Forgiveness* (Madison: University of Wisconsin Press): 46–62.

61.   Eugenia Zorbas (2004), "Reconciliation in Post-Genocide Rwanda," *African Journal of Legal Studies* 1: 29-52.

62.   Rory Carroll (18 December 2003), "Genocide Witnesses 'Killed to Stop Testimony'" (retrieved at http://www.guardian.co.uk/world/2003/dec/18/rorycarroll).

63.   Jon Silverman (29 January 2004), "Rwanda's Song of Reconciliation," *BBC News* (Retrieved at http://news.bbc.co.uk/2/hi/programmes/from_our_own_correspondent/3439525.stm).

64.   P. Kanyangara, B. Rime, P. Philippot and V. Yzerbyt (2007), "Collective Rituals, Emotional Climate and Intergroup Perception: Participation in 'Gacaca' Tribunals and Assimilation of the Rwandan Genocide," *Journal of Social Issues* 63: 387-403.

65.   Ibid., p. 401.

66.   Adelman and Suhrke, *The Path of a Genocide*.

CHAPTER 6: THE NATURE OF GOODNESS

1.   Daniel Batson (1991), *The Altruism Question: Toward a Social-Psychological Answer* (Hillsdale: Lawrence Erlbaum Associates).

2.   Desmond Tutu and Mpho Tutu (2010), *Made for Goodness: And Why This Makes All the Difference* (New York: Harper Collins), p. 5.

3.   Dacher Keltner Jeremy Adam Smith and Jeremy Marsh eds. (2010), *The Compassionate Instinct: The Science of Human Goodness* (New York: W.W. Norton & Company).

4.   Stephen G. Post and Jill Neimark (2007), *Why Good Things Happen to Good People* (New York: Broadway Books).

5.   Nel Noddings and Paul J. Shore (1984), *Awakening the Inner Eye: Intuition in Education* (New York: Teachers College Columbia University).

6.   Svetlana Broz (2004), *Good People in an Evil Time: Portraits of Complicity and Resistance in the Bosnian War,* translated by Ellen Elias-Bursac (New York: Other Press).

7.   Pumla Godobo-Madikizela and Chris Van Der Merwe eds. (2009), *Memory, Narrative, and Forgiveness: Perspectives on the Unfinished Journeys of the Past* (Cambridge: Cambridge Scholars Publishing).

8.   Samuel P. Oliner (2003), *Do Unto Others: Extraordinary Acts of Ordinary People* (Boulder: Westview Press), p. 100.

9.   Mother Teresa (2010), "All Great Quotes" (Retrieved from http://www.allgreat-quotes.com/love_quotes209.shtml on November 22, 2010).

10.   Stephen G. Post (2003), *Unlimited Love: Altruism, Compassion, and Service* (Philadelphia: Templeton Foundation Press).

11.   Samuel P. Oliner and Pearl M. Oliner (1988), *The Altruistic Personality* (New York: The Free Press)

12.   Viktor Frankl (1959), *Man's Search for Meaning* (Washington: Washington Square Press).

13.   Dean Ornish (1998), *Love and Survival: The Scientific Basis for the Healing Power of Intimacy* (New York: Harper Collins).

14.   Ibid., 189.

15.   Emile Durkheim (1951), *Suicide* (Illinois: The Free Press).

16.   Pitirim Sorokin (1954), *The Ways and Power of Love* (Boston: Beacon Press).

17.   Kalyan Sen Gupta (2005), *The Philosophy of Rabindranath Tagore* (Vermont: Ashgate Publishing Company), p. 14.

18.   World Economic Forum (2005) "Trust in Governments, Corporations and Global Institutions Continues to Decline" (Retrieved from http://www.weforum.org/en/media/Latest%20Press%20Releases/PRESSRELEASES87 on September 20, 2010)

19. Paul Ekman (2008), "Can I Trust You," in *The Greater Good* 5: 20-25, p. 25.

20. Pamela Paxton and Jeremy Smith (2008), "America's Trust Fall," in *The Greater Good* 5: 14-17.

21. Gordon Anderson (2009), *Life, Liberty, and the Pursuit of Happiness: Version 4.0* (St. Paul: Paragon House), p. xviii.

22. Robert Putnam (2000), *Bowling Alone: The Collapse and Revival of American Community* (New York: Simon and Schuster).

23. Michael Kosfeld et al. "Oxytocin Increases Trust in Humans," in *Nature* June 2005: 673-676.

24. Ibid., p. 673.

25. Oliner, *Do Unto Others.*

26. Ibid.

27. Ervin Staub (2003), *The Psychology of Good and Evil: Why Children, Adults, and Groups Help and Harm Others* (Cambridge: Cambridge University Press) and N.C. Briggs, J. Piliavin, D. Lorentzen, and G. Becker (1986), "On Willingness to be a Bone Marrow Donor," in *Transfusion* 26: 234-330.

28. Mitch Albom (1997) *Tuesdays with Morrie: An Old Man, a Young Man, and Life's Great Lesson* (New York: Doubleday).

29. Kyle Irwin, Tucker Mcgrimmon and Brent Simpson (2008), "Sympathy and Social Order," in *Social Psychology Quarterly* 71: 379-397.

30. Harold G. Koenig (2001), *Handbook of Religion and Health* (New York: Oxford University Press) and Harold G. Koenig (2002), *Spirituality in Patient Care: Why, How, When, and What* (Philadelphia: Templeton Foundation Press).

31. Lauren Wispe (1986), "The Distinction Between Sympathy and Empathy: To Call Forth a Concept, A Word Is Needed," in *Journal of Personality and Social Psychology* 50, 2: 314-321, p. 314.

32. Oliner, *Do Unto Others.*

33. N. Allen and J. Phillippe Rushton (1983), "Personality Characteristics of Community Mental Health Volunteers: A Review," in *Journal of Voluntary Action Research* 12: 36-49.

34. Allen M. Omoto and Mark Snyder (2002), "Considerations of Community: The Context and Process of Volunteerism," in *American Behavioral Scientist* 45: 846-867.

35. J. Dancy & M.L. Wynn-Dancy (1995), "The Nature of Caring in Volunteerism

within Geriatric Settings," in *Activities, Adaptation, and Aging* 20: 5-12.

36. Omoto and Snyder, "Considerations of Community."

37. Ibid.

38. Oliner, *Do Unto Others.*

39. Omoto and Snyder, "Considerations of Community."

40. N. Eisenberg, C. Valiente & C. Champion (2004), "Empathy Related Responding: Moral, Social, and Socialization Correlates," in A. G. Miller ed. *The Social Psychology of Good and Evil* (New York: Guilford Press): 386-415.

41. Ibid., 397.

42. Elliot Aronson (2004), "Reducing Hostility and Building Compassion: A Lesson from the Jigsaw Classroom," in A. G. Miller ed. *The Social Psychology of Good and Evil* (New York: Guilford Press): 469-488.

43. Anne Colby and William Damon (1992), *Some Do Care: Contemporary Lives of Moral Commitment* (New York: The Free Press).

44. Ibid., p. 298

45. Simon Wiesenthal (1998), *Sunflower: On the Possibilities and Limits of Forgiveness* (New York: Schocken Books).

46. Ibid., p. 54.

47. Rudolf Vrba (1964), *I Cannot Forgive* (Vancouver: Regent College Publishing).

48. Andrew Weil (2003), *Self Healing: Creating Natural Health for your Body and Mind* (New York: Harper Collins), p.1.

49. Samuel Oliner (2008), *Altruism, Intergroup Apology, Forgiveness, and Reconciliation* (St. Paul: Paragon House), p. 72.

50. Chris Salierno (June 1997), "Sempo Sugihara: A "Righteous Person" in *An End to Intolerance*: p. 5.

51. *Samuel Eliot Morison (1975), History of United States Naval Operations in World War II, Volume I: The Battle of the Atlantic 1939-1943 (London: Little, Brown and Company).*

52. Barry M. Sax (2003), "Higher Duty," *Reformed Judaism*, 67-76.

53. Yad Vashem, "Metropolitan Chrysostomos: Mayor Lucas Karreri," *The Righteous Among the Nations* (Retrieved from http://www1.yadvashem.org/yv/en/righteous/stories/chrysostomos_karreri.asp on September 20, 2010).

54. International Children's Surgical Foundation, "Why We Do It" (Retrieved from http://www.icsfoundation.org/why-we-do-it on October 4, 2009).

55. Rigoberta Menchu (1998), *Crossing Borders* (New York: Verso).

56. Habitat for Humanity (2010) "Habitat for Humanity" (Retrieved from http://www.habitat.org/ on October 6, 2010).

57. Wangari Maathi (2007), *Unbowed* (New York: Anchor Books).

58. Michael McCullough, Kenneth I. Pargament, Carl E. Thoresen (1999), *"Forgiveness: Theory, Research, and Practice"* (New York: The Guilford Press).

CHAPTER 7: THE WORLD OF HEROES

1. Anthony Giddens (1984), *The Constitution of Society: Outline of the Theory of Structuration* (Berkeley: University of California Press) and William H. Sewell (1992), "A Theory of Structure: Duality, Agency, and Transformation," in *The American Journal of Sociology* 98, 1: 1-29.

2. Sewell, "A Theory of Structure," p. 4.

3. Vincent Jeffries (1998), "Virtue and the Altruistic Personality," in *Sociological Perspectives* 41, 1: 151-166.

4. Bill Berkowitz and J. Macaulay eds. (1970) *Altruism and Helping Behavior: Social Psychological Studies of Some Antecedents and Consequences* (New York: Academic Press).

5. J.P. Rushton (1980), *Altruism, Socialization and Society* (New Jersey: Prentice Hall).

6. Peter Gibbon (2003), *A Call to Heroism: Renewing America's Vision of Greatness* (New York: Grove Press).

7. Ernest Becker (1971), *The Birth and Death of Meaning* (New York: The Free Press).

8. Joseph Campbell (1949), *Hero with a Thousand Faces* (Bollinger Series XVII: Princeton University Press).

9. Miriam Polster (1992), *Eve's Daughters: The Forbidden Heroism of Women* (San Francisco: Josse-Bass Publisher).

10. Anne Colby and William Damon (1992), *Some Do Care: Contemporary Lives of Moral Commitment* (New York: The Free Press) and Selwyn Becker and Alice Eagly (2004), "The Heroism of Women and Men," in *American Psychological Association* 59, 3: 163–178.

11. Oliner and Oliner, *The Altruistic Personality*.

12. Oliner, *Do Unto Others.*

13. Ibid.

14. Oliner and Oliner, *The Altruistic Personality.*

15. Goode, *The Celebration of Heroes*, p. 345.

16. Sorokin, *The Ways and Power of Love*, p. 328.

17. "Maimonides" *Wikipedia* (Retrieved on August 23, 2010 from http:// en.wikipedia.org/wiki/Maimonides).

18. Vincent Jeffries (2005), "Pitirim A. Sorokin's Integralism and Public Sociology," *The American Sociologist* 36, 3-4: 66-87.

19. Oliner, et al. *Embracing the Other.*

20. Iris Murdock (1970), *The Sovereignty of Good* (London: Routledge and Kegan Paul).

21. Paul Tillich (1968), *A Complete History of Christian Thought* (New York: Harper & Row).

22. Ibid., p. 3.

23. Ibid.

24. Kathleen Noble (1994), *The Sound of a Silver Horn: Reclaiming the Heroism in Contemporary Women's Lives* (New York: Ballantine Books), p. 5.

25. Becker and Eagly, "The Heroism of Women and Men."

26. Vicky Anderson (1993), "Gender Differences in Altruism among Holocaust Rescuers" in *Journal of Social Behavior and Personality* 8: 43–58 and Oliner and Oliner, *The Altruistic Personality.*

27. Carol Gilligan (1982), *In a Different Voice: Psychological Theory and Women's Development.* (Cambridge: Harvard University Press), p. 7.

28. Donna Rosenberg (2001), *World Mythology* (Lincolnwood: National Textbook Co.).

29. Ann McGovern (1990), *The Secret Soldier: The Story of Deborah Sampson* (New York: Scholastic Inc.).

30. Ruth Sidel (2006), *Unsung Heroines: Single Mothers and the American Dream* (Berkeley: University of California Press).

31. Ibid., p. 80.

32. Kathryn Bel Monte (1998), *African-American Heroes and Heroines of America:*

150 True Stories of African-American Heroism (Lifetime Books).

33. Colby and Damon, *Some Do Care*.

34. Ibid., p. 283.

35. Oliner, *Do Unto Others*.

36. Cara Buckley, "Man is Rescued By Stranger on Subway Tracks," *New York Times*, January 3, 2007 (Retrieved on September 22, 2010 at http://www.nytimes.com/2007/01/03/nyregion/03life.html).

37. "The Village of Le Chambon-sur-Lignon: André & Magda Trocmé, Daniel Trocmé," *The Righteous Among the Nations* (Retrieved on October 4, 2009 at http://www1.yadvashem.org/yv/en/righteous/stories/trocme.asp) and Oliner, *The Altruistic Personality*.

38. Becker and Eagly, "The Heroism of Women and Men."

39. Oliner, *Do Unto Others*.

40. Ibid.

41. Ibid.

42. Bill Berkowitz (1987), *Local Heroes* (Maryland: Lexington Books).

43. Ibid.

44. Robert N. Bellah, Richard Madsen, William M.Sullivan, Ann Swindler & Steven M. Tipton (1985), *Habits of the Heart: Individualism and Commitment in American Life* (New York: Harper Row).

45. Ibid., p. 153.

46. Allan H. Pasco (1997), *Sick Heroes* (England: University of Exeter Press).

47. Eugene Weber (1995), *The Western Tradition* (Lexington: D.C. Heath and Company).

48. John W. Roberts (1989), *From Tricksters to Bad Men: The Black Folk Hero in Slavery and Freedom* (Philadelphia: University of PA Press).

49. Gibbon , *A Call to Heroism*, p. 9.

50. Thomas Carlyle (1966), *On Heroes, Hero-Worship and the Heroic in History* (Nebraska: University of Nebraska Press).

51. Sidney Hook (1980), *Philosophy and Public Policy* (Illinois: Southern Illinois University Press), p. 158.

52. Campbell, *Hero with a Thousand Faces*.

53.   Becker, *The Birth and Death of Meaning*.

54.   Ibid., p. 78.

55.   Ibid., p. 76-77.

CHAPTER 8: SUMMARY AND CONCLUSION

1.   Martin Buber (1958), *I and Thou* (New York: Charles Scribner's Sons).

2.   Baran Zeyno & Onur Sazak, "The Ambassador: How a Turkish diplomat Saved 20,000 Jews during the Holocaust," *The Weekly Standard* (Reprinted in *Together* April 2009, p. 10).

3.   Peter Singer (2009), *The Life You Can Save* (New York: Random House) (Reprinted in *Newsweek* March 2009, p. 48).

4.   Peggy Begley (4 March 2009), "Adventures in Good and Evil," *Newsweek*: 46.

5.   Ervin Staub (1989), *The Roots of Evil: The Origins of Genocide and Other Group Violence* (Cambridge: Cambridge University Press).

6.   Herbert C. Kelman (1973), "Violence Without Moral Restraint: Reflections on the Dehumanization of Victims and Victimizer," in *Journal of Social Issues* 29: 25-61.

7.   Robert J. Lifton (1986), *The Nazi Doctors: Medical Killing and the Psychology of Genocide* (New York: Basic Books).

8.   Rollo May (1967), *Psychology and the Human Dilemma* (New York: W.W. Norton and Company, Inc.).

9.   Ibid., p. 286.

10.   Ibid., p. 300.

11.   Philip Zimbardo (2007), *The Lucifer Effect: Understanding How Good People Turn Evil* (New York: Random House).

Bibliography

Chapter 1: Follow the Leader

Aho, James A. 1994. *This Thing of Darkness: A Sociology of the Enemy.* Seattle: University of Washington Press.

Baron, Lawrence. 1988. "The Historical Context of Rescue." In *The Altruistic Personality.* Ed. Samuel P. Oliner and Pearl M. Oliner. New York: Free Press, 13-48.

Bauer, Y. 1982. *A History of the Holocaust.* New York: Franklin Watts.

Browning, Christopher. 1992. *Ordinary Men.* New York: Harper Collins.

Dawidowicz, Lucy. 1975. *The War Against the Jews: 1933-1945.* New York: Hole, Rinehart and Winston.

Des Forges, Alison. 1999. *Leave None to Tell the Story.* New York: Human Rights Watch.

Felice, Renzo De. 1976. *Fascism: An Informal Introduction to its Theory and Practice.* New Jersey: Transaction Books.

Gilbert, M. 1985. *The Holocaust: A History of the Jews of Europe During the Second World War.* New York: Holt, Rinehart & Winston.

Goldhagen, Daniel. 1996. *Hitler's Willing Executioners.* London: Abacus.

Hay, Malcolm. 1951. *The Foot of Pride: The Pressure of Christendom on the People of Israel for 1900 Years.* Boston, MA: Beacon Press.

Hilberg, Raul. 1961. *The Destruction of European Jews.* New York: Quadrangle Books Inc.

Hogan, Kevin and James Speakman. 2006. *Covert Persuasion: Psychological Tactics and Tricks to Win the Game.* New Jersey: John Wiley and Sons, Inc.

Julius, Anthony. 2010. *Trials of the Diaspora: A History of Anti-Semitism in England.* USA: Oxford University Press.

Lipstadt, Deborah. 1994. *Denying the Holocaust: The Growing Assault on Truth and Memory.* New York: Plume.

Miller, Alice. 1984. *For Your Own Good: Hidden Cruelty in Child-Rearing and the Roots of Violence*. New York: Farrar, Straus and Giroux.

Oliner, Samuel. 2008. *Altruism, Intergroup Apology, Forgiveness and Reconciliation*. St. Paul: Paragon House.

Oliner, Samuel. 2003. *Do Unto Others: Extraordinary Acts of Ordinary People*. Boulder: Westview Press.

Oliner, Samuel P. and Pearl M. Oliner. 1995. *Toward a Caring Society: Ideas into Action*. Westport: Praeger.

Oliner, Samuel P. and Pearl M. Oliner. 1988. *The Altruistic Personality*. New York: Free Press.

Opotow, S. 1990. "Deterring Moral Exclusion." *Journal of Social Issues*, 46: 173-182.

Staub, Ervin. 1989. *The Roots of Evil: The Origin of Genocide and Other Group Violence*. New York: Cambridge University Press.

Toland, John. 1977. *Adolph Hitler*. New York: Ballantine Books.

Wiesel, Elie. 1960. *Night*. New York: Hill and Wang.

Wistrich, Robert E. 2010. *A Lethal Obsession: Anti-Semitism from Antiquity to the Global Jihad*. New York: Random House.

Wyman, D.S. 1984. *The Abandonment of the Jews: America and the Holocaust, 1941-1945*. New York: Pantheon Books.

Zimbardo, Philip. 2007. *The Lucifer Effect: Understanding How Good People Turn Evil*. New York: Random House.

CHAPTER 2: HOW COULD THEY DO THAT?

Aho, James A. 1994. *This Thing of Darkness: A Sociology of The Enemy*. Seattle: University of Washington Press.

Alexander, Jeffrey C. 2003. *The Meanings of Social Life: A Cultural Sociology*. New York: Oxford University Press.

Alexander, Jeffrey C. 2001. "Toward a Sociology of Evil: Getting Beyond Modernist Common Sense about the Alternative to the Good." in *Rethinking Evil*, edited by Maria Pia Lara. Ewing, NJ: University of California Press, 153-172.

Arendt, Hannah. 1963. *Eichmann in Jerusalem: A Report on the Banality of Evil*. New York: The Viking Press.

Aristotle. n.d.. *Nicomachean Ethics.* Accessed online on February 16, 2006 at http://plato.stanford.edu/entries/aristotle-ethics/.

Asch, Solomon E. 1951. "Effects of Group Pressure upon the Modification and Distortion of Judgement." In *Groups, Leadership and Men,* edited by Harold S. Guetzkow. Pittsburgh: Carnegie Press.

Bandura, Albert. 1990. "Selective Activation and Disengagement of Moral Control." *Journal of Social Issues* 46: 27:46.

Barnett, Victoria J. 1999. *Bystanders: Conscience and Complicity during the Holocaust.* Westport: Greenwood Press.

Bauman, Zygmunt. 1989. *Modernity and the Holocaust.* New York: Cornell University Press.

Baumeister, R. F. 1997. *Evil: Inside Human Violence and Cruelty.* New York: Freeman.

Bellah Robert. 1971. "Evil and American Ethos." *Sanctions for Evil.* eds. Nevitt Samdord and Craig Comstock. San Francisco: Jossey-Bass.

Browning, Christopher. 1992. *Ordinary Men: Reserve Police Battalion 101 and the Final Solution in Poland.* New York: Harper Collins.

Broz, Svetlana. 2004. *Good People in an Evil Time.* New York: Other Press.

Carey, Benedict. 2005. "For the Worst of Us, the Diagnosis May be Evil." *New York Times,* Tuesday, February 8, D1.

Carey, Benedict. 2006. "When Death Is on the Docket, The Moral Compass Wavers." *New York Times,* Tuesday, February 7, D1.

Cohen, Elie A. 1953. *Human Behavior in the Concentration Camp.* New York: Grosset and Dunlap.

Coles, Robert. 1989. *The Call of Stories: Teaching and the Moral Imagination.* Boston: Houghton Mifflin Co.

Dawidowicz, Lucy S. 1975. *The War Against the Jews 1933-1945.* New York: Holt, Rinehart and Winston.

Doob Leonard. 1978. *Panoramas of Evil.* Connecticut: Greenwood Press.

Freud, A. 1936. *Ego and the Mechanisms of Defense.* London: Hogarth.

Fromm, Erich. 1973. *The Anatomy of Human Destructiveness.* London: Macmillan Press.

Frontline. 1985. "A Class Divided." WGBH Educational Foundation video presentation of the 1968 Jane Elliott experiment. Yale University Films, broadcast March 26, 1985.

Goldhagen, Daniel Jonah. 1996. *Hitler's Willing Executioners: Ordinary Germans and The Holocaust.* New York: Alfred A. Knopf.

Gross, Jan T. 2002. *Neighbors: The Destruction of the Jewish Community in Jedwabne, Poland.* New York: Penguin Books.

Haley, Alex. 1976. *Roots.* New York: Doubleday.

Hay, Malcolm. 1951. *The Foot of Pride: The Pressure of Christendom on The People of Israel for 1900 Years.* Boston: Beacon Press.

Hick , John. 1985. *Evil and the God of Love.* London: Macmillan/Palgrave Press.

Janis, Irving. 1982. *Victims of Groupthink.* Boston: Houghton Mifflin.

Janis, Irving. 1971. "Groupthink Among Policy Makers." *Sanctions for Evil.* eds. Nevitt Sanford and Craig Comstock. San Francisco: Jossey-Bass.

Kelman, Herbert C. 1973. "Violence Without Moral Restraint: Reflections on the Dehumanization of Victims and Victimizers." *Journal of Social Issues* 29 (4): 25-62.

Klein, Richard Libowitz, Marcia Sachs Little, and Sharon Steeley. St. Paul, MN: Paragon House.

Lara, Maria Pia. 2001. "Introduction: Contemporary Perspectives." in *Rethinking Evil*, edited by Maria Pia Lara. Ewing, NJ: University of California Press, 1-14.

Leitenberg, Milton. 1997. "Rwanda and Burundi Genocide: A Case Study of Neglect and Indifference." in *Race, Ethnicity, and Gender*, edited by Samuel P. Oliner and Phillip T. Gay. Dubuque: Kendall-Hunt Publishing Company, 253-279.

Lieb, Julian. 2006. "Hatred Often Lurks in the Shadows of Mania." Accessed online on March 1, 2006 at http://www.codoh.com/newrevoices/nrandom/nrando-mania.html.

Lifton, R.J. 1986. *The Nazi Doctors: Medical Killing and The Psychology of Genocide.* New York: Basic Books.

Lorenz, Konrad. 1963. *On Aggression.* Florida: Harcourt Brace & Company.

Milgram, Stanley. 1969. *Obedience to Authority: An Experimental View.* New York: Harper Colophon Books.

Miller, A. (2004). "What can the Milgram obedience experiments tell us about the Holocaust? Generalizing From the Social Psychology Laboratory." In *The Social Psychology of Good and Evil*, ed. A. Miller. New York: Guilford, 193-239.

Miller, Alice. 1983. *For Your Own Good: Hidden Cruelty in Child-Rearing and the Roots of Violence.* New York: Farrar Strauss Giroux.

Miller, Alice. n.d. Interview with Natural Child Project. Accessed online on February 15, 2006 at http://www.naturalchild.com/alice_miller/roots_violence.html.

Patterson, David. 2005. "The Complicity of Modern Philosophy in the Extermination of the Jews." in *The Genocidal Mind: Selected Papers from the 32nd Annual Scholars' Conference on the Holocaust and the Churches*, edited by Dennis B. 105-123. St. Paul: Paragon House.

Plato. [1999]. Timaeus. Translated by Benjamin Jowett. Hazelton, PA: Pennsylvania State University Electronic Classics Series. Accessed online on January 10, 2006 at http://www2.hn.psu.edu/faculty/jmanis/plato/timaeus.pdf.

Power, Samantha. 2004. "Dying in Darfur." *The New Yorker*. Accessed online on March 8, 2006 at http://www.newyorker.com/fact/content/?040830fa_fact1.

Prunier, Gerard. n.d. "Interview with Fergal Keane." *Frontline*. PBS. Accessed online on March 9, 2006 at http://www.pbs.org/wgbh/pages/frontline/shows/rwanda/etc/interview.html.

Rosenberg, Marshall. 1999. *Nonviolent Communication: A Language on Compassion*. Encinitas: Puddle Dancer Press.

Rosenthal, Ludwig. 1979. *The Final Solution to the Jewish Question*. Berkeley: Western Jewish History Center: Judah L. Magnes Memorial Museum.

Rubenstein, Richard L. 1975. *The Cunning of History: The Holocaust and the American Future*. New York: Harper & Row.

Sanford, N. 1971. "Authoritarianism and Social Destructiveness." *Sanctions for Evil* eds. N. Sanford and C. Comstock San Francisco: Jossey-Bass.

Sarbin, Theodore R. 1986. "The Narrative as Root Metaphor for Psychology." in *Narrative Psychology: The Storied Nature of Human Conduct*, edited by Theodore R. Sarbin. New York: Praeger, 3-21.

Shirer, William L. 1941. *Berlin Diary: The Journal of a Foreign Correspondent*. New York: Alfred A. Knopf.

Staub, Ervin. 2000. "Preventing Genocide: Activating Bystanders, Helping Victims and the Creation of Caring." *The (e)Journal of Cultural Criticism*. Accessed online on March 6, 2006 at http://www.othervoices.org/2.1staub/preventing.html.

Staub, Ervin. 1989. *The Roots of Evil: The Origins of Genocide and Other Group Violence*. Cambridge: Cambridge University Press.

Taylor, Richard. 2000. *Good and Evil*. New York: Prometheus Books.

Tiger, Lionel. 1987. *The Manufacture of Evil: Ethics, Evolution, and the Industrial*

System. New York: Harper & Row Publishers.

Toland, John. 1977. *Adolf Hitler*. London: Book Club Associates.

Tulving, Endel. 1983. *Elements of Episodic Memory*. New York: Oxford University Press.

University of Arkansas. 2004. "But is it Really Cheating?" UA Researcher Examines Moral Judgment vs. Behavior in College Classrooms." Accessed online February 20, 2006 at http://listserv.uark.edu/scripts/wa.exe?A2=ind0409&L=daily_headlines&P=906.

Valentina's Nightmare. 1997. *Frontline*. (Videotape). Produced by BBC Television, April 1, 1997. Transcript accessed online on March 2, 2006 at http://www.pbs.org/wgbh/pages/frontline/shows/rwanda/etc/script.html.

Vincent, Paul. 2005. "The Genocidal Mind: In Search of a Definition." in *The Genocidal Mind: Selected Papers from the 32nd Annual Scholar's Conference on the Holocaust and the Churches*, Dennis B. Klein, Richard Libowitz et al. 39-59. St. Paul: Paragon House.

Vitz, Paul C. 1990. "The Use of Stories in Moral Development: New Psychological Reasons for an Old Education Method." *American Psychologist* 45 (6): 709-720.

Vogt, Hannah. 1965. *The Burden of Guilt: A Short History of Germany 1914-1945*. New York: Oxford University Press.

Waller, James. 2007. *Becoming Evil: How Ordinary People Commit Genocide and Mass Killing*. Oxford: Oxford University Press.

Wiesel, Elie. 1969. *Night*. New York: A Discuss Book/Avon Books.

Yale Law School. 1998. "Nuremberg Trial Page." The Avalon Project. Accessed online on February 10, 2006 at http://www.yale.edu/lawweb/avalon/imt/proc/naeve.htm.

Zimbardo, Phillip G. 2007. *The Lucifer Effect: Understanding How Good People Turn Evil*. Random House. New York

Zimbardo, Philip G. 2004. "A Situationist Perspective on the Psychology of Evil: Understanding How Good People are Transformed into Perpetrators." In *The Social Psychology of Good and Evil: Understanding Our Capacity for Kindness and Cruelty,* edited by Arthur Miller. New York: Guilford Publishers.

Zimbardo, Philip G. 2000. "The Psychology of Evil." *Eye on Psi Chi* Fall 16-19.

Zimbardo, Philip G. 1991. *Quiet Rage: The Stanford Prison Study*. (Videotape). Stanford: Leland Stanford Junior University: Academic distribution, Stanford University, 1992.

CHAPTER 3: SILENTLY STANDING BY

Arendt, Hannah. 1979. *The Origins of Totalitarianism*. San Diego: Harcourt Brace Jovanovich.

Associated Press. 2008. *7 Bosnian Serbs Guilty of Genocide 4 Others Acquitted in Srebrenica Massacre*. Retrieved on August 6, 2008 (http://www.sfgate.com/cgi-bin/article.cgi?f=/c/a/2008/07/30/MN7S121D1I.DTL&hw=bosnia+leader+sentenced&sn=002&sc=659).

Barnett, Michael N. 2002. *Eyewitness to A Genocide: The United Nations and Rwanda*. Ithaca: Cornell University Press.

Barnett, Victoria J. 1999. *Bystanders: Conscious and Complicity During the Holocaust*. Westport: Greenwood Press.

Bar-On, D. 2001. "The Bystander in Relation to the Victim & the Perpetrator: Today and During the Holocaust." *Social Justice Research* 14 (2): 125-148.

Barr, Dennis J. 2005. "Early Adolescents' Reflection on Social Justice: Facing History and Ourselves in Practice and Assessment." *Intercultural Education* 16 (2):145-160.

Bar-Zohar, Michael. 1998. *Beyond Hitler's Grasp: The Heroic Rescue of Bulgaria's Jews*. Massachusetts: Adams Media Corporation.

Bauman, Zygmunt. 1989. *Modernity and the Holocaust*. Ithaca, NY: Cornell University.

Beaman, A. L., Barnes, P. J., Klentz, B. & McQuirk, B. (1978) "Increasing helping rates through information dissemination: teaching pays." *Personality and Social Psychology Bulletin*, 4(3), 406–411.

Bell, Michael, M. 2004. *Farming for Us All: Practical Agriculture and the Cultivation of Sustainability*. University Park: The Pennsylvania State University Press.

Berry, Wendell. 1977. *The Unsettling of America: Culture and Agriculture*. San Francisco: Sierra Club Books.

Blumer, Herbert. 1969. *Symbolic Interactionism: Perspective and Method*. New Jersey: Prentice- Hall.

Broz, Svetlana. 2006. "Courage Under Fire." *Greater Good*, Fall/Winter, 10-13.

Cesarani, David and Paul A. Levine. 2002. *Bystanders to the Holocaust: A Re-evaluation*. Portland: Frank Cass.

Chew, Sing. 2001. *World Ecological Degradation: Accumulation, Urbanization, and Deforestation 3000 B.C.– A.D. 2000*. New York: Rowman & Littlefield Publishers.

Chomsky, Noam. 1991. *Media Control: The Spectacular Achievements of Propaganda*. New York: Seven Stories Press.

Cushman, Thomas and Stjepan Gabriel Meštrović. 1996. *This Time We Knew: Western Responses to Genocide in Bosnia*. New York: New York University Press.

Darley, J and Latané, B 1968. "Bystander Intervention in Emergencies: Diffusion of Responsibility." *Journal of Personality and Social Psychology* 8 (4): 377-383.

Douglas, Mary. 1986. *How Institutions Think*. Syracuse: Syracuse University Press.

Durkheim, Emile. [1933] 1984. *The Division of Labor in Society*. New York: Free Press.

Forsyth, Don. 2004. "Big Ball of Blame." *Style Weekly*. Retrieved August 5, 2009 (http://oursocialworld.blogspot.com/).

Freeman, Naomi, J. 2006. "Socioeconomic Status and Belief in a *Just World*: Sentencing of Criminal Defendants." *Journal of Applied Social Psychology* (36): 2379-2394.

Gahm, Gregory A., Barbara A. Lucenko, Paul D. Retzlaff, and Seiya Fukuda. 2007. "Relative Impact of Adverse Events and Screened Symptoms of Posttraumatic Stress Disorder and Depression Among Active Duty Soldiers Seeking Mental Health Care," *Journal of Clinical Psychology* 63 (3): 199-211.

Glazer, Sarah. 2004. "Stopping Genocide: Should the U.S. and U.N. Take Action in Sudan?" *The CQ Researcher* 14 (29): 685-708.

Goldhagen, Daniel Jonah. 1996. *Hitler's Willing Executioners: Ordinary Germans and the Holocaust*. New York: Alfred A. Knopf.

Greene-Shortridge, Tiffany M., Thomas W. Britt, and Carl A. Castro. 2007. "The Stigma of Mental Health Problems in the Military," *Military Medicine* 172 (2): 157-161.

Grünfeld, Fred and Anke Huijboom. 2007. *The Failure to Prevent Genocide in Rwanda: the Role of Bystanders*. Boston: Martinus Nijhoff.

Hodge, Charles W, Artin Terhakopian, Carl A. Castro, Stephen C. Messer, and Charles C. Engel. 2007. "Association of Posttraumatic Stress Disorder with Somatic Symptoms, Health Care Visits, and Absenteeism Among Iraq War Veterans," *American Journal of Psychiatry* 164 (1): 150-153.

Kodas, Michael. 2008. *High Crimes: The Fate of Everest in an Age of Greed*. New York: Hyperion Books.

Lambert, Alan, J. and Katherine Raichle. 2000. "The Role of Political Ideology in Mediating Judgments of Blame in Rape Victims and Their Assailants: A Test of the Just World, Personal Responsibility, and Legitimization Hypotheses." *Personality and Social Psychology Bulletin* (26): 853-86.

Latané, B and Darley, J. 1970. *The Unresponsive Bystander: Why Doesn't He Help?* New York: Appleton- Century- Crofts.

_____. 1975. *Help in a Crisis: Bystander Response to an Emergency.* Morriston: General Learning Press.

Latané, B. & Nida, S. 1981. "Ten Years of Research on Group Size and Helping." *Psychological Bulletin* 89 (2): 308-324.

LeBor, Adam. 2006. *"Complicity with Evil": The United Nations in the Age of Modern Genocide.* New Haven: Yale University Press.

Levine, R.M. 1999. Rethinking Bystander Non-Intervention: Social Categorisation and The Evidence of Witnesses at The James Bulger Murder Trial. *Human Relations* 52: 1133-1155.

Levine, Lloyd E. 2007. "One Step Closer to Lights Out for the Incandescent." *California Progress Report.* Retrieved August 5, 2009 (http://www.californiaprogressreport.com/2007/04/one_step_closer.html).

Lyons, Robert and Scott Straus. 2006. *Intimate Enemy: Images and Voices of the Rwandan Genocide.* Cambridge: Zone Books.

Lyson, Thomas A. 2004. *Civic Agriculture: Reconnecting Farm, Food, and Community.* Lebanon: Tufts University Press.

Manning, R., Levine, M. & Collins, A. 2007. "The Kitty Genovese Murder and the Social Psychology of Helping: The Parable of the 38 Witnesses" *American Psychologist* 62 (6): 555-562.

May, Larry. 1990. "Collective Inaction and Shared Responsibility." *Nous* 24 (2): 269-277.

Mino, Tamaki. 2006. *"Ijime* (Bullying) in Japanese Schools: A Product of Japanese Education Based on Group Conformity." Presented at the Second Annual Rhizomes: Re-Visioning Boundaries Conference of The School of Languages and Comparative Cultural Studies, February 24-25, Brisbane, Australia.

Morton, Lois W. 2003. "Rural Health Policy." Pp. 290-302 in *Challenges for Rural America in the Twenty-First Century*, edited by David L. Brown and Louis E. Swanson. University Park, PA: The Pennsylvania State University.

Mueller, John. 2000. "The Banality of 'Ethnic War'." *International Security.* 25: 42-70.

Oliner, Samuel P. 2008. *Altruism, Intergroup Apology, Forgiveness and Reconciliation.* St. Paul: Paragon House.

_____. 2003. *Do Unto Others: Extraordinary Acts of Ordinary People.* Boulder: Westview Press.

Oliner, Samuel and Pearl Oliner. 1988. *The Altruistic Personality: Rescuers of Jews in Nazi Europe*. New York: The Free Press.

Oliver, Pamela and Gerald Marwell. 1993. *The Critical Mass in Collective Action: A Micro-Social Theory*. New York: Cambridge University Press.

Power, Samantha. 2003. *A Problem from Hell: America and the Age of Genocide*. New York: Basic Books.

Pratkanis, Anthony and Elliot Aronson. 1992. *Age of Propaganda: The Everyday Use and Abuse of Persuasion*. New York: Henry Holt and Co.

RefugeeInternational.org. 2005. *Washington Circle Luncheon with Author Samantha Power*. Retrieved on July 7, 2007 (http://www.refugeesinternational.org/ content/event/detail/5027/).

Reicher, S., Cassidy, C., Hopkins, N. & Levine, M. 2006. "Saving Bulgaria's Jews: An Analysis of Social Identity and the Mobilisation of Social Solidarity. *European Journal of Social Psychology* 36: 49-72.

Reisner, Ann. 2003. "Newspaper Construction of a Moral Farmer." *Rural Sociology* (68): 46-63.

Ridgeway, Cecilia L. 1993. "Gender, Status, and the Social Psychology of Expectations" in *Theory on Gender/Femenism on Theory*, edited by Paula England. New York: Aldine de Gruyter, 175-197.

Shaffer, Jack and Samuel Oliner. 1995. "Disaffiliation from Hate Groups." Presented at Pacific Sociological Association, 1995.

Shotland, Lance R. and Charles A. Stebbins. 1983. "Emergency and Cost as Determinants of Helping Behavior and the Slow Accumulation of Social Psychological Knowledge." *Social Psychology Quarterly* 46 (1): 36-46.

Simons, Marlise and Neil MacFarquhar. 2009. "Court Issues Arrest Warrant for Sudan's Leader." *The NewYork Times*. Retrieved May 15, 2009 (http://www. nytimes.com/2009/03/05/world/africa/05court.html).

Singh, Vishavjit. 2002. "A Nation of Bystanders." *Sikh Spectrum*. Retrieved May 15, 2009 (http://www.sikhspectrum.com/102002/nation.htm).

Sprinz, Detlef F., and Tapani Vaahtoranta. 1994. The Interest-Based Explanation of International Environmental Policy. *International Organization* 48 (1):77-105.

Staub, Ervin. 1996. "Responsibility, Helping, Aggression, and Evil." *Psychological Inquiry* 7 (3): 252-254.

_____. 1989(a). *The Roots of Evil: The Origins of Genocide and Other Group Violence*. New York: Cambridge University Press.

_____. 1989(b)."The Evolution of Bystanders, German Psychoanalysts, and Lessons for Today." *Political Psychology* (10): 39-52.

_____. 1985. "The Psychology of Perpetrators and Bystanders." *Political Psychology* 6 (1): 61-85.

Starr, Amory. 2004. "How Can Anti-Imperialism Not Be Anti-Racist? The North American Anti-Globalization Movement." *Journal of World Systems Research* 10 (1): 118-151.

Steinfeldt, Irena. 2002. *How Was it Humanly Possible?: A Study of Perpetrators and Bystanders During the Holocaust: Pedagogical Guidebook.* Jerusalem: International School for Holocaust Studies Beth Shalom Holocaust Memorial Centre.

Stephen, Lynn. *Zapata Lives!: History and Cultural Politics in Southern Mexico.* Berkeley: University of California Press.

Syed M. Ahmed, Jeanne P. Lemkau, Nichol Nealeigh, Barbara Mann. 2001. "Barriers to Healthcare Access in a Non-Elderly Urban Poor American Population." *Health & Social Care In the Community* 9 (6): 445–453.

Tice, Dianne M. and Roy F. Baumeister. 1985. "Masculinity Inhibits Helping in Emergencies: Personality Does Predict the Bystander Effect." *Journal of Personality and Social Psychology* 49 (2): 420-428.

Toye, Suelan. 2005. "Silent Bystanders No More: Movie Inspires Teachers, Students to Act (Teachers, Students Send Stern Message to UN.)" *News @ University of Toronto, Social Sciences, Business, and Law.* Retrieved on March 6, 2006 (http://www.news.utoronto.ca/bin6/050429-1307.asp).

United States Holocaust Memorial Museum. 2010. "Overview: Sudan." Retrieved on August 3, 2010 (http://www.ushmm.org/genocide/take_action/atrisk/region/sudan).

VandeHei, Jim. 2005. "In Break with U.N., Bush Calls Sudan Killings Genocide." *Washington Post,* June 2, p. A19. Retrieved June 8, 2007 (http://www.washingtonpost.com/wp-dyn/content/article/2005/06/01/AR2005060101725.html).

Van Herp, Michel, Veronique Parqué, Edward Rackley, and Nathan Ford. 2003. "Mortality, Violence, and Lack of Access to Healthcare in the Democratic Republic of Congo," *Disasters* 27 (2): 141–153.

Vetlesen, Arne Johan. 2000. "Genocide: A Case for the Responsibility of the Bystander." *Journal of Peace Research* (37) 4: 519-532.

Chapter 4: Paving the Way to Resistance

Ainsztein, Reuben. 1974. *Jewish Resistance in Nazi-Occupied Eastern Europe*. New York: Barnes and Nobles Books.

Alexy, Trudi. 1993. *The Mezuzah in the Madonna's Foot: Marranos and Other Secret Jews*. San Francisco: Harpers.

Arendt, H. 1965. *Eichman in Jerusalem*. New York: Viking Compass.

Barbalet, J.M. 1985. "Power and Resistance." *The British Journal of Sociology* 36: 531-548.

Bauer, Yehuda. 2001. *History of the Holocaust*. New York: Holmes and Meier.

Bender, Sara. 2008. *The Jews of Bialystok During World War II and the Holocaust*. New Hampshire: University Press of New England.

Berenbaum, Michael. 1993. *The World Must Know: The History of the Holocaust as Told in the United States Holocaust Memorial Museum*. Boston: Little, Brown.

Bettelheim, B. 1971. *The Informed Heart: Autonomy in a Mass Age*. New York: Avon.

Blatt, Toivi Thomas. 1997. *From the Ashes of Sobibor A Story of Survival*. Illinois: Northwestern University Press.

Blatt, Toivi Thomas. 2004. *Sobibor The Forgotten Revolt A Survivors Report*. Issaquah, Washington: Fifth paperback printing.

Bowman, Steven. 2006. *Jewish Resistance in Wartime Greece*. Portland: Vallentine Mitchell.

Cohen, Rich. 2000. *The Avengers: A Jewish War Story*. New York: Borzoi Books.

Dawidowicz, Lucy S. 1976. *A Holocaust Reader*. New York: Behrman House Inc.

Deschner, Gunther. 1972. *Warsaw Rising*. New York: Ballantine Books Inc.

Dimsdale, Joel E. 1980. *Survivors, Victims, and Perpetrators Essays on the Nazi Holocaust*. New York: Hemisphere Publishing Corporation.

Duffy, Peter. 2003. *The Bielski Brothers The True Story of Three Men Who Defied The Nazis, Saved 1,200 Jews, and Built a Village in the Forest*. New York: Harper Collins Publishers Inc.

Eckman, Lester and Lazar, Chaim. 1977. *The Jewish Resistance: The History of the Jewish Partisans in Lithuania and White Russia under Nazi Occupation, 1940-45*. New York: Shengold.

Feig, G. Konnilyn. 1979. *Hitler's Death Camps: The Sanity of Madness*. New York: Holmes and Meier Publishers.

Fein, Helen. 1997. "Genocide by Attrition 1939-1993: The Warsaw Ghetto, Cambodia, and Sudan: Links between Human Rights, Health, and Mass Death." *Health and Human Rights* 2: 10-45.

Frankl, Viktor. 2006. *Man's Search for Meaning*. Boston: Beacon Books.

Garlinski, Jozef. 1975. *Fighting Auschwitz*. Connecticut: Faswcett Crest Books.

Gilbert, Martin. 1985. *The Holocaust: A History of the Jews in Europe During the Second World War*. New York: Holt, Rinehart & Winston.

Gutman, Israel. 1994. *Resistance The Warsaw Ghetto Uprising*. New York: Miles Lerman Center for the Study of Jewish Resistance of the United States Holocaust Memorial Museum.

Halivni, T.H. 1979. "The Birkenau Revolt: the Poles Prevent a Timely Insurrection." *Jewish Social Studies*. 41: 123-154.

Hanania, Joseph. 2005. "When Risk Taking Becomes a Victim." *Forward.com*. Retrieved on August 17, 2010. http://www.aceupoursleeve.com/downloads/ForwardOpEd.pdf.

Harff, Babara, Ted Robert Gutt. 1988. "Toward Empirical Theory of Genocide and Politicides: Identification and Measurement of Cases Since 1945." *International Studies Quarterly* 32: 359-371.

Hemmendinger, Judith and Robert Krell. 2000. *The Children of Buchenwald Child Survivors of the Holocaust and Their Post-war Lives*. Jerusalem, Israel: Gefen Publishing.

Henry, Patrick. 2007. *We Only Know Men: The Rescue of Jews in France During the Holocaust*. Washington D.C: The Catholic University of America Press.

Hilberg, Raul. 1961. *The Destruction of European Jews*. New York: Quadrangle Books.

Holocaust Education and Research Team. 2007. "The White Rose." Retrieved from http://www.holocaustresearchproject.org/revolt/whiterose.html.

Katz, Stephen T. 1983. *Post-Holocaust Dialogues: Critical Studies in Modern Jewish Thought*. New York: New York University Press.

Krakowski, S. 1983. *The War of the Doomed: Jewish Armed Resistance in Poland 1942-1944*. New York: Holmes and Meier.

Kelman, Herbert C. 1973. "Violence Without Moral Restraint: Reflections on the Dehumanization of Victims and Victimizers." *Journal of Social Issues*. 29: 25–61.

Kulka, E., ed. 1976. *Collection of Testimonies and Documents on the Participation of Czechoslovak Jews in the Second World War*. Jerusalem: Yad Vashem.

Kurzman, Dan. 1976. The *Bravest Battle: The 28 Days of the Warsaw Ghetto Uprising*. Los Angeles: Pinnacle.

Lampe, David. 1957. The *Danish Resistance: A History of Five Years of Secret Warfare Against The Nazi Occupation*. New York: Ballantine Books.

Landau, Ronnie S. 1992. *The Nazi Holocaust*. Chicago: Ivan R, Dee.

Langer, Lawrence L. 1982. *Versions of Survival: The Holocaust and the Human Spirit*. New York: State University of New York Press.

Latham, Michelle. 2000. *Economic Motives for Total Genocide: A Comparison of the Armenian, the Holocaust and Rwandan Genocides. Unpublished Master's Thesis Boston College, Boston*.

Lazare, Lucien. 1996. *Rescue as Resistance: How Jewish Organizations Fought the Holocaust in France*. New York: Columbia University Press.

Lee, Lydia. May 2, 2003. "Warsaw Ghetto survivor recalls hunger, fear and grief." Retrieved on August 17, 2010. http://www.jweekly.com/article/full/19799/warsaw-ghetto-survivor-recalls-hunger-fear and-grief/.

Levin, Nora. 1968. *The Holocaust: The Destruction of European Jewry 1933-1945*. New York: Schocken Books.

Malinowski, R. Wladyslaw. 1944. "Patterns of Underground Resistance." *Annals of the American Academy of Political and Social Science* 232: 126-133.

Mark, Ber. 1975. *Uprising in the Warsaw Ghetto*. New York: Schocken Books.

Marrus, M. R. and Paxton, R.O. 1983. *Vichy France and the Jews*. New York: Schocken.

Melson, Robert. 1992. *Revolution and Genocide: On the Origins of the Armenian Genocide and the Holocaust*. Chicago: University of Chicago Press.

Milton, Sybil. 1979. *The Stroop Report*. New York: Pantheon Books.

Muckelbauer, John. 2000. "On Reading Differently: Through Foucault's Resistance." *College Englis*h 63: 71-94.

Novitch, Miriam. 1980. *Sobibor*. New York: Holocaust Library.

Oliner, Samuel P. 2003. *Do Unto Others: Extraordinary Acts of Ordinary People*. Boulder: Westview Press.

Oliner, Samuel and Kathleen Lee. 1996. *Who Shall Live: The Wilhelm Bachner Story*. Chicago: Academy Chicago Publishers.

Oliner, Samuel P. 1998. "Rescuers of Jews During the Holocaust: A Portrait of Moral Courage. In Michael Berenbaum and Abraham Peck eds. *The Holocaust and*

History: The Known, the Unknown, the Disputed, and the Reexamined. Indiana: Indiana University Press. 678-690.

Pechersky, Alexander. 1967. "Revolt in Sobibor." In Yuri Suhl ed. *They Fought Back.* New York: Schocken Books. 7-30.

Poliakov, L. 1979. *Harvest of Hate.* New York: Holocaust Library.

Rajzman, Samuel. 1945. *Uprising in Treblinka* in U.S. Congress. House Committee on Foreign Affairs. *Punishment of War Criminals.* 79th Cong., 1st sess. Washington D.C.: GPO, 120-125.

Rings, Wener. 1982. *Life with the Enemy: Collaboration and Resistance in Hitler's Europe, 1939-1945.* New York: Doubleday.

Rohrlich, Ruby. 1998. *Resisting the Holocaust.* New York: Oxford International Publishers Ltd.

Rosenblum, Joe. 2001. *Defy The Darkness: A Tale of Courage in the Shadow of Mengele.* Wesport: Praeger Publishers.

Rossiter, Margaret L. 1986. *Women in the Resistance.* New York: Praeger Publishers.

Rozett, Dr. Robert. 1990. as quoted in *Encyclopedia of the Holocaust.* New York: Macmillan Publishing Company.

Scislowska, Monika. 2010. "Former inmate recalls daring escape from Auschwitz." *SFGate*.com. Retrieved on August 17, 2010. http://articles.sfgate.com/2010-07-20/world/21991462_1_auschwitz-warehouse-gas-chambers.

Seden, Othniel J. 1980. *The Survivor of Babi Yar.* Boulder: Enkidu Press.

Smoliar, Hersh. 1966. *Resistance in Minsk.* Oakland: Judah L. Magnes Memorial Museum.

Stadtler, Bea. 1973. *The Holocaust: A History of Courage and Resistance.* New York: Behrman House Inc.

Steiner, Jean-Francois. 1967. *Treblinka.* New York: The New American Library, Inc.

Sterling, Eric. Ed. 2005. *Life in the Ghettos During the Holocaust.* New York: Syracuse University Press.

Suhl, Yuri. 1967. *They Fought Back: The Story of The Jewish Resistance in Nazi Europe.* New York: Schocken Books.

Tec, Nechama. 1990. *In The Lion's Den: The Life of Oswald Rufeisen.* New York: Oxford University Press.

Tec, Nechama. 1993. *Defiance: The Bielski Partisans.* New York: Oxford University Press.

Thalhammer, Kristina, Paul L. O'Loughlin, et al. 2007. *Courageous Resistance: The Power of Ordinary People.* New York: Palgrave Macmillan.

Trunk, Isaiah. 1979. *Jewish Responses to Nazi Persecution Collective and Individual Behavior in Extremis.* New York: Scarbrough.

Vrba, Rudolf. 1964. *I Cannot Forgive.* Vancouver: Regent College Publishing.

Wittenstein, George W. 1997. *Memories of the White Rose.* Retrieved from http:// www.historyplace.com/pointsofview/white-rose1.htm

Wolfe, Robert. 1980. "Putative Threat to National Security as a Nuremberg Defense for Genocide." *Annals of the American Academy of Political and Social Science* 450: 46-67.

Yad Vashem. 1999. *Studies XXVVII.* Jerusalem, Israel.

CHAPTER 5: PRECONDITIONS OF RESISTANCE

Adalian, Rouben Paul. *Musa Dagh.* Retrieved August 13, 2009. (http://www.arme-nian-genocide.org/musa_dagh.html).

Adelman, Howard and Astri Suhrke. 2000. *The Path of a Genocide: The Rwanda Crisis from Uganda to Zaire.* London: Transaction Publishers.

African Rights. 2002. *A True Humanitarian.* Retrieved on January 12, 2010. http:// www.humanrightsblog.org/reports/Wilkens.pdf.

Akcam, Taner. 2006. *A Shameful Act: The Armenian Genocide and the Question of Turkish Responsibility.* New York: Holt.

Ali, M. Taisiler. 1999. *Civil Wars in Africa: Roots and Resolution.* London: McGills-Queen's University Press.

Attallah, Maral. N. 2007. *Choosing Silence: The United States, Turkey and the Armenian Genocide.* Unpublished Master's Thesis, Humboldt State University, Arcata.

Barker, Greg. 2004. "The Man Everyone Remembers." *Frontline.* Retrieved on January 12, 2010. http://www.pbs.org/wgbh/pages/frontline/shows/ghosts/video/mbaye.html.

Balakian, Peter. 2003. *The Burning Tigris: The Armenian Genocide and America's Response.* New York: Harper Collins.

Barton, James L. 1930. *The Story of Near East Relief.* New York: MacMillan.

Carroll, Rory. 18 December 2003. "Genocide Witnesses 'Killed to Stop Testimony.'" Retrieved from http://www.guardian.co.uk/world/2003/dec/18/rorycarroll.

Chaliand, Gerard and Yves Ternon. 1983. *The Armenians: From Genocide to Resistance.* London: Zed Press.

Dadrian, N. Vahakn. 1995. *The History of the Armenian Genocide: Ethnic Conflict from the Balkans to Anatolia.* Providence: Berghahn Book.

Dallaire, Romeo General. 2003. *Shaking Hands with the Devil.* Canada: Random House.

Davison, Roderic H. 1948. "The Armenian Crisis, 1912-1914." *American Historical Review* 53, 10: 481-505.

Doyle, Mark. "Memories of Captain Mbaye Diagne" *Frontline: Ghosts of Rwanda.* Retrieved on August 17, 2010. http://www.pbs.org/wgbh/pages/frontline/shows/ghosts/video/capt.html.

Des Forges, Alison. 1999. *Leave None to Tell the Story.* New York: Human Rights Watch.

Enright, Robert D., Suzanne Freedman and Julio Rique, 1998. "The Psychology of Interpersonal Forgiveness", in Robert Enright and Joanna North, eds, *Exploring Forgiveness.* Madison: University of Wisconsin Press (46–62).

Frontline. 2004. "Interview General Romeo Dallaire." *Frontline: Ghosts of Rwanda.* Retrieved on August 12, 2010. http://www.pbs.org/wgbh/pages/frontline/shows/ghosts/interviews/dallaire.html.

Gaillard, Philippe. 2004. "Interview Philippe Gaillard." *Frontline.* Retrieved on January 12, 2010. http://www.pbs.org/wgbh/pages/frontline/shows/ghosts/interviews/gaillard.html.

Graber, G. S. 1996. *Caravans to Oblivion: The Armenian Genocide, 1915.* New York: J. Wiley.

Helmick, Raymond G. and Rodney L. Petersen. eds. 2001. *Forgiveness and Reconciliation: Religion, Public Policy, and Conflict Transformation.* Pennsylvania: Templeton Foundation Press.

Henry Morgenthau Sr. quoted in "Armenian Genocide Quotes." *Armeniapedia.* Retrieved on August 17, 2010. http://www.armeniapedia.org/index.php?title=Armenian_Genocide_Quotes#Henry_Morgenthau_Sr.

Hovannisian, G. Richard. 1992. *The Armenian Genocide: History, Politics, Ethics.* New York: St. Martin's Press.

Hovannisian, Richard G. "The Question of Altruism during the Armenian Genocide of 1915." In *Embracing the Other.* 1992. Eds. Pearl Oliner, Samuel Oliner, et al. New York: New York University Press. 282-305.

Kanyangara, P. Rime, B. Philippot, P. Yzerbyt, V. 2007. "Collective Rituals, Emotional Climate and Intergroup Perception: Participation in 'Gacaca' Tribunals and Assimilation of the Rwandan Genocide." *Journal of Social Issues.* 63: 387-403.

Keane, Fergal. 1995. *Season of Blood: A Rwandan Journey.* New York: Penguin Books.

Klinghoffer, Arthur. 1998. *The International Dimension of Genocide in Rwanda.* New York: New York University Press.

Kuperman, J. Alen. 2001. *The Limits of Humanitarian Intervention: Genocide in Rwanda.* Washington D.C: Brookings Institution Press.

Lampe, David. 1957. The *Danish Resistance: A History of Five Years of Secret Warfare Against The Nazi Occupation.* New York: Ballantine Books.

Latham, Michelle. 2000. "Economic motives for total genocide: A comparison of the Armenian, the Holocaust and Rwandan genocides." Unpublished Master's Thesis Boston College, Boston.

Mamdani, Mahmood. 2001. When *Victims Become Killers: Colonialism, Nativism, and the Genocide in Rwanda.* Princeton: Princeton University Press.

Melson, Robert. 1992. *Revolution and Genocide: On the Origins of the Armenian Genocide and the Holocaust.* Chicago: University of Chicago Press.

Miller, E. Donald and Lorna Touryan Miller. 1993. *Survivors: An Oral History for the Armenian Genocide.* Berkeley: University of California Press.

Prunier, Gerard. 1995. *The Rwandan Crisis: History of A Genocide.* New York: Columbia University Press.

"Rwandan Genocide Acts of Rescue." Retrieved on January 12, 2010. http://www.vhec.org/images/pdfs/rwanda.pdf.

Rosoux, Valerie. 2006. "The Figure of the Righteous Individual in Rwanda." *International Social Science Journal.* 58: 491-499.

Rusesabagina, Paul. 2006. *An Ordinary Man.* New York: Penguin Group.

Staub, Erwin, Laurie Ann Pearlman, et. al. 2005. "Healing, Reconciliation, Forgiving and the Prevention of Violence after Genocide or Mass Killing: An Intervention and its Experimental Evaluation in Rwanda." *Journal of Social and Clinical Psychology.* 24: 297-334.

Taisier, Alim M., et al. eds. 1999. *Civil Wars in Africa: Roots and Resolution.* Canada: McGill-Queen's University Press.

Taylor, C. Christopher. 1999. *Sacrifice as Terror: The Rwandan Genocide of 1994.* New York: Oxford International Publishers Ltd.

Ternon, Yves. 1990. *The Armenians: History of A Genocide*. Delmar: Caravan Books.

Uvin, Peter. 1998. *Aiding Violence: The Development Enterprise in Rwanda*. West Harford: Kumarian Press.

Verwimp, P. 2000. "Peasant ideology and genocide in Rwanda under Habyarimana." http://research.yale.edu/ycias/database/files/GS19.pdf.

Werfel, Franz. 1933. *Forty Days of Musa Dagh*. New York: Carroll & Graf Publishers.

Zorbas, Eugenia. 2004. "Reconciliation in Post-Genocide Rwanda." *African Journal of Legal Studies*. 1: 29-52.

Chapter 6: The Nature of Goodness

Allen, N. and J. Phillippe Rushton. 1983. "Personality Characteristics of Community Mental Health Volunteers: A Review." *Journal of Voluntary Action Research* 12: 36-49.

Aronson, Elliot. 2004. "Reducing Hostility and Building Compassion: A Lesson From the Jigsaw Classroom." in A. G. Miller ed. *The Social Psychology of Good and Evil*. New York: Guilford Press, 469-488.

Batson, Daniel. 1991. *The Altruism Question: Toward a Social-Psychological Answer*. Hillsdale: Lawrence Erlbaum Associates.

Briggs, N.C., J. Piliavin, D. Lorentzen, and G. Becker. 1986. "On Willingness to be a Bone Marrow Donor." *Transfusion* 26: 234-330.

Cancian, Francesca. 1995. Truth and Goodness: Does the Sociology of Inequality Promote Social Betterment? *Sociological Perspectives On Inequality*: Papers from the 56th Annual Meeting 38: 339-356.

Colby, Anne and William Damon. 1992. *Some Do Care: Contemporary Lives of Moral Commitment*. New York: The Free Press.

Dancy, J., & Wynn-Dancy, M. L. 1995. The Nature of Caring in Volunteerism within Geriatric Settings. *Activities, Adaptation, and Aging*. Vol. 20, 5-12.

Durkheim, Emile. 1951. *Suicide*. Illinois: The Free Press.

Eisenberg, N., Valiente, C. & Champion, C. 2004. "Empathy Related Responding: Moral, Social, and Socialization Correlates." in A. G. Miller ed. *The Social Psychology of Good and Evil*, 386–415. New York: Guilford Press.

Ekman, Paul. 2008. "Can I Trust You?" In *The Greater Good* Vol. 5: 20-25.

Engel, Beverly. 2001. *The Power of Apology: Healing Steps to Transform All Your Relationships*. New York: John Wiley and Sons, Inc.

Frankl, Viktor. 1959. *Man's Search for Meaning*. Washington: Washington Square.

Habitat for Humanity. 2010. "Habitat for Humanity." Retrieved from http://www. habitat.org/ on October 6, 2010.

International Children's Surgical Foundation. 2005-2010. "Why We Do It." Retrieved from http://www.icsfoundation.org/why-we-do-it on October 4, 2009.

Irwin Kyle, Tucker Mcgrimmon and Brent Simpson. 2008. "Sympathy and Social Order." *Social Psychology Quarterly*. Vol. 71 379-397.

Kielburger, Craig and Marc Kielburger. 2004. *Me to We: Finding Meaning in a Material World*. Canada: Wiley Publishing.

Koenig, Harold G. 2001. *Handbook of Religion and Health*. New York: Oxford University Press.

Koenig, Harold G. 2002. *Spirituality in Patient Care: Why, How, When, and What*. Philadelphia: Templeton Foundation Press.

Maathi, Wangari. 2007. *Unbowed*. New York: Anchor Books.

Michael Kosfeld et al. "Oxytocin Increases Trust in Humans." *Nature* (June 2005): 673-676.

McCullough, Michael E., Kenneth I. Pargament, Carl E. Thoresen. 1999. *"Forgiveness: Theory, Research, and Practice."* New York: The Guilford Press.

Menchu, Rigoberta. 1998. *Crossing Borders*. New York: Verso.

Morison, Samuel Eliot. 1975. *History of United States Naval Operations in World War II, Volume I The Battle of the Atlantic 1939-1943*. London: Little, Brown.

Noddings, Nel. 2010. *The Maternal Factor: Two Paths to Morality*. Berkeley: University of California Press.

Noddings, Nel, and Paul J. Shore. 1984. *Awakening the Inner Eye: Intuition in Education*. New York: Teachers College Columbia University.

Oliner, Samuel. 2008. *Altruism, Intergroup Apology, Forgiveness and Reconciliation*. St. Paul: Paragon House.

Oliner, Samuel P. 2003. *Do Unto Others: Extraordinary Acts of Ordinary People*. Boulder: Westview Press

Oliner, Samuel and Pearl Oliner, 1988. *The Altruistic Personality*. New York: The Free Press.

Omoto, Allen M. and Mark Snyder, 2002. "Considerations of Community: The Context and Process of Volunteerism." *American Behavioral Scientist* 45: 846-867

Snyder, M., Omoto, A. M., & Lindsay, J. J. 2004. "Sacrificing Time and Effort for the Good of Others: The Benefits and Costs of Volunteerism." in A. G. Miller ed. *The Social Psychology of Good and Evil* New York: The Guilford Press, 444-468.

Ornish, Dean. 1998. *Love and Survival: The Scientific Basis for the Healing Power of Intimacy.* New York: Harper Collins.

Paxton, Pamela and Jeremy Smith. 2008. "America's Trust Fall". *Greater Good.* 5: 14-17.

Post, Stephen G. and Jill Neimark. 2007. *Why Good Things Happen to Good People.* New York: Broadway Books.

Post, Stephen G. 2003. *Unlimited Love: Altruism, Compassion, and Service.* Philadelphia: Templeton Foundation Press.

Salierno, Chris. June 1997. "Sempo Sugihara: A "Righteous Person," *An End to Intolerance*: 5.

Sax, Barry M. 2003. "Higher Duty." *Reformed Judaism*, 67-76.

Sen Gupta, Kalyan. 2005. *The Philosophy of Rabindranath Tagore.* Vermont: Ashgate Publishing Company.

Smedes, Lewis. 1996. *The Art of Forgiving: When You Need to Forgive and Don't Know How.* New York: Ballantine Books.

Sorokin, Pitirim. 1954. *The Ways and Power of Love.* Boston: Beacon Press.

Staub, Ervin. 2003. *The Psychology of Good and Evil: Why Children, Adults, and Groups Help and Harm Others.* Cambridge: Cambridge University Press.

Tutu, Desmond and Mpho Tutu. 2010. *Made for Goodness*: *And Why This Makes All the Difference.* New York: Harper Collins.

Vrba, Rudolf. 1964. *I Cannot Forgive.* Vancouver: Regent College Publishing.

Weil, Andrew. 2003. *The Gift of Forgiveness. Self Healing: Creating Natural Health for Your Body and Mind.* New York: Harper Collins.

Wiesenthal, Simon. 1998. *Sunflower: On the Possibilities and Limits of Forgiveness.* New York: Schocken Books.

Wispe, Lauren. 1986. "The Distinction Between Sympathy and Empathy: To Call Forth a Concept, A Word Is Needed" in *Journal of Personality and Social Psychology.* 50 (2), 314-321.

World Economic Forum. 2005. "Trust in Governments, Corporations and Global Institutions Continues to Decline," Retrieved from http://www.weforum.org/en/media/Latest%20Press%20Releases/PRESSRELEASES87 on September 20, 2010.

Yad Vashem. "Metropolitan Chrysostomos: Mayor Lucas Karreri," *The Righteous Among the Nations*. Retrieved from http://www1.yadvashem.org/yv/en/righteous/stories/chrysostomos_karreri.asp on September 20, 2010.

CHAPTER 7: THE WORLD OF HEROES

Anderson, Vicky. (1993). "Gender Differences in Altruism Among Holocaust Rescuers." *Journal of Social Behavior and Personality*, 8, 43–58.

Becker, Ernest. 1971. *The Birth and Death of Meaning*. New York: The Free Press.

Becker, Selwyn and Eagly, Alice . 2004. "The Heroism of Women and Men." *American Psychological Association*. 59, 3: 163–178

Bellah, Robert N., Richard Madsen, William M.Sullivan, Ann Swindler, and Steven M. Tipton. 1985. *Habits of the Heart: Individualism and Commitment in American Life*. New York: Harper Row.

Bel Monte, Kathryn. 1998. *African-American Heroes and Heroines of America: 150 True Stories of African-American Heroism*. Lifetime Books.

Berkowitz, Bill. 1987. *Local Heroes*. Maryland: Lexington Books.

Buckley, Cara "Man is Rescued By Stranger on Subway Tracks." *New York Times*. January 3, 2007 (Retrieved on September 22, 2010 at http://www.nytimes.com/2007/01/03/nyregion/03life.html).

Campbell, Joseph. 1949. *Hero with a Thousand Faces*. Bollinger Series XVII, Princeton University Press.

Carlyle, Thomas. 1966. *On Heroes, Hero-Worship, and the Heroic in History*. Nebraska: *University of Nebraska Press*.

Colby, Anne and William Damon. 1992. *Some Do Care: Contemporary Lives of Moral Commitment*. New York: The Free Press.

Gibbon, Peter. 2003. *A Call to Heroism: Renewing America's Vision of Greatness*. New York: Grove Press.

Giddens, Anthony. 1984. *The Constitution of Society: Outline of the Theory of Structuration*. Berkeley: University of California Press.

Gilligan, Carol. 1982. *In a Different Voice: Psychological Theory and Women's Development*. Cambridge: Harvard University Press.

Goode, William. 1978. *The Celebration of Heroes: Prestige as a Social Control System*. Berkeley: University of California Press.

Hook, Sidney. 1980. *Philosophy and Public Policy*. Illinois: Southern Illinois University Press.

Jeffries, Vincent. 2005. "Pitirim A. Sorokin's Integralism and Public Sociology." *The American Sociologist* 36, 3-4: 66-87.

Jeffries, Vincent. 1998. "Virtue and the Altruistic Personality." *Sociological Perspectives.* 41,1: 151-166.

Macauley, J. & Berkowitz, L. 1970. *Altruism and Helping Behavior.* New York: Academic Press.

McGovern, Ann. 1990. *The Secret Soldier: The Story of Deborah Sampson*. New York: Scholastic Inc.

Murdock, Iris. 1970. *The Sovereignty of Good*. London: Routledge and Kegan Paul.

Noble, K. 1994. *The Sound of a Silver Horn: Reclaiming the Heroism in Contemporary Women's Lives.* New York: Ballantine Books.

Oliner, Samuel P. and Pearl M. Oliner. 1988. *The Altruistic Personality*. New York: The Free Press.

Oliner, Samuel P. and Kathleen Lee. 1996. *Who Shall Live: The Wilhelm Bachner Story*. Chicago: Academy Chicago Publishers.

Oliner, Pearl M., Samuel P. Oliner, Lawrence Baron, Lawrence A. Blum, Dennis L. Krebs, and M. Zuzanna Smolenska. 1992. *Embracing the Other: Philosophical, Psychological, and Historical Perspectives on Altruism*. New York: New York University Press.

Oliner, Samuel P. 2003. *Do Unto Others: How Altruism Inspires True Acts of Courage*. Cambridge: Westview Press.

Pasco, Allan H. 1997. *Sick Heroes*. England: University of Exeter Press.

Polster, Miriam. 1992. *Eve's Daughters: The Forbidden Heroism of Women*. San Francisco: Josse-Bass Publisher.

Roberts, John W. 1989. *From Tricksters to Bad Men: The Black Folk Hero in Slavery and Freedom*. Philadelphia: University of PA Press.

Rosenberg, Donna. 2001. *World Mythology*. Lincolnwood: National Textbook Co.

Rushton, JP. 1980. *Altruism, Socialization and Society*. New Jersey: Prentice Hall.

Sewell, William H. 1992. "A Theory of Structure: Duality, Agency, and Transformation." *The American Journal of Sociology*. 98, 1: 1-29.

Sidel, Ruth. 2006. *Unsung Heroines: Single Mothers and the American Dream*. Berkeley: University of California Press.

Sorokin, Pitirim. 1954. *The Ways and Power of Love*. Templeton Press, 2002.

"The Village of Le Chambon-sur-Lignon: André & Magda Trocmé, Daniel Trocmé," The Righteous Among the Nations retrieved on October 4, 2009 http://www1. yadvashem.org/yv/en/righteous/stories/trocme.asp).

Tillich, Paul. 1968. *A Complete History of Christian Thought*. New York: Harper & Row.

Weber, Eugene. 1995. *The Western Tradition*. Lexington: D.C. Heath and Company.

"Deborah Sampson: How She Served as a Soldier in the Revolution—Her Sex Unknown to the Army." *New York Times*, October 8. Retrieved October 31, 2007.

CHAPTER 8: SUMMARY AND CONCLUSION

Begley, Peggy. "Adventures in Good and Evil." *Newsweek*, March 4, 2009 p. 46.

Buber, Martin. 1958. *I and Thou*. New York: Charles Scribner's Sons.

Kelman, Herbert C. 1973. "Violence Without Moral Restraint: Reflections on the Dehumanization of Victims and Victimizers." *Journal of Social Issues*, 29: 25-61.

Lifton, Robert J. 1986. *The Nazi Doctors: Medical Killing and the Psychology of Genocide*. New York: Basic Books.

May, Rollo. 1967. *Psychology and the Human Dilemma*. New York: W.W. Norton and Company, Inc..

Salierno, Chris. 1997. "Sempo Sugihara: A Righteous Person." *An End to Intolerance*, 5 (Retrieved from http://iearn.org/hgp/aeti/aeti-1997/sempo-sugihara.html on September 27, 2010).

Singer, Peter. 2009. *The Life You Can Save*. New York: Random House. Reprinted in *Newsweek* March 2009 p. 48.

Staub, Ervin. 1989. *The Roots of Evil: The Origins of Genocide and Other Group Violence*. Cambridge: Cambridge University Press.

2010. "Top Ten Evil People of All Time" (Retrieved from http://www.bahrainonline. org/showthread.php?p=856833 on September 27, 2010).

Waite, Robert G. 1977. *The Psychopathic God: Adolf Hitler*. New York: New American Library.

Zeyno Baran & Onur Sazak. "The Ambassador: How a Turkish Diplomat Saved 20,000 Jews during the Holocaust" *The Weekly Standard* 14, (2009). Reprinted in *Together* April 2009 p. 10.

Zimbardo, Philip. 2007. *The Lucifer Effect: Understanding How Good People Turn Evil*. New York: Random House.

Index

C

S

X

Y

Z